NO-BRAINER'S GUIDE TO JESUS

NO-BRAINER'S
GUIDE TO
JESUS

WRITTEN BY **JAMES S. BELL,** JR. AND **STAN CAMPBELL**

TYNDALE HOUSE PUBLISHERS, INC., WHEATON, ILLINOIS

Visit Tyndale's exciting Web site at www.tyndale.com

Library of Congress Cataloging-in-Publication Data

Bell, James S.
  No-brainer's guide to Jesus / by James S. Bell and Stan Campbell.
    p. cm.
  ISBN 0-8423-5427-1 (pbk.)
  1. Jesus Christ—Person and offices. I. Campbell, Stan. II. Title.
BT203 .B45 2001
232—dc21   00-066638

Printed in the United States of America

06 05 04 03 02 01
6   5   4   3   2   1

CONTENTS

CHAPTER ONE

"WHO WAS THAT MASKED MAN, JED? HE AIN'T FROM THESE PARTS."

Who *Was* That Masked Man?

JESUS: AN INTRODUCTION

Jesus Christ.

Perhaps no other three syllables of the English language (including "I love you") have caused as much discussion, debate, dissension, deep thought, adoration, wonder, and confusion. To some people, these two words are little more than an addition to an already well-stocked arsenal of profanities and verbal outbursts. To others, they represent the answer for all that's ailing today's world. And for millions of people in between, they may be a source of delight or disgust.

Was Jesus Christ a well-conceived myth, perpetrated by a few men eager to elevate their own positions in the eyes of others?

Was He a historical reality, yet just a man who accidentally fulfilled some of the prophecies of the Messiah who was to come?

Was Jesus a wise and righteous prophet of the times, no more or less important than Buddha, Mohammed, Confucius, and others?

Was He who He said He was . . . the Son of God? Or did He really *say* that's who He was?

Whatever you currently believe about Jesus, you can find yourself

1

in good company. Opinions about Jesus are as broad as they are deeply held. Here are just a few quotations that reflect the wide spectrum of beliefs concerning who Jesus was:

"Had there been a lunatic asylum in the suburbs of Jerusalem, Jesus Christ would infallibly have been shut up in it at the outset of his public career. That interview with Satan on a pinnacle of the temple would alone have damned him, and everything that happened after could but have confirmed the diagnosis."—*Havelock Ellis*

"Christ preached the greatness of man: We preach the greatness of Christ. The first is affirmative; the last negative."—*Ralph Waldo Emerson*

"We believe in God, and in that which has been sent down on us and sent down on Abraham, Ishmael, Isaac and Jacob, and the Tribes, and that which was given to Moses and Jesus and the Prophets, of their Lord; we make no division between any of them, and to Him we surrender."—*The Koran*

"The Mosaic religion had been a Father religion; Christianity became a Son religion. The old God, the Father, took second place; Christ, the Son, stood in His stead, just as in those dark times every son had longed to do."—*Sigmund Freud*

"Jesus of Nazareth was the most scientific man that ever trod the globe. He plunged beneath the material surface of things, and found the spiritual cause."—*Mary Baker Eddy*

"The three greatest dolts in the world: Jesus Christ, Don Quixote, and I."—attributed to *Simón Bolívar*

These few opinions only begin to represent who Jesus was in the eyes of various key people throughout history. We will print more quotes throughout this book in a sidebar we're calling "Opinion Poll." (The authors and publishers don't necessarily endorse all of the opinions expressed. They are merely a sampling of what has been written about Jesus throughout the past couple of millennia.)

As you can see, the psychiatrists try to analyze the world's fasci-

nation with Jesus. The Christian Scientists focus on the "scientific" aspects of Jesus. Other religions tend to cast him as merely another teacher among many. And some people don't even try to hide their contempt for and/or skepticism about the importance of Jesus Christ.

While the authors hope to address a variety of opinions and philosophies concerning the person of Jesus, it is not our attempt to make this book an objective piece of research. We all have our favorite sources we prefer to consult. Some people enjoy the *Wall Street Journal* over breakfast every morning. Others prefer the *National Enquirer.* We have the freedom to decide what's more important to us at any given time, whether it's the current return on money market accounts or the latest sighting of alien creatures who look like Elvis.

Similarly, as we look at the topic of Jesus, we could choose a number of primary sources, but our goal will be to try to present a clearer picture of the *biblical* Jesus. Yet even if we consult the Bible as the single most authoritative source of information, it will still be no easy task to get a clear picture of Jesus—at least, not as clear as we might like. Even within the context of Scripture, we get what may seem to be a lot of variance as to who this Jesus person was . . . and is . . . and will be.

The book you're reading is called a *No-Brainer's Guide,* but if you truly want a no-brain experience, you would do well to blindly pick any theory about Jesus and boldly stick to it without bothering with facts or justification. (This seems to be the method of choice for lots of people today.) But if you really desire to better understand who Jesus is, you're going to have to engage that brain of yours. However, it will be the goal of the authors to simplify the concepts as much as possible. We're no geniuses ourselves, but we've been working in the Christian publishing field for decades. And while we may not be any smarter than anyone else, we do hear a lot of the questions being asked. As you join us in a search for satisfactory answers, we'll try to have a lot of fun as we explore.

OPINION POLL

"The foundation of Christian belief is the biblical picture of Christ, not the historical Jesus."—*Paul Tillich*

Can You See the Real Me?

All the confusion about Jesus should come as no surprise. Aren't we all a bit inconsistent as we relate to the various people in our lives? Even as kids we learn to adjust our behavior depending on the situation. And though your behavior may be a bit inconsistent from person to person, it makes perfect sense to you. And that's just little ol' *you*. As we will see in this book, Jesus was considerably more complex than the average human being. If His enemies saw Him in one light while His disciples saw Him in another, where's the mystery in that? Wouldn't the same be true of you . . . or of anyone?

But in addition, the confusion about Jesus is wrapped within a couple of other layers. To begin with, He was something of a celebrity in His time. We will see that after He began His public ministry, He was almost continually barraged by people hoping to see signs, receive healing, or simply hear what He had to say. It was as close as anyone in the first-century world could come to dealing with the *paparazzi*, and we know how difficult it is to get an accurate perception of someone by focusing primarily on his or her public life. You can witness every public act of the President of the United States or your favorite actress, but you'll still have a very limited understanding of the depth of the person.

Thankfully, the Bible also provides several "behind the scenes" descriptions of Jesus when the crowds weren't around. We'll try to look at a broad assortment of small-group interactions and one-on-one conversations, as well as how He dealt with crowds.

Claim Check

Another complication in getting a clear view into the person of Jesus are His claims to be God. We've seen what happens when people make similar claims today. They have their group of followers, to be sure, but many others look on in skepticism and disbelief. It wasn't much different for Jesus. We will look at many of the claims concerning Jesus' deity—both His own declarations and those made by other people. You may or may not agree that His claims are valid, and it stands to reason that He would have had numerous detractors in His time (as well as in ours). We urge you to examine the accounts for yourself and come to your own conclusions.

(The authors' pro-Jesus convictions are likely to come through from time to time. We hope you won't take offense, because we're not trying to hide them. We want you to know up front that we're churchgoing, believing Christians who work with some of the leading pastors and seminary teachers of our time. Yet this is not meant to convert you into a believer in Jesus' claims. We will attempt to be as objective as possible as we look at the biblical presentation of Jesus. You can see for yourself what the Bible has to say and take it from there.)

OPINION POLL

"If ever the Divine appeared on earth, it was in the person of Christ."—*Johann Wolfgang von Goethe*

What If . . . ?

But suppose for a moment that Jesus *was* who He said He was. Suppose that God Himself stepped out of heaven, willfully choosing to take a sabbatical from being Lord of the Universe long enough to live a short lifetime as a human being—progressing from baby to teenager to adult. His connection with God the Father would be considerably restricted, yet still much stronger than anyone else's on earth. From the beginning of time, He had known what it was like to be God. But for the first time, He would experience firsthand the horrors of living in a sin-tainted world. He still had access to the full power of God, to be sure, but it seems that His self-imposed rule was that He wouldn't use it for His own benefit. He wasn't willing to use supernatural power to dodge the pain, fear, shame, sorrow, or other emotions inherent in the human experience. While it's impossible for us to empathize with such a situation, try to imagine it.

Readers younger than the authors may not recall the old "Lone Ranger" shows starring Clayton Moore. No one really knew what the Lone Ranger looked like because he was always disguised somehow. He usually wore his famous mask, but some of the best shows were when he would go into town dressed as an old prospector or in some other getup. The viewers realized the townspeople didn't know

"If the life and death of Socrates are those of a philosopher, the life and death of Jesus Christ are those of a God."
—Jean-Jacques Rousseau

whom they were dealing with. The Lone Ranger could outshoot them, outfight them, and outthink them. But in his grungy disguise, his peers would frequently look down on him. And even in his mask, they almost always assumed he was a bad guy. Yet he would always save the day, and at the end of each episode some confused soul was pondering the same old question: "Who was that masked man?"

As Jesus spent 33 years in human society under those conditions, don't you suppose most people would be a bit confused as to His secret identity? Although He was God (according to our supposition), Jesus looked like any guy from a dusty first-century Middle East country. Some people failed to see through this disguise. Others, however, couldn't help but see that beneath this costume of skin and bone was a Presence that was more than human.

Jesus' cloak of humanity worked to His advantage at times, however. The fact that He was God wasn't something He wished to broadcast indiscriminately. The truth would be told in time, but people needed an opportunity to catch on slowly—beginning with His rather dense disciples. This news was simply too incredible to absorb quickly.

Those who believe Jesus was fully God realize that He was God "in a mask." He was someone special, but His full glory was not visible. It's probably a good thing, because God told Moses in the Old Testament: "You may not look directly at my face, for no one may see me and live" (Exodus 33:20). If Jesus had arrived without some kind of mask to shield His divinity, perhaps we would have been far too frightened to learn as much about Him as we know now.

At Christmas you might sing, "Hark! The Herald Angels Sing" without thinking much about the words. For example, part of the song includes the phrase, "Veiled in flesh the Godhead see, Hail th' incarnate deity." It's not Greek or Latin, though it may as well be. Rather, it's a poetic way of saying that when we look at Jesus incarnate (in the flesh), we see God behind a veil. Jesus was in every sense a true and accurate portrayal of God, but in His humanity He did not overpower us with the incomprehensible and frightening fullness of God.

The Personal Touch

We don't want you to blindly accept that Jesus was God. We simply ask you to be objective as you see what the Bible records about Him. Make your own observations, discoveries, and interpretations. If you are at least open to the possibility, you'll probably get a lot more out of this book. And be ready for a few surprises along the way.

Another thing to keep in mind as you go through this book is that the biblical accounts of Jesus are not for our reading pleasure only. Encounters with Jesus call for some kind of response. We'll see some people eagerly walk away from everything else for an opportunity to learn at the feet of the Master. We'll see others vehemently oppose what He is saying. Some will reject Him, but reluctantly. Others will desperately want to believe but will struggle to do so. All these options are still valid responses. But the one option we don't have is to sit by as a spectator. Jesus will expect us to go one way or the other.

The pursuit of the biblical Jesus is not a matter of dry theology, but of dynamic relationships. To those who choose to respond, Jesus holds out numerous challenges, promises, and hopes. It's a personal matter just between you and Him. The authors will be bringing to light many of the biblical facts and opinions about Jesus, but what you do with them is up to you. If you take them to heart as well as to mind, you will be able to interact with the material on a whole new level.

Belly Up to the (Side)Bar

We will be using a relatively new Bible translation known as the New Living Translation. Even some of the most familiar Bible passages may sound a bit different than you're accustomed to, but that can be beneficial. If a newer translation causes us to stop and think about Scriptures that may have become *too* familiar, the passages can take on a fresh new meaning. If you're hearing some of these things for the first time, this translation is not at all hard to understand. And if

OPINION POLL

"If Jesus Christ were to come today, people would not even crucify him. They would ask him to dinner, . . . hear what he had to say, and make fun of it."
—*Thomas Carlyle*

7

"Christ is the most unique person in history. No man can write a history of the human race without giving first and foremost place to the penniless teacher of Nazareth."—*H. G. Wells*

you're hearing it for the thousandth time, perhaps you'll respond to it in a new, enlightening way.

As we continue through this book, you'll also see a number of recurring sidebars. These include:

Opinion Poll

We mentioned this one already. It will include quotes about Jesus.

Something Old, Something New

These sidebars will connect prophecies or events in the Old Testament with their fulfillment or parallel in the New Testament. Frequently the significance cannot be fully understood unless this connection is made.

W.D.J.D.?

Perhaps you've seen T-shirts, bumper stickers, bracelets, and such with the W.W.J.D. logo, which stands for "What would Jesus do?" But it's hard to know what Jesus would do today if we don't know what He did in the past. So we will target specific circumstances and situations where we want to stop and ask, "What *did* Jesus do?"

In Jesus' Name

At one point Jesus told His disciples, "You can ask for anything in my name, and I will do it" (John 14:13). But the Bible provides a number of different names and titles that are applied to Jesus. As we come to them, we'll take a look at these names and their significance. Each of the names provides another bit of additional insight into the totality of who Jesus is.

In addition, in the Appendix of this book you will find a concise timeline of the life of Jesus Christ and a topical index of verses that give you a sampling of some of the things Jesus told his followers.

Jesus liked to say, "He who has ears, let him hear," which is also translated, "Anyone who is willing to hear should listen and understand." So from this point on, the watching and listening begins. Let's see what we can discover about this mysterious God-Man known as Jesus Christ.

Questions to Ponder and/or Discuss

Look for this section at the end of each chapter. You'll find about three questions to prompt more in-depth personal consideration. You can dwell on these questions privately if you wish. Or if you are going through this book with a partner or small group, you can use them as discussion questions.

1. If everything to be known about Jesus were symbolized by the amount of water in the Pacific Ocean, what quantity of water do you think represents your current knowledge of Him?

2. You read several quotes about Jesus in this chapter. If you were asked for a quote about Him, what would you say?

3. Which of the following best describes your current opinion about Jesus:

- He was an ordinary guy who got a lot of good PR.
- He was a good man, possibly a prophet, but no more.
- He was an ambitious but confused leader.
- He was 100 percent God in human form.
- Other: _____

"HI, HONEY. YOU REMEMBER THE JOHNSONS . . . DINNER . . . TONIGHT . . . OUR HOUSE AT SIX?"

Company's Coming!

JESUS IN PROPHECY

When, exactly, do adults get so lousy at the art of anticipation? As kids, we "just can't wait" for a big event. The month between Thanksgiving and Christmas is approximately a century long in kid time. And then, as soon as the anticipation of Christmas morning has finally paid off in explosions of sheer joy and unparalleled contentment, we start counting the days until we are out of school and summer vacation arrives. A kid's whole life is anticipation of the next landmark event.

But somewhere along the way we become adults, and growing up ruins everything. Perhaps it starts when we get married. Yes, we look forward to the wedding ceremony, of course. Yet it seems no matter how much time we allow, we're never quite ready when the day comes. The sheer joy of anticipation is replaced with a feeling of panic as the date doesn't dangle in the future as much as it hurtles toward the present.

Or maybe it simply gets to the point in our lives where we may have less future than past, so we start resisting it. But for whatever the reason, many adults lose the childlike thrill of anticipating big events.

SOME THINGS YOU'LL DISCOVER IN THIS CHAPTER

1. The Old Testament gave us many clues as to what Jesus would be like.

2. The prophecies of the Old Testament aren't simple or clear, but they can be interpreted.

3. Old Testament kings prefigured Jesus, the coming eternal ruler.

"MESSIAH" (John 4:25)
"CHRIST" (Ephesians 1:22)
"ANOINTED ONE" (Psalm 2:2)

Messiah comes from Hebrew. *Christ* comes from the Greek language. Both words mean "anointed one." All three terms are used frequently throughout Scripture in reference to Jesus.

"DELIVERER" (Romans 11:26-27)

During Israel's history the nation had sought deliverance from Philistines, Midianites, Babylonians, Persians, Greeks, Romans, and numerous other opponents. But Jesus came to deliver His people from even bigger enemies—sin, death, and Satan.

Back in the Good Old Testament

If you were one of God's people living during the days of the Old Testament (the books of the Bible that were written many years before Jesus came to earth), you should have had an ongoing sense of anticipation for the coming of a *messiah*. After the reigns of David and Solomon, the line of kings contained desperately few decent people, but the prophets promised a wonderful and powerful ruler would one day arise from the line of David. No matter how bad your life might get, you had the promise that in the future things would get better.

Various passages in the Old Testament describe how the once-great nations of Israel and Judah both experienced tragic defeats after they turned away from God and began to worship various idols. Israel fell first, and most of the people were absorbed into the Assyrian Empire. Not long afterward, a siege on Judah resulted in the Babylonians storming in, looting the temple, and taking charge. They took everything of value, including the more promising people, and left only the poorer folks to tend the land for them. The circumstances God's people faced during this period were frequently horrifying. When food supplies ran out during the sieges, they grew desperate and ate donkey heads (2 Kings 6:25), and some even resorted to cannibalism (Lamentations 2:20; 4:10). Their military losses resulted in their enemies mutilating their leaders and raping their women (2 Kings 25:7; Lamentations 5:11-15).

Yet throughout the bleak years and the heartbreaking conditions, God's promise was that after a 70-year exile in Babylon, the people would return to their homeland. And beyond that, it was foretold that one day someone would arrive and make things right on a more permanent basis. The situation might have seemed completely hopeless without such anticipation of a savior and deliverer.

The Old Testament is filled with prophecies, descriptions, and images of this coming Messiah. We will see in the next chapter that in spite of all the promises and preparation, the world had lost much of its anticipation by the time this Messiah, Jesus, finally arrived. But that certainly wasn't the fault of all the faithful and persistent prophets of the Old Testament. Let's take a look at what they had to say about the Messiah. We will see that even in the Old Testament, there is much said about Jesus, the primary figure of the New Testament.

Before the Beginning

Even before the world is spoken into existence, we get a clue that Jesus is around. You probably know something of the creation story, of how God created the world in six days and rested on the seventh. But sometimes we don't pay enough attention to the pronouns in the story. We read that "God" created heavens, earth, plants, and animals. But when we get to the creation of human beings, we discover that "God" is not singular: "Then God said, 'Let *us* make people in *our* image, to be like *ourselves*' " (Genesis 1:26, italics added).

A couple of explanations are suggested for this wording. Some people suggest that God was speaking to those present in heaven at the time (His attending angels). It's like you might say, "Let's throw a party," intending to do all the work yourself but inviting others within voice range to participate.

Another possibility is that God is sort of talking to Himself. In the concept of the Trinity, the church affirms that God is one, although He expresses Himself in three distinct Persons: Father, Son, and Holy Spirit. This statement in Genesis may suggest that the Persons of the Godhead are agreeing to create the human race. If so, then from the first chapter of the first book of the Bible, Jesus is a prominent figure.

Then, before we even get to the end of Genesis 3, Adam and Eve have already made a big mess of everything. They've listened to a deceitful serpent and have gone their own way instead of God's. As God is explaining what's going to happen to them, He pronounces a curse on the serpent, and we have our first official prophecy about Jesus: "Because you have done this, you will be punished. You are singled out from all the domestic and wild animals of the whole earth to be cursed. You will grovel in the dust as long as you live,

OPINION POLL

"By a Carpenter mankind was made, and only by that Carpenter can mankind be remade."—*Desiderius Erasmus*

IN JESUS' NAME
"ELOHIM"

This name for God is used in Genesis 1 and more than 2,500 other places in Scripture, but only in the Old Testament. It is a plural noun, yet is consistently used with singular verb forms, suggesting that it might represent a "plural of majesty" to describe God's unlimited and unsurpassed authority. In other words, perhaps it is plural to suggest not *more than* one, but rather a *more intense* one. The literal translation is debated, but *Elohim* is frequently interpreted as "The Strong One."

13

crawling along on your belly. From now on, you and the woman will be enemies, and your offspring and her offspring will be enemies. He will crush your head, and you will strike his heel" (Genesis 3:14-15).

We later learn that Satan is "a liar and the father of lies" (John 8:44), beginning with this biggie in the Garden of Eden. His evil influence will continue to "strike the heel" of humanity with all kinds of temptation and sin. But paired with this original sin of Adam and Eve is an original promise of eventual redemption. Some day a descendant of the woman will "crush [the] head" of Satan, putting an end to his wicked rule over humanity. Since the first mentioned descendant of Eve (Cain) was only able to crush the head of his brother (Abel), we must assume the prophecy referred to another person. The only descendant of Eve capable of such a feat was Jesus. (We'll see more about this in chapters 11 and 12.)

No sooner do His newly created human beings sin than God promises to do something about it! In addition, the sin in the garden foreshadows *how* Jesus will deal with the sin problem. God knew that the fig leaves Adam and Eve were using to cover their nakedness would dry up and become useless, so He provided them with clothing from animal skins instead (Genesis 3:21). This is the first hint we have of death . . . of blood. It certainly won't be the last.

Profiting from Propheting

We could do an entire book on the prophecies about Jesus in the Old Testament, but let's start with just a few of the no-brainer ones. Many of the prophets have important things to say about the coming Messiah, but the primary writer in this respect is Isaiah. The following passages are from his book:

> "Look! The virgin will conceive a child! She will give birth to a son and will call him Immanuel—'God is with us'" (Isaiah 7:14).

> "The people who walk in darkness will see a great light. . . . For a child is born to us, a son is given to us. And the

government will rest on his shoulders. These will be his royal titles: Wonderful Counselor, Mighty God, Everlasting Father, Prince of Peace. His ever expanding, peaceful government will never end. He will rule forever with fairness and justice from the throne of his ancestor David. The passionate commitment of the Lord Almighty will guarantee this!" (9:2, 6-7)

"'Comfort, comfort my people,' says your God. 'Speak tenderly to Jerusalem. Tell her that her sad days are gone and that her sins are pardoned. Yes, the Lord has punished her in full for all her sins.' . . . Yes, the Sovereign Lord is coming in all his glorious power. He will rule with awesome strength. See, he brings his reward with him as he comes. He will feed his flock like a shepherd. He will carry the lambs in his arms, holding them close to his heart. He will gently lead the mother sheep with their young" (40:1-2, 10-11).

"Look at my servant, whom I strengthen. He is my chosen one, and I am pleased with him. I have put my Spirit upon him. He will reveal justice to the nations. He will be gentle—he will not shout or raise his voice in public. He will not crush those who are weak or quench the smallest hope. He will bring full justice to all who have been wronged. He will not stop until truth and righteousness prevail throughout the earth. Even distant lands beyond the sea will wait for his instruction. . . . I, the Lord, have called you to demonstrate my righteousness. I will guard and support you, for I have given you to my people as the personal confirmation of my covenant with them. And you will be a light to guide all nations to me. You will open the eyes of the blind and free the captives from prison. You will release those who sit in dark dungeons" (42:1-4, 6-7).

"He was despised and rejected—a man of sorrows, acquainted with bitterest grief. We turned our backs on him and looked the other way when he went by. He was

OPINION POLL

"The one who keeps his eyes on the head and the origin of the whole universe has them on the perfection of virtue, on truth, on justice, on morality, and on everything else that is good, because Christ is goodness itself."
—*Gregory of Nyssa*

IN JESUS' NAME
"THE LORD IS OUR RIGHTEOUSNESS" (Jeremiah 23:6)

Righteousness is a state of "right-ness" before God—a status sinful people cannot achieve on their own efforts. As this name clearly expresses, Jesus is the source of righteousness, able to allow sinful people to connect with a perfect God.

despised, and we did not care. Yet it was our weaknesses he carried; it was our sorrows that weighed him down. And we thought his troubles were a punishment from God for his own sins! But he was wounded and crushed for our sins. He was beaten that we might have peace. He was whipped, and we were healed! . . . He was oppressed and treated harshly, yet he never said a word. He was led as a lamb to the slaughter. And as a sheep is silent before the shearers, he did not open his mouth. . . . He had done no wrong, and he never deceived anyone. But he was buried like a criminal; he was put in a rich man's grave" (53:3-5, 7, 9).

But Isaiah was by no means the only person used by God to prepare people for the coming of the Messiah. Here are some additional samples taken from various Old Testament books:

"'For the time is coming,' says the Lord, 'when I will place a righteous Branch on King David's throne. He will be a King who rules with wisdom. He will do what is just and right throughout the land. And this is his name: 'The Lord Is Our Righteousness'" (Jeremiah 23:5-6).

"But you, O Bethlehem Ephrathah, are only a small village in Judah. Yet a ruler of Israel will come from you, one whose origins are from the distant past" (Micah 5:2).

"Give justice to the king, O God, and righteousness to the king's son. Help him judge your people in the right way; let the poor always be treated fairly. May the mountains yield prosperity for all, and may the hills be fruitful, because the king does what is right. Help him to defend the poor, to rescue the children of the needy, and to crush their oppressors. May he live as long as the sun shines, as long as the moon continues in the skies. Yes, forever! . . . May he reign from sea to sea, and from the Euphrates River to the ends of the earth" (Psalm 72:1-5, 8).

"I saw someone who looked like a man coming with the clouds of heaven. He approached the Ancient One and was led into his presence. He was given authority, honor, and royal power over all the nations of the world, so that people of every race and nation and language would obey him. His rule is eternal—it will never end. His kingdom will never be destroyed" (Daniel 7:13-14).

"Rejoice greatly, O people of Zion! Shout in triumph, O people of Jerusalem! Look, your king is coming to you. He is righteous and victorious, yet he is humble, riding on a donkey—even on a donkey's colt" (Zechariah 9:9).

OPINION POLL

"Christ came when all things were growing old. He made them new."
—*Augustine of Hippo*

Ask the Proph-essors

So what do Isaiah and his peers have to tell us? Let's look at what seem to be some clear lessons.

Lesson #1: Some Old Testament prophecies clearly refer to the life, death, and resurrection of Jesus.

The prophets of the Old Testament foretold that the Messiah would be born of a virgin, in Bethlehem, and would be known for His righteousness. He would suffer and even die yet would have an everlasting kingdom that included not only the Jewish nation but the outsiders—the Gentiles—as well. As we will soon see, the New Testament account of Jesus will confirm all these things.

Lesson #2: Some Old Testament prophecies refer to a time beyond the life of Jesus.

Here are a couple of additional prophecies concerning the Messiah:

"Out of the stump of David's family will grow a shoot—yes, a new Branch bearing fruit from the old root. . . . In that day the wolf and the lamb will live together; the leopard and the goat will be at peace. Calves and yearlings will be safe among lions, and a little child will lead them all. The cattle will graze among bears. Cubs and calves will lie down together. And lions will eat grass as the livestock do. Babies

17

will crawl safely among poisonous snakes. Yes, a little child will put its hand in a nest of deadly snakes and pull it out unharmed" (Isaiah 11:1, 6-8).

"Watch, for the day of the Lord is coming when your possessions will be plundered right in front of you! . . . On that day his feet will stand on the Mount of Olives, which faces Jerusalem on the east. And the Mount of Olives will split apart, making a wide valley running from east to west, for half the mountain will move toward the north and half toward the south. . . . On that day the sources of light will no longer shine, yet there will be continuous day! Only the Lord knows how this could happen! There will be no normal day and night, for at evening time it will still be light. On that day life-giving waters will flow out from Jerusalem, half toward the Dead Sea and half toward the Mediterranean, flowing continuously both in summer and in winter. And the Lord will be king over all the earth. On that day there will be one Lord—his name alone will be worshiped" (Zechariah 14:1, 4, 6-9).

Wow! Have we missed something? Assuming Jesus has come to earth and ascended back to heaven, at what point did the Mount of Olives go seismic? And when can our kids start playing around the cobra pits?

In Jesus' lifetime, He didn't "reign from sea to sea" as Psalm 72 suggested. Men of every language didn't worship Him, as Daniel predicted. These and other prophecies apparently refer to a *future* rule of Jesus. We will find out more about it in later chapters.

Lesson #3: Some Old Testament prophecies require more speculation and interpretation than others.

While certain prophecies are spelled out clearly, others are more obscure and symbolic. Such passages allow for various translations and interpretations. For example, take a look at this one:

"I see him, but not in the present time. I perceive him, but far in the distant future. A star will rise from Jacob; a scep-

ter will emerge from Israel. It will crush the foreheads of Moab's people, cracking the skulls of the people of Sheth" (Numbers 24:17).

Clearly, this prophecy refers to a person, but does it also refer to a literal star? Since a star was instrumental in the story of the birth of Jesus, some people interpret this prophecy as a prediction of the celestial body seen by the wise men in the Christmas story. Not everyone is comfortable with allowing so much leeway for interpretation. But that's exactly why some of the Old Testament prophecies are subject to debate and varied opinions.

Lesson #4: Many Old Testament prophecies served dual purposes.

Some prophecies address Old Testament events that took place before the arrival of Jesus. Other prophecies referred to the life and ministry of Jesus and were fulfilled during a 33-year span early in the first century. Other prophecies seem to apply to a time yet in the future, frequently referred to as "the day of the Lord."

It's not always easy to differentiate between these prophecies as we read through the Old Testament—especially if it's all rather new to us. In many cases, a prophecy is true both for a soon-to-occur event and also for a more distant one. For example, the "ruler who would come out of Jacob" mentioned in the previous prophecy was fulfilled in large part when David rose to power under God's plan, took the throne, and defeated all of Israel's enemies. Yet in a more permanent sense, Jesus was the ruler out of Jacob who did away with the power of sin. When interpreting Old Testament prophecy, it's frequently difficult to determine whether the message was primarily short-term, more long-range and messianic, or both.

Lesson #5: Sometimes Scripture connects prophecies with their fulfillment.

As we move to the New Testament, we're going to look for places that tell us certain prophecies have been fulfilled. Sometimes such facts are clearly stated, and it's not too hard to make the connection. Here's one example:

"This is what the Lord says: 'A cry of anguish is heard in Ramah—mourning and weeping unrestrained. Rachel weeps

OPINION POLL

"It ain't those parts of the Bible that I can't understand that bother me, it is the parts that I do understand."—*Mark Twain*

for her children, refusing to be comforted—for her children are dead'" (Jeremiah 31:15).

Sounds a bit obscure, doesn't it? Nothing is said, or even hinted, about Jesus. You might come across this verse while reading through Jeremiah, stop long enough to scratch your head in confusion, and move quickly ahead. But now let's take a look at a New Testament passage:

> "Herod was furious when he learned that the wise men had outwitted him. He sent soldiers to kill all the boys in and around Bethlehem who were two years old and under, because the wise men had told him the star first appeared to them about two years earlier. Herod's brutal action fulfilled the prophecy of Jeremiah: 'A cry of anguish is heard in Ramah—weeping and mourning unrestrained. Rachel weeps for her children, refusing to be comforted—for they are dead'" (Matthew 2:16-18).

Thanks to the New Testament, we have a clear understanding of what Jeremiah had predicted.

These insights are rather common in the New Testament. Many will be highlighted from now on in our ongoing sidebar called "Something Old, Something New."

Anticipation: Best If Used before 4 B.C.

In the next chapter we will turn to the New Testament and begin to get a clearer look at Jesus. We'll see if these prophecies turn out to be accurate, and we'll make a close examination to see what else we can find out about Him.

But we haven't given up on the Old Testament. In addition to the prophecies about Jesus, the Old Testament is filled with symbolic events and perhaps even personal appearances that are very significant. It's a bit premature to introduce them at this point, but we don't want to overlook them. We'll get back to several more of them in Chapter 16.

At this point, just keep in mind that the significant amount of prophetic material in the Old Testament *should* have prepared the people for the coming of Jesus. Perhaps you're too young to remember, but at one time in our society, two words could shift an entire household into an immediate frenzy of cleaning and anticipation: "Company's coming." In those two words, the kids knew they were supposed to clean their rooms and their faces, put on some decent clothes, and then report to the living room to see what else needed to be done. Meanwhile, the adults would be tidying up, making meal preparations, and so forth.

In one sense, the Old Testament served as a message to the Jewish people that "Company's coming." They were to be prepared, vigilant, and on their best behavior. But after a few centuries of waiting, during which they faced some incredible national turbulence, their anticipation eventually deteriorated into apathy. Besides, when their guest showed up around 4 B.C. (according to the best estimates of the experts), He didn't exactly fulfill all their expectations.

So, beginning in the next chapter, we'll start looking at various aspects of the life of Jesus. But first, be sure to stop for a moment to anticipate what *you* might discover.

OPINION POLL

"Read the prophetic books without seeing Christ in them, and how flat and insipid they are! See Christ there, and what you read is fragrant."
—*John Chrysostom*

Questions to Ponder and/or Discuss

1. In what ways, if at all, is your faith affected by knowing that so much about the life of Jesus had been prophesied centuries before?

2. What is your opinion about biblical prophecy?

- It's too confusing to fool with.
- It's kinda cool. Wish I knew more.
- I enjoy the challenge of figuring out as much as I can.
- Other: _____

3. On a scale of 1 (least) to 10 (most), what would you say is your current level of anticipation in regard to spiritual things?

CHAPTER THREE

"I SAID *DON'T* PULL THE RED TAB!"

A Gift Sent Special Delivery

J E S U S   T H E   B A B Y

What would life be like without Christmas? Although many people in our society have stripped away most vestiges of its religious significance, the holiday continues to be one of the brightest spots in the year. And even people who don't choose to acknowledge Jesus during the Christmas season find themselves thinking about noble qualities: peace, joy, love, giving, and so forth. For those of us in Chicago and other frigid places, Christmas is an inner warm spell to relieve the outer cold. Yet if the original Source of Christmas is given a prominent place in the celebration, the significance of Christmas becomes even more thrilling.

The Very First Noel

But if you think Christmas is a special occasion now, you should have seen the first one! God had been planning that celebration for centuries—from the moment Adam and Eve sinned in the Garden of Eden.

The human race was facing a problem only God could solve. Even those who considered themselves God's people had by and

SOME THINGS YOU'LL DISCOVER IN THIS CHAPTER

1. What the world's first "Christmas party" was like

2. The dilemma Joseph faced regarding his fiancée, Mary

3. Insights into the various groups of people that first saw Jesus

large rejected Him in the past, but God never stopped loving them. After all, they were being born into a world steeped in sin. The spiritual forces who resisted God were active and vigilant in creating numerous and powerful temptations among God's people, attempting with all the power of hell to turn them away from the truth.

The current crew of professing believers in God no longer had judges, kings, or prophets to lead them. They were under the thumb of the Roman Empire yet were reasonably free to practice their religion. The religious leaders motivated them to remain faithful in their annual sacrifices and celebrations, but most of them missed the point that God was more interested in personal, heartfelt relationships than empty ceremonies.

So God did what no other being was capable of doing. He sent His Son to become the final, perfect, ultimate sacrifice to deal with the sin that permeated humanity. The problem would be dealt with once and for all.

God could have parted the clouds, made a brief statement from heaven, and gotten the nasty business over with in a matter of seconds. He could have seen that His beloved Son was placed in the finest palaces and kept in utmost comfort until the time was right. He could even have changed His mind and decided that we rebellious human beings didn't deserve such a sacrificial action on His part. That was the choice of God the Father.

Now shift your perspective from that of God the Father to God the Son. One moment Jesus was in the splendor of heaven with His Father, but by an act of will, the next moment He found Himself growing up on earth instead.

And it didn't take long to discover that Jesus was no ordinary earthling. He had a great amount of power at His disposal. Think of the thrill of being able to bail yourself out of any jam or to wreak havoc on any or all of your enemies. If He chose, Jesus would never have to suffer or do without until the time came for His final sacrifice. While earth is certainly no picnic compared to heaven, Jesus could have created a pretty good vacation package here, ensuring His continual peace and comfort.

Yet according to the Bible, God the Son didn't demand special treatment during His time on earth as a human being. If anything, it was just the opposite. God the Father chose an extremely poor couple to bring up His Son. Without even the privacy of a hotel room, Jesus was born in a stable and placed in a feeding trough, not a padded crib. He came not as a power-obsessed conqueror, but as a helpless baby. He chose to experience everything other poor human beings face during infancy, puberty, adolescence, and adulthood. Though He had access to God's incredible power, He used it only for the good of others.

OPINION POLL

"He was made what we are, that He might make us what He is Himself."
—*Irenaeus*

By Invitation Only

The birth of Jesus is remembered as the world's first Christmas celebration. When most people plan a big Christmas party, they put a lot of thought into the guest list. They try to achieve a certain level of commonality, hoping their guests will get along with each other and feel comfortable. (For example, we might not want people from work to meet Uncle Bob.) But the "invitation list" for the world's first Christmas party was a peculiar one indeed. Let's take a look at who was there.

Mary (Luke 1:26-38)

The young woman chosen by God to be the mother of Jesus seemed to have an inordinate amount of faith and courage. When approached by the angel Gabriel and told what was about to happen, she at first was "confused and disturbed" (Luke 1:29). Besides, she was already engaged, so her future was somewhat secure. She was certainly perplexed as to how pregnancy could occur since she was a virgin. But by the end of the conversation, she said, "I am the Lord's servant, and I am willing to accept whatever he wants. May everything you have said come true" (Luke 1:38).

Joseph (Matthew 1:18-25)

While Mary was called to perform an incredible act of service for God, Joseph was called to stand by and do nothing. Did Mary not tell Joseph about her angelic visit and the news Gabriel had

IN JESUS' NAME
"SON OF THE MOST HIGH"
(Luke 1:32)
"THE SON OF GOD"
(Luke 1:35)

Even though Jesus was only months away from becoming a human being, these angel-designated names reflected His divine stature.

SOMETHING OLD,
SOMETHING NEW

Isaiah 7:14 . . . Matthew 1:22

As if most husbands-to-be aren't stressed out enough, poor Joseph heard that his *virgin* fiancée was going to have a baby whose father was God Himself. Not only would Joseph soon be a husband, but he would also immediately become a father. Or would that be a stepfather? or godfather? . . . The facts of what he was being told must have certainly taken a while to sink in. So the angel reminded him of an old prophecy: "Look! The virgin will conceive a child! She will give birth to a son, and he will be called Immanuel."

delivered? Or did Joseph not believe her? Either way, Joseph soon found himself with a pregnant fiancée.

Today an unmarried, pregnant teenager is regarded as just another "statistic," but in this first-century Jewish culture, Mary's pregnancy would have been humiliating and scandalous. Joseph would certainly be assumed to be the father, yet he would have little of the joy that should have been associated with having a firstborn son—a major event in this society. To his credit, Joseph was planning to give Mary a quiet divorce rather than make a scene. But he too had an angel encounter. The angel explained what God was doing, and Joseph agreed to the plan. Joseph and Mary were married before Jesus was born, but Scripture makes it clear that the two had no sexual relations until after the birth of Jesus (Matthew 1:24-25).

The Shepherds (Luke 2:8-20)

You might remember that Joseph and Mary were from Nazareth but had traveled to Bethlehem to comply with a Roman census (Luke 2:1). Away from friends and immediate family, they probably had no one to celebrate Jesus' birth with them, although the news of her premature pregnancy might have made them unwelcome guests anyway. But this event was too great to go unheralded. A group of shepherds were doing their usual job outside the city. One moment they were trying to keep from stepping in sheep by-products in the dark, and the next a brilliant angel was in their midst. Then, before they knew it, the skies were filled with angels. Upon hearing the news of the birth of a Savior, the shepherds rushed to see Him. And as they returned to their flocks, they were quick to spread the word about what they had witnessed.

The Wise Men (Matthew 2:1-12)

Meanwhile, a group of Eastern astrologers were winding their way toward Bethlehem. Somehow they had figured out that a particular star over Bethlehem would lead them to "the newborn king of the Jews" (Matthew 2:2). When they arrived in Bethlehem, they stopped to pay their respects to the local authority, King Herod, but the possibility of a new king was not something the *current* king was eager to hear.

Herod summoned a group of religious leaders, who told him the Messiah was to be born in Bethlehem (about five miles away). Herod feigned excitement. He was hoping to use the wise men (also called Magi) as his henchmen to return and tell him the exact location of his new competition so he could send someone to have the child killed. But God warned the wise men in a dream of Herod's plot, and they went home by a different route. While visiting Jesus, the Magi gave Him gifts: gold, incense, and myrrh.

The Bible doesn't say how many wise men traveled to see Jesus. It doesn't say they were kings. They aren't named. And they almost certainly weren't standing around the manger with the shepherds, as we like to pose them on our lawns at Christmas. By the time they got to Bethlehem, Jesus was in a "house" (Matthew 2:11). Based on Herod's edict to kill all male children, Jesus might have been as old as two years when the wise men first saw him.

The Angels (Luke 2:8-14)

While there may not have been a lot of human beings present to celebrate the birth of Jesus, "the armies of heaven" had come to earth to proclaim the event. One major role of angels is to deliver messages from God. Usually one is all it takes, but in this case "a vast host" of them showed up.

Anna and Simeon (Luke 2:21-38)

We don't hear as much about these two people as we do the others at Christmas, but they shouldn't be overlooked as we consider the birth of Jesus. Simeon was a faithful and godly man who had been promised he would not die until he had seen "the Lord's Messiah." When Jesus arrived, Simeon prophesied about what would happen to Him, and he blessed Jesus' parents. Anna was 84 years old—a long-time widow who never left the temple as she "stayed there day and night, worshiping God with fasting and prayer." She too was given insight into the significance of the young child.

IN JESUS' NAME
"JESUS" (Matthew 1:21)
"IMMANUEL" (Matthew 1:23)

The names for the Messiah were both very relevant. "Jesus" was the Greek form of the Hebrew "Joshua," which means *savior.* "Immanuel" means "God with us." While God's continual presence is assured throughout the Old Testament, this would be the first time since Eden that He would make Himself available to be seen and touched.

SOMETHING OLD,
SOMETHING NEW
Micah 5:2 ... Matthew 2:3-6

When Herod wanted to know where the Messiah was going to be born, he had the religious authorities consult the Old Testament prophecies. And sure enough, the wise men went to Bethlehem and confirmed what Micah had written centuries before.

Everybody in!

So there you have it, the invitation list for the first Christmas celebration. What an odd mix! Mary, who had her first child before she had ever slept with a man; Joseph, who had to feel like the "odd man out" while helping his new wife through this incredibly difficult time; the shepherds, smelling of manure (and possibly booze), who wouldn't have seemed out of place around a manger; the angels, who had come the longest distance to be present; the wise men, who had used knowledge and signs to find their way; and Anna and Simeon, whose regular, daily faithfulness to God paid off in an enormous blessing.

These people represented rich and poor, wise and ignorant, Jew and Gentile, devout believers and new seekers. Most of them had sacrificed something to be there (reputation, time, jobs, etc.). Yet their commitment confirmed that Jesus was (and would be) someone worth checking out.

In gym at school, when kids play dodgeball or some other elimination sport, perhaps no cry is as welcome as "Everybody in!" Even though you might have been "out" and doomed to sit idly and watch, the "Everybody in!" command gives you a new chance. This was the message of the first Christmas: Everybody is in.

The Jewish religious leaders had gotten proficient at placing people outside, making them feel not quite good enough to approach God. But from the first moments of Jesus' life, we see an inclusion of everyone willing to come—and even a connection between the spiritual forces of heaven and the human beings on earth.

And in an ironic twist, we also need to take note of who *wasn't* there at the manger. Did you notice as you read the previous accounts? Some of the top religious leaders of the country, those chosen by King Herod to advise him, had actually looked up the prophecy and had heard from the wise men that it was coming true. Of everyone on earth, those should have been the guys with the greatest sense of anticipation for the birth of a Messiah. Why didn't they tag along with their Eastern visitors? Was it too much trouble to go five miles if there was a chance they would find the Savior

who had been prophesied for centuries? Was their time too valuable? Was it mere laziness? And more importantly, do we find ourselves relating more with these guys than with the others who eventually found their way to the Christ child?

Why in the World?

For some reason, God chose to have His Son come to earth as a poor, seemingly insignificant baby. The tiny child was His most special gift. Yet only Mary and perhaps a few others realized what a special delivery this was. Most of the world had no idea what was going on. Why didn't God do more to make the birth of Jesus a major, worldwide, newsworthy event?

In His infinite wisdom, perhaps God knew that He could do even more than have Jesus die for our sins. Jesus could also show us what God was like. As we see how Jesus acted and related to others, we can get surprising insight into the nature of God.

In addition, Jesus would serve as a model of how to live. While His actions revealed God's character to us, they also showed us how much fuller and more complete our lives can be if we more faithfully devote ourselves to God the Father. This role of Jesus as a model of servanthood is covered in the next chapter.

Questions to Ponder and/or Discuss

1. To what extent is Christmas a spiritual time for you? Do any past Christmas celebrations stand out as extra-special to you? Why?

2. Which of the characters involved at the birth of Jesus do you most relate to? Why?

- Shepherds
- Mary
- Anna
- Wise men
- Joseph

OPINION POLL

"The characteristics of God Almighty are mirrored for us in Jesus Christ. Therefore, if we want to know what God is like we must study Jesus Christ."
—*Oswald Chambers*

- Simeon
- Angels
- Herod/Advisers
- The rest of the world (who didn't have a clue what was going on!)

3. Where would you say you are right now in the "game" of life?

- Still in it and loving every minute.
- I *was* in, but I think I've been knocked out.
- I'm on the sidelines, eager to hear the "Everybody in" signal.
- You mean there's a game going on somewhere?
- Other: _____

CHAPTER FOUR

At Your Service

JESUS THE SERVANT

"What do you want to be when you grow up?"

It's a question that adults are fond of asking small children. And good parents usually encourage their kids to think big—astronauts, musicians, cowboys, presidents, professional quarterbacks, ballerinas, explorers, inventors, and so forth. It's normal for a child to go through several stages before getting to college and choosing a major.

The answers you don't expect to hear to the question might include waiters, maids, cage cleaners at the zoo, sewer workers, roofers, etc. Some jobs don't have the same glory (or paycheck) as others, although they may be just as important. We yearn for the high-profile, rewarding careers without a lot of toil and sweat. If we are forced to take other courses in life, we usually feel we are forced to "settle."

Yet without people willing to work in the service professions, our world would cease to function as smoothly as it does now. What if we had no one to call when our sump pumps fail, our toilets need snaking, the air conditioning goes out in the middle of a summer

SOME THINGS YOU'LL DISCOVER IN THIS CHAPTER

1. Jesus and John the Baptist were similar in some ways.

2. The disciples of Jesus had different purposes and roles.

3. Jesus became the model of servanthood for His disciples.

31

heat wave, the car's transmission falls out while on vacation, or skunk colonies decide to build condominiums beneath the house? How would you like to personally handle every problem that comes along? Only occasionally do we recognize the great value of people in service professions—but at those times their worth seems priceless.

As Joseph and Mary looked at the tiny baby they had placed in the manger, they no doubt had big hopes and dreams for their child—probably bigger than most, based on what the angels had told them. But as Jesus grew and began to pursue His own path in life, it soon became clear that He had chosen to be a servant.

Cousin John

Very little is said of Jesus' childhood or adolescence. It is assumed that He led a very normal life, probably taking up carpentry as a trade because that's how Joseph earned a living. Perhaps He also spent this time discovering who He was and determining God's will for His earthly life. Since Jesus came to earth as a baby, it is unlikely He was born with all knowledge. He probably had to study and learn as all youngsters do. But somewhere along the way, in God's perfect timing, the Father made all things known to Him (John 5:19-20).

When Jesus was about 30, He began His public ministry (Luke 3:23). But He didn't have to start from scratch. John the Baptist was already hard at work, living in the desert and telling people to repent of their sins because "the Kingdom of Heaven is near" (Matthew 3:1-2). As people confessed their sins, John would baptize them in the Jordan River. But he spoke boldly of someone to follow him who would baptize not with water, but "with the Holy Spirit and with fire" (Matthew 3:11).

Jesus and John were related through their mothers (Luke 1:36), and had had a bond since before their births. When the pregnant Mary visited the pregnant Elizabeth, the unborn baby who would become John the Baptist "jumped for joy" in Elizabeth's womb in recognition of the not-yet-born Christ (Luke 1:39-45).

But more than their blood relationship, Jesus and John were alike in other ways. Both lived simple lives. Both taught people about God's kingdom. Both had some clashes with the established religious leaders. Some of Jesus' original disciples had first been disciples of John the Baptist (John 1:35-42). Eventually John stood before a high-ranking Roman official and accused him of sexual impropriety, for which he was jailed and eventually beheaded (Matthew 14:1-12). Jesus would stand before Pilate and Herod just prior to being crucified.

Jesus' respect for John was clear. At one point Jesus told a crowd of people: "I tell you, of all who have ever lived, none is greater than John. Yet even the most insignificant person in the Kingdom of God is greater than he is!" (Luke 7:28) John the Baptist, like Jesus, consciously chose to be a servant of God.

So as Jesus began His public ministry, He went down to the Jordan River to be baptized by John. At this point, John was one of the only people who knew Jesus' "secret identity," and he was reluctant to baptize Him. But at Jesus' insistence, John consented.

Prior to the baptism, John had identified Jesus as "the Lamb of God who takes away the sin of the world" (John 1:29). And right after Jesus was baptized, other signs verified that He was indeed someone special. The Holy Spirit came down from heaven "like a dove" and rested on Him. In addition, a voice from heaven said, "This is my beloved Son, and I am fully pleased with him" (Matthew 3:16-17). Some people point out that this is one of the Bible's clearest examples of the Trinity: Jesus is beginning His ministry, the Holy Spirit is present for the event, and God the Father speaks from heaven.

W.D.J.D.?

Why did Jesus get baptized? We are told that people were baptized by John after confessing their sins (Matthew 3:6). Jesus had no sins to confess. What was His need for baptism? Perhaps as much as anything, He was baptized to identify with the people to whom He had come to minister. A good servant does things not required of him, and this action is only one of many that Jesus did for our benefit rather than His own. In addition, the ceremony seemed to serve as a spotlight for Jesus' step into public ministry. And it provided an ideal opportunity for God the Father to publicly endorse His Son.

Obedience Is a Full-Time Job; Don't Accept a Tempt (Matthew 4:1-11)

With the affirmations by John and His heavenly Father, perhaps Jesus' baptism was a high point in His life. But not long afterward, Jesus went into the desert to be tempted by the devil. It seems that Satan waited 40 days until Jesus was good and hungry before making the first offer. And as he had done with Adam and Eve, the devil began by attempting to plant a seed of doubt: "If you are the Son of

W.D.J.D.?

Like any of us, Jesus was beset by numerous strong temptations during a moment of physical weakness. What did He do? In each instance, He quoted an appropriate Scripture from the Old Testament (Deuteronomy 8:3; 6:16; 6:13) that reminded Him to remain faithful.

God, change these stones into loaves of bread." ("If" is a big two-letter word when it comes to daring someone to do something.) But Jesus refused to comply. He was intentionally fasting, the purpose of which is to get closer to God on a spiritual level by denying one's physical desires for a period of time. He was focusing on God's will rather than His own during this time.

Next the devil tried to get Jesus to throw himself from the highest point of the temple and depend on God's angels to miraculously deliver him from harm. Perhaps the intent was for a lot of people to see that Jesus was indestructible and attract a crowd. But Jesus realized that He was here to be a servant, not a circus attraction. He would certainly draw crowds of people to Himself as He began to display the power of God on *their* behalf. But He wasn't going to try to *manipulate* people into following Him as if He were a rock star or pro wrestler. Just because Satan was daring Jesus to do foolish things didn't mean Jesus was about to dare His Father to act on His behalf. Jesus made His point clearly: "Do not test the Lord your God."

Finally, the devil held out the promise of power and splendor, but Jesus again refused. He would, of course, have those things in the end. But Jesus' path would take Him to the Cross so that all human beings could share in His kingdom. How many of us would have done the same if offered the option of a selfish shortcut that eliminated all the pain?

Apparently, even the devil will quote the Bible if it serves his purposes. (Compare Matthew 4:6 with Psalm 91:11-12.) Jesus demonstrates how important it is to know more than just a few scattered verses. Otherwise, we will always be vulnerable to those who attempt to twist Scripture for their own benefit. The more familiar we become with the Bible, the more certainty we have that God is there to help us withstand any problem or temptation.

Twelve of One Group, Six Dozen of Another
(Matthew 10; Luke 9:1-9; 10:1-24)

Jesus' devotion to seeking God's will would be crucial to His success as a servant. When the time came to select His disciples, He spent the

night praying before selecting the 12 men who would be closer to Him than anyone else (Luke 6:12-16). And of all the people who might have desired to follow Him in support of His ministry, He selected 12 to be his closest disciples. These would be the ones with whom He would spend the most time. They heard everything He taught. They witnessed the miracles and healings. They traveled with Him down dusty roads and in storm-tossed ships. They learned first-hand what it was like to be a servant under all conditions.

OPINION POLL

"Christ's deeds and examples are commandments of what we should do." —*John Wycliffe*

To be honest, the disciples weren't very good at it at first. They didn't "get it" when Jesus started telling parables. They sometimes opposed Him on key issues. They displayed an embarrassing lack of faith at times. They even argued over which of them was the greatest. But after three years of training, this was the group of people who carried on in Jesus' place during a difficult transition.

A couple of times we are told of Jesus sending out teams of disciples to get some practice at being good servants. At least once He sent out the Twelve. Before He did He "gave them authority to cast out evil spirits and to heal every kind of disease and illness" (Matthew 10:1). He told them to focus on the Jewish people, which is where they would have been most comfortable. He told them not to take much money; instead, he told them to find good people who would take care of their housing and food needs while on the road.

The disciples were to be servants but not doormats. If they encountered a home or town that refused to welcome or listen to them, they were to "shake off the dust of that place from your feet" and go elsewhere. At this point, with all the people eager to hear the good news of the kingdom of God, Jesus didn't want His disciples butting heads with stubborn opponents or wasting time in meaningless debate. Jesus wanted His servant-disciples to use their heads as well as their hearts. He told them to "be as wary as snakes and harmless as doves."

Jesus didn't want a group of starry-eyed hangers-on. He wanted more than an entourage. He told His followers to be on guard against those who would have them arrested and beaten. He told them to expect to be hated because of their association with Him.

W.D.J.D.?

When Jesus had a big decision to make, what did He do? We know that prior to choosing His disciples, He prayed all night long. Even though He was an extremely busy person, He would frequently seek out a solitary place to spend time talking to His Father—even if he needed to get up "long before daybreak" to do so (Mark 1:35).

OPINION POLL

"It is high time that the ideal of success should be replaced by the ideal of service."—*Albert Einstein*

Yet he also encouraged them not to be afraid. Although Jesus came with a message of hope and comfort for all people, He realized that as people had different responses to this message, homes would be divided. But everyone who put Him first would be rewarded, as would anyone who even offered a cup of cold water to those doing Jesus' business.

Later Jesus sent out 72 of His followers with similar instructions and warnings. He realized they would be "lambs among wolves," but He also empowered them to survive among the hostility they might encounter. When the 72 returned, it was with a sense of joy and wonder. They reported, "Lord, even the demons obey us when we use your name!"

Holding Serve

From beginning to end, Jesus modeled servanthood with His life. Even his birth was orchestrated to place Him in a humble setting where service was both learned and practiced. His baptism demonstrated that He was at the service of His Father. His temptations were met head-on, in a way that creates hope and determination for any who choose to use the same methods to avoid sin. And the people He chose as followers were quickly given opportunities to go into their surrounding communities and begin to serve others.

Lots of religious leaders were *talking* about service to God. But Jesus was essentially the only one who was able to suggest, "Do as I say *and* as I do." He modeled everything He taught.

In the following chapter we'll see how the theme of servanthood infused Jesus' teachings, miracles, and entire life. He was even willing to stoop and wash His disciples' feet, and then in a final act of service, to give His life for others. (More on these acts of service later.)

For anyone who desires to be a servant even today, His lessons and His model still stand.

Questions to Ponder and/or Discuss

1. Consider the following roles:

(D)   Dictator with unquestioned authority

(M)   Monarch who receives input from others but retains
      final say

(T)   Team player

(R)   Reluctant servant

(W)   Willing servant

(O)   Other: _____

For each of the following relational categories, determine
which of the above roles comes most naturally to you. Indicate
your choice by placing an X beneath the appropriate letter.
(Skip the ones that don't apply to you.) Also indicate any
changes you would like to make by placing a check mark
beneath the role you *wish* to have in each category.

D   M   T   R   W   O

Work Relationships

School Relationships

Relationship with Parents

Relationship with Children

Church/Spiritual Relationships

Friendships

2. What is your usual attitude toward people in the service
professions (waiters/waitresses, flight attendants, repair people,
etc.)? Do you tend to encourage them and make their jobs more
enjoyable, or do you tend to look down on them?

3. On a scale of 1(least) to 10 (most), how good are you at
knowing Scripture and applying it to specific situations you
face?

CHAPTER FIVE

"YES, MRS. EDWARDS, YOUR SON WAS WEARING
CLEAN UNDERWEAR WHEN THEY BROUGHT HIM IN."

See Me, Feel Me, Touch Me, Heal Me

JESUS THE HEALER

Perhaps you can recall certain times during your school days when it seemed all your teachers had gotten together to see just how much work they could dump on you simultaneously. Or maybe in a work setting you have found yourself reporting to more than one person (or client), and you simply don't have enough hours in the week to make everyone happy.

In the last chapter we looked at the service mindset of Jesus. Life as a servant isn't too bad if the master is a good one who doesn't overwork the servant. But when a servant has more than one master, life can get very complicated. Certainly, Jesus came to serve His heavenly Father. But He was also a servant to people, which left Him with thousands who were determined to benefit from His service.

As soon as people found out Jesus had unusual power, they flocked to Him in droves. Hurting people sought Him out for healing. His disciples were trying to figure out what was going on and pressed Him for more details about the things He was teaching. The religious authorities regularly engaged Jesus in debate and interrogation, hoping to trick Him into saying or doing something for

SOME THINGS YOU'LL DISCOVER IN THIS CHAPTER

1. Jesus performed many types of healings among people of different backgrounds.

2. Evil spirits were also cast out of people, demonstrating that Jesus had power over the devil.

3. Death itself was overcome in the raising of Lazarus.

which they could arrest (and preferably kill) Him. And others seemed to follow Him simply hoping to see a good show.

Jesus the servant took it all in stride. Throughout it all He maintained a private spiritual life, a social life with regular visits to close friends, a family life with appropriate care for His mother, and a seemingly endless ministry. In this chapter we want to take a closer look at some of the things He was doing that attracted so much attention.

And the foremost attention-getting thing that Jesus did was to heal people who were sick. These days people debate the reality of miracles, but the Bible states them as fact and never suggests a reason to doubt the events. As God saw fit, He would provide power to be used on His behalf by certain people. In the Old Testament, Moses had parted the Red Sea and summoned water for about a million people by striking a rock. Elijah and Elisha were prophets who performed numerous miracles, including calling down fire from heaven and raising people from the dead.

Numerous other people performed great miracles for God. But no one represented God like Jesus did. God's power flowed through Him to person after person who was hurting—many who had suffered for years or even decades. It was clear that He was no con man or illusionist. As we will see, no malady was too difficult for Him to heal.

Touch and Go

In numerous accounts of Jesus' healing miracles, it is recorded that He physically touched the person who was hurting. In our society, caring people have to think twice about touching people in vulnerable states of mind. Certainly, touch is misused by many people, creating suspicion and fear rather than comfort for the victim. And in our litigious culture, many of us choose a complete "hands-off" policy rather than risk a lawsuit.

But Jesus embraced little children with no fear of abuse charges. In fact, He was their biggest supporter. He reached out to hurting women and men alike, and He allowed people to approach and touch Him (John 12:1-3). Sometimes a hug is the best medicine for what's hurting a person, and Jesus could minister with touch without doing anything in the least disconcerting or inappropriate.

A Man with Leprosy (Mark 1:40-45)

One time a leper came to Jesus, begging on his knees for healing. Put yourself in the place of this poor guy. Lepers were kept separate from "proper" society. Not only was theirs a physical illness, but the disease created social and spiritual isolation as well. (Leprosy prevented the "ritual cleanness" required for worship.) Unable to make a living, many lepers were required to beg. And when they chanced to come near other people, they were supposed to announce their uncleanness.

Yet when Jesus saw this man, He was "moved with pity." Not only did He give the command to "Be healed!" but He also reached right out and touched the guy. Immediately the man was cured of his leprosy.

This was early in Jesus' ministry, and He asked the man not to tell anyone other than the priest (who would have needed to verify the cure and proclaim the man "clean" again). But the healed leper just couldn't help it. Instead, "he spread the news, telling everyone what had happened to him." This would be a recurring pattern in Jesus' early ministry. Newly healed people simply couldn't keep quiet about what He had done for them. As a result, Jesus could hardly enter a city without being mobbed, and He "had to stay out in the secluded places." Still, people sought Him out wherever He was.

Two Blind Men (Matthew 9:27-31)

A couple of blind men began to follow Jesus and beg Him to have mercy on them. Jesus took them indoors, though Scripture doesn't say why. (For more privacy to attend to their needs? So He could try to keep a low profile? So their eyes could adjust more gradually after He healed them?)

Jesus touched their eyes as He praised their faith. After their sight was restored, He "sternly warned them" not to tell anyone. But they went through their entire community, blabbing to everyone about what had been done for them.

SOMETHING OLD,
SOMETHING NEW
**Leviticus 13:1-46; 14:1-32 …
Mark 1:40-45**

If you don't think people in this culture took leprosy seriously, go back and read all the Old Testament detail involved in identifying and treating skin diseases. When you see what diseased people had to endure back then, you might not be quite so critical about your HMO.

OPINION POLL

"Miracles are God's *coup d'état.*"
—Anne-Sophie Swetchine

SOMETHING OLD,
SOMETHING NEW
Leviticus 15:19-33 . . . Mark 5:25-34

It should come as no surprise that if infectious skin diseases (such as leprosy) would render someone "unclean," then bleeding was just as bad or worse. Menstruating women, and anyone who touched them, had the same ceremonial limitations as lepers.

A Woman with a Bleeding Problem (Mark 5:25-34; Luke 8:43-48)

At least one time, Jesus healed someone who touched *Him.* He was on His way to see a dying 12-year-old girl at her father's request, and as usual, He was beset by crowds of people pushing toward Him. In that crowd was a woman who had suffered from a hemorrhage for 12 years—perhaps an ongoing menstrual or uterine problem. She had been to numerous doctors and had spent all her money attempting to cure the problem.

But when Jesus came by, she got close enough to reach out in faith and touch the hem of His clothing, assuming the crowd would provide her with anonymity. She was instantly healed and probably hoped to slip away undetected. But Jesus sensed a transferal of His power and asked who had touched Him. His disciples thought it was a foolish question given the conditions, but the woman came forward and confessed what she had done. Jesus affectionately addressed her as "Daughter" and confirmed that it was her faith that had freed her (perhaps just in case anyone thought His clothes had magic powers).

In these and other stories in the Gospels, miraculous healing was prompted by touch. But lest we suspect that Jesus used sleight of hand or misdirection to convince naive people that He had power He didn't actually possess, consider the variety of conditions he cured. He healed leprosy, fever (Matthew 8:14-15), bleeding, blindness, deafness (Mark 7:31-37), swollen limbs (Luke 14:1-6), and even a severed ear (Luke 22:47-51)! In addition, He did most of these things before a large aggregation of witnesses. Had He been a con man, surely someone would have noticed. Instead, His "patients" were so enthralled that they went out telling everyone what had happened—even after Jesus had urged them not to.

You Have My Word

Even though Jesus had a nice "touch" when it came to helping hurting people, the Bible also makes it clear that physical contact wasn't necessary when it came to healing. Let's look at a few examples.

A Royal Official and His Son (John 4:46-54)

As soon as Jesus started healing people, word spread rapidly about His power. One early request for healing came from a royal official whose son was near death. He tracked Jesus down and begged Him to come to his house. But instead of going with the man, Jesus said, "Go back home. Your son will live!"

As the official was on his way back, his servants met him and told him his son was well. The boy's fever had broken at exactly the time Jesus had spoken. As a result, the man and his household believed in Jesus.

The Centurion and His Servant (Luke 7:1-10)

A similar event took place with a Roman centurion. Centurions were officers in charge of 100 Roman soldiers. In this passage, a centurion showed great compassion for one of his slaves who was so sick he was about to die. The centurion sent Jewish elders asking Jesus to come and heal the servant. The Jews attested to the centurion's concern for them and their people, a striking statement since there was no love lost for Romans in general. Jesus started for the man's house but was met along the way by messengers of the centurion.

The centurion, of course, was familiar with authority and the issuing of commands. He had suggested that Jesus save a trip and merely "say the word from where you are" to heal the servant. Jesus was astounded at the faith of this Roman soldier—greater than anything He had witnessed among His own people. By the time the centurion's messengers got back, the servant was well.

A Paralyzed Man and His Friends (Mark 2:1-12)

In another story, someone's desire to see Jesus went through the roof (literally). Jesus was speaking in a house, and the place was so packed that no one could even get near the entrance. A group of men had brought a friend of theirs who was paralyzed. Since they couldn't go through the door, they hoisted their friend onto the roof, dug through the ceiling, and lowered his mat down to where Jesus was.

Jesus was touched by the faith of these men. He naturally had the

W.D.J.D.?

Encounters with religious leaders were to become a recurring struggle for Jesus. He realized He was saying and doing things they didn't necessarily approve of, but rather than avoiding them or attempting to work behind their backs, He did what He wanted and needed to do. After all, Jesus' message and ministry were to any of them who might choose to believe as well. How many of us would have been as bold, knowing of the conflicts and consequences that would surely result?

OPINION POLL

"I should not be a Christian but for the miracles."—*Augustine of Hippo*

attention of the crowd at this point, so He said to the man, "My son, your sins are forgiven." The religious leaders in the group naturally thought it was pretentious (and downright blasphemous) of Jesus to presume to forgive sins. Jesus knew their thoughts and asked them which was easier: (1) to tell the guy his sins were forgiven, or (2) to tell the man to get up and walk. Obviously, anyone there could have spoken the words to tell the man he was forgiven. After all, what external proof was there?

But Jesus wasn't finished. He went ahead and told the man, "Stand up, take your mat, and go on home, because you are healed." The man stood, took his mat, and walked out through the crowd.

As we see from these examples, a word from Jesus was all it took to effect healing—both physical and spiritual. When people supplied the faith, Jesus was liberal in using the power of God on their behalf.

Acting in Faith

So far, the healings we have seen have required little from the participants other than belief in Jesus and the faith that He could do something to help. But at other times, Jesus asked for a particular response from the people He was helping. Their actions of faith only served to accentuate the miracles that were taking place.

Ten Lepers (Luke 17:11-19)

While traveling one day, Jesus was entering a village when 10 men called out, "Jesus, Master, have mercy on us!" The men were lepers and wanted His help. But this time, instead of touching and healing them, Jesus told them to "Go show yourselves to the priests." As they did, their leprosy miraculously disappeared. One of the men stopped when he saw what had happened. He came back, threw himself at Jesus' feet, and thanked Him. Jesus commended the man's faith, but expressed dismay that only one person of the 10 had bothered to say thanks. (The man's example was even more noteworthy because he was a Samaritan—not a full-blooded Jew.)

The Jews who were better versed in the law and more in tune with religious teachings should have set the example but failed to do so.

Blind Bartimaeus (Mark 10:46-52)

Bartimaeus was a blind beggar beside the road when Jesus came along one day. (Perhaps you know this story from the song about him, a traditional spiritual.) He had heard of Jesus, and when he realized who was nearby, Bartimaeus began to shout, "Son of David, have mercy on me!" People tried to get him to shut up, but he would not be silent. Jesus called him forward and asked, "What do you want me to do for you?" It seems like an obvious question, but Bartimaeus quickly replied, "I want to see!"

Jesus said, "Go your way. Your faith has healed you." Immediately Bartimaeus regained his sight and began to follow Jesus down the road.

An Invalid at a Pool (John 5:1-15)

People who experience ongoing pain and distress often reach a level of desperation that drives them to seek help in any form they can find it. One particular pool in Jerusalem during Jesus' time was thought to have healing powers. People apparently believed an angel of God would come from time to time to stir up the water, after which the first person in the pool would be cured of whatever was wrong. Consequently, sick and injured people would gather at this location in large numbers. One man who was camped out at this pool had been an invalid for 38 years. But he had no friends to help him, and being an invalid made it impossible for him to be first into the pool.

Jesus sensed this man's desperation and asked if he wanted to get well. Then He told him, "Stand up, pick up your sleeping mat, and walk!" The man did as he was told and discovered he had been healed. Later Jesus found the man again and added, "Now you are well; so stop sinning, or something even worse may happen to you."

All these people and others acted in faith before healing took place. Whether it was going to the priests or washing in a particular

W.D.J.D.?

Jesus told ten guys to do something, and nine of them did exactly as He instructed. Yet He expressed disappointment with those nine and commended the single leper who, on his own initiative, first insisted on expressing gratitude for being healed. What are we to learn from this story? Perhaps that Jesus desires for us to develop proper (thankful) attitudes toward Him rather than attempting to mechanically heed the letter of the law with little thought about why those rules and regulations exist.

IN JESUS' NAME
"SON OF DAVID" (Mark 10:47)

David was Israel's greatest king. He defeated the nation's enemies, united the 12 tribes, and established a throne in Jerusalem. The title signified that Jesus was a flesh-and-blood descendant of David, and that He, too, would conquer strong enemies and establish peace.

OPINION POLL

"Jesus' cures have nothing to do with magic and sorcery, where the person is overpowered against his will. They are an appeal for faith, which itself sometimes appears to be the real miracle by comparison with which the cure is of secondary importance. The healing stories of the New Testament must be understood as stories of faith."
—*Hans Küng*

IN JESUS' NAME

"THE HOLY ONE SENT FROM GOD" (Luke 4:34)

Although this was early in Jesus' ministry and few people had any inkling that Jesus was "sent from God," He was already being acknowledged by the demonic forces. To be *holy*, in essence, means to be "set apart" from sin. So Jesus was absolutely holy, yet He was sent from God to live among sinful people.

body of water (John 9), these people obeyed Jesus' instructions and benefited as a result. It seems that miracles of God couldn't be taken for granted. Sometimes acts of faith were required as catalysts for God's healing power. In such cases, laws of physics were bent a bit. It seems that when faith is involved, some actions have quite an *unequal* (and miraculous) reaction.

Demon-strative Spirits

In certain cases, Jesus connected spiritual health to physical healing. He was willing and able to cure any physical problem, but He was more concerned about spiritual healing. Physical health was temporary and would come to an eventual end with the death of the person. But spiritual cleansing through a belief in Him would have eternal benefits.

In that respect, a significant part of Jesus' healing ministry was directed toward people who had the worst possible spiritual problems—possession by evil spirits (or "demons," depending on your Bible translation). Most Bible scholars believe demons are fallen angels who chose to follow Lucifer (Satan) in his rebellion against God. While Jesus was on a mission to save humanity from sin and convince people to follow Him to salvation and eternal life in heaven, His enemy was hard at work to enlist recruits as well.

Below are some of Jesus' encounters with people who had been overpowered by evil spirits.

A Man in a Synagogue (Luke 4:31-37)

A synagogue seems like a strange place to find a demon-possessed person, but that's where this man happened to be one day when Jesus was teaching. The spirit inside the man began to heckle Jesus: "Go away! Why are you bothering us, Jesus of Nazareth? Have you come to destroy us? I know who you are—the Holy One sent from God."

Jesus sternly commanded the spirit to be quiet and to come out of the man. As people watched, the evil spirit threw the man to the ground, but did not harm him as it left. The people in attendance were amazed that anyone would have the "authority and power" to give orders even to spirits.

People with Physical Side Effects

Apparently, possession by evil spirits is sometimes accompanied by assorted physical problems. As Jesus eliminated the negative spiritual presence from certain people, their other symptoms disappeared as well. For example, Jesus cast out an evil spirit from a man who couldn't speak, but his speech was fine afterward (Matthew 9:32-33).

OPINION POLL

"We must remember that Satan has his miracles, too."—*John Calvin*

In another instance, a possessed man was both blind and mute. The expulsion of the demon eliminated the physical limitations of the man (Matthew 12:22-23).

And lest we believe that possession was a gender-related problem, a woman was brought to Jesus who was unable to stand straight, having been "crippled by an evil spirit" for 18 years. Jesus placed His hand on her and told her, "Woman, you are healed of your sickness!" Right away she straightened up and began to praise God (Luke 13:10-13).

In many of these cases, the observing Pharisees accused Jesus of being in league with Beelzebub (Satan). This relationship, they said, gave Him power to rid people of evil spirits. But Jesus pointed out that such an accusation didn't make any sense. He told them, "Any kingdom at war with itself is doomed. A city or home divided against itself is doomed. And if Satan is casting out Satan, he is fighting against himself. His own kingdom will not survive. And if I am empowered by the prince of demons, what about your own followers? They cast out demons, too, so they will judge you for what you have said. But if I am casting out demons by the Spirit of God, then the Kingdom of God has arrived among you" (Matthew 12:25-28).

In other words, Jesus obviously had power to drive out evil spirits, but the power was not from Satan. Yet if it was from God, the religious leaders were clearly going to be in hot water if they continued to oppose Him.

A Man Possessed with a "Legion" of Spirits (Luke 8:26-39)

One of the most spectacular exorcisms took place after Jesus and the disciples landed at a region across the Sea of Galilee. Jesus was

IN JESUS' NAME
"SON OF THE MOST HIGH GOD"
(Luke 8:28)

Again, it is noteworthy that the forces of evil expressed this insight into the nature of Jesus before most people did. Although He was a long way from "home," Jesus' true identity was no mystery to Satan's followers.

W.D.J.D.?

Sometimes we are led to believe that Jesus wants His followers to roam all over the world preaching, teaching, and doing difficult things. But here He instructed the man to go home and simply be a reminder of God's goodness. In addition, the man hadn't had a normal life in a long time. Rather than take him away from his home, Jesus thought it better that he stay and get reacquainted with his family and friends. So doing God's will is sometimes fulfilled in the most logical and practical course of action.

met by a demon-possessed man whose life was far from normal. He had not worn clothes for a long time, and he was living among the tombs rather than in a home. He had been chained and guarded, probably for his own protection, but had such strength that he could break the chains. The spirit within him drove him into the wilderness and away from those who might want to help him.

The evil spirit recognized Jesus as "Son of the Most High God." When Jesus asked for demon's name, it replied "Legion," which indicated a great many demons within the man. The demons begged Jesus not to torture them or send them to "the Bottomless Pit." (See Revelation 9:1-11; 20:1-3.) Instead, they begged Jesus to send them into a large herd of pigs feeding nearby.

Jesus did as they requested. But as the demons left the man and entered the pigs, the entire herd rushed down a steep bank into the lake and drowned. The men tending the pigs ran to tell the townspeople what had happened. By the time everyone returned to check it out, the formerly possessed man was clothed and in his right mind, sitting at Jesus' feet. Frankly, the local people were scared silly and asked Jesus to leave. (In addition to the spiritual consequences, He wasn't doing much for their economy.)

The man who had been freed was the exception. He begged to go with Jesus. However, Jesus asked that he remain at home with his friends and family to "tell them all the wonderful things God has done for you."

O Lord, I Feel Like I'm Dying . . .

So Jesus showed that He could heal any sickness and cure any disease. He could remove evil spirits from people—no matter how numerous or how long they had been entrenched within the person. What else could He do to prove He had the power of God? How about a few resurrections?

The Son of the Widow of Nain (Luke 7:11-17)

As Jesus was entering a town called Nain, He came upon a funeral procession. The dead person was the only son of a widow, which would have been especially tragic in this culture. (With little opportunity for women to make a living, this poor woman now had neither husband nor son to care for her.) The Gospel notes that when Jesus saw the woman, "his heart overflowed with compassion."

Although a large crowd of people was present, He told the woman not to cry. Then he touched the coffin and said, "Young man, get up!" The man sat right up and began to talk. Not surprisingly, those present determined that Jesus was a great prophet sent by God to help His people. News about Him spread throughout the land.

Jairus's Daughter (Mark 5:21-24, 35-43)

A synagogue ruler named Jairus sought out Jesus one day because his 12-year-old daughter was very ill. He asked Jesus to accompany him to his house, so Jesus started with him. But along the way, men came from Jairus's home to inform him that his daughter had died. Therefore, "there's no use troubling the Teacher [Jesus] now."

Jesus told Jairus, "Don't be afraid. Just trust me." When they got to Jairus's home, you can imagine the scene with people crying and wailing loudly. Speaking over the din of the mourners, Jesus said, "Why all this weeping and commotion? The child isn't dead; she is only asleep."

That changed the tone of the group. They went from crying for the girl to laughing at Jesus. But Jesus had everyone leave the room except the girl's parents and three of His disciples. Then He reached out, touched the girl's hand, and told her to get up. Immediately she stood up and began to walk. Jesus told the parents to give the girl something to eat. (Perhaps they were too stunned to think of doing so on their own?) He also gave strict orders not to tell what had happened.

Lazarus (John 11:1-44)

This resurrection was more personal. Lazarus, along with his sisters Mary and Martha, were close friends of Jesus. The two sisters sent word to Jesus that Lazarus was sick. But after hearing the news, Jesus stayed where He was for two more days. He realized Lazarus had died by that time, but told His disciples, "I will go and wake him up."

W.D.J.D.?

A good friend had died. Jesus was surrounded by grieving friends and relatives of the dead man. What did He do? "Jesus wept" (John 11:35). Some people state boldly that faith in God should get us through any crisis and seem to suggest that tears and fears show lapses in genuine belief. Jesus knew exactly what He was going to do, yet expressed His sadness publicly. (Some people speculate that Jesus wept because He realized He was bringing Lazarus back from a much better place.)

OPINION POLL

"Miracles are God's signature, appended to his masterpiece of creation."
—*Ronald Knox*

When He got to their home, a large crowd of mourners had assembled to comfort Mary and Martha. By that time, Lazarus had been in a tomb for four days. Both sisters expressed confidence that Jesus could have done something if He had arrived earlier. Others in the crowd questioned why Jesus was away opening eyes of the blind, yet hadn't helped His friend.

Jesus instructed people to remove the stone from the tomb. Martha didn't think that was such a good idea, because after four days in the heat of the Middle East, the odor was a concern. But Jesus insisted. First, He thanked God for what was about to happen and that this event would cause many people to believe that the Father had sent Jesus. Then Jesus called loudly, "Lazarus, come out!"

It wasn't an easy task when wrapped tightly in linen strips, but Lazarus came stumbling from the tomb. Jesus told bystanders to help remove the grave clothes. While Lazarus' family and friends were glad to welcome him back to the land of the living, this very public resurrection triggered an intensely hostile reaction from the religious leaders. Those who were already at odds with Jesus intensified their efforts to have Him put to death. And since a living Lazarus was a reminder of what had occurred, the chief priests even schemed to put *him* to death as well (John 12:10).

The Road to Health Is Paved with Good Interventions

This chapter hasn't covered all of the healings of Jesus presented in the Bible, but it lists many of them. Yet keep in mind that scholars estimate that Scripture only informs us of about 40 days in Jesus' three-year ministry. As John concludes his gospel, he tells us, "I suppose that if all the other things Jesus did were written down, the whole world could not contain the books" (John 21:25).

Jesus came to earth as a servant, and a major element of His service was to heal and restore people to both physical and spiritual health. Wherever Jesus went, people's lives were changed for the

better. As you read these accounts from the Bible, you will see how frequently it is noted that the people were amazed, and they flocked to be around Him. Yet we know that eventually Jesus was put to death. So what happened?

In the next couple of chapters, we will see how it was possible for people to forsake Jesus, even though His miraculous healings seemed to display irrefutable power from God.

Questions to Ponder and/or Discuss

1. Which of Jesus' healing miracles do you find most impressive? Which (if any) do you find most difficult to comprehend and/or believe?

2. Would you consider Jesus' miracles to be acts of service? Why or why not?

3. If Jesus were walking through your neighborhood, how do you think you would respond?

- Keep watching "Who Wants to Be a Millionaire?" and not give Him a second look.
- Stand at a distance and watch Him work.
- Try to strike up a conversation. (What would you talk about?)
- Ask for a miraculous favor. (What would you ask for?)
- Other: _____

CHAPTER SIX

"OH, THAT'S MR. WILSON. HE'S A FRESHMAN SUBSTITUTE TEACHER."

The No-Substitute Teacher

JESUS THE TEACHER, PART 1

SOME THINGS YOU'LL DISCOVER IN THIS CHAPTER

1. Many people liked the physical and material things Jesus provided but not the implications of His spiritual teachings.

2. Jesus was concerned not only about outward behavior but also about the attitude of the heart.

3. Jesus stood out as a teacher because of what He said and the authority He exerted.

What we learn as we go through school is in no small degree influenced by the teachers we get. Good teachers aren't simply interested in drilling a series of facts and figures into the mushy minds of their students. Rather, experienced teachers realize the importance of creating interest, rewarding progress with praise, and so on. And most people have one or two special teachers who are credited with life-changing attitudes toward school, life, and the world in general.

When the Bible refers to "teachers of the law," the description that follows isn't usually a pleasant or positive one. The Pharisees are most often mentioned, but there were also the Sadducees (chief priests) and a few other groups. The main groups didn't even share the same theology. For example, the Sadducees didn't believe in the resurrection of the dead or in angels and spirits. Yet *all* these groups exerted strict authority over the common people.

Not all of these religious teachers were inherently bad or evil, but many were arrogant, insensitive, hypocritical, and very legalistic. The Pharisees had dissected the Old Testament law into 248 "do's"

and 365 "don'ts." And they liked to give the impression that *they* fulfilled every single commandment.

But suddenly Jesus showed up and started teaching. The comment is made frequently that He "taught as one who had real authority—quite unlike the teachers of religious law" (Matthew 7:29 and other places). To some people, Jesus was like the cool, creative substitute teacher who shows up when your regular stodgy teacher has to have bile removal surgery.

To other people, however, Jesus' unusual teachings got just a little bit *too* unusual. He sometimes taught difficult lessons, and from time to time He would toss out a difficult concept for people to ponder. If they thought about it for a while and caught on to what He was teaching, they would be rewarded for their efforts. If they didn't want to work that hard or were simply coming out to see what Jesus might do on any given day, they might miss out on something important.

Today's Assignment: Read Chapter 6 of the Book of John

The sixth chapter of John provides an encapsulated example of what Jesus had to contend with. As we saw in the last chapter, Jesus performed no shortage of healing miracles during His travels. He did other miracles, as we will see later. One of the more public ones was feeding more than 5,000 people with five small loaves of bread and two fish. John 6 opens with this account and explains that Jesus' miracles were the very reason the people had turned out in droves to see Him. In fact, after He fed them all in such a miraculous way, the intention of the crowd was to take Him by force and make Him their king (John 6:14-15), but Jesus knew what was on their minds and retreated before they could act.

The chapter continues to describe Jesus walking on the water to meet His disciples in a boat. Meanwhile, the huge crowd saw that Jesus was no longer in the same location and went to track Him down. When they found Him, He told them, "The truth is, you want to be with me because I fed you, not because you saw the miracu-

lous sign. But you shouldn't be so concerned about perishable things like food. Spend your energy seeking the eternal life that I, the Son of Man, can give you. For God the Father has sent me for that very purpose" (John 6:26-27).

Then Jesus began to teach and take their questions. The more He talked, the more they resisted what He was saying. As long as He fed them and healed them, they were happy. But when He identified *Himself* as "the bread from heaven" and tried to get them to think in spiritual rather than physical terms, they quickly became disagreeable. And when Jesus began talking (symbolically) about them eating His flesh and drinking His blood, they were repulsed.

As a result of the crowd's change of heart about Jesus, "many of his disciples turned away and deserted him" (John 6:66). Jesus could heal any disease. He could feed hungry crowds using the most meager of meals. He could walk on water and display the power of God in various ways. But in spite of all these things that attracted people to Him, many still refused to listen to what He was trying to teach them.

So let's take a closer look at some of Jesus' teachings. Perhaps some of us have yet to make the decision whether to believe what He's saying or to join those who turn and walk away.

Mountain Hearing (Matthew 5–7)

Jesus' best-known body of teaching is perhaps the Sermon on the Mount. Some people suggest it's a "best of" collection of Jesus' teachings rather than a single sermon. But however you look at it, the material was cutting edge stuff back then and remains fresh and applicable today.

The Beatitudes

Jesus was being followed by crowds of people, so He went up on a mountainside, perhaps so His voice would carry better. The biblical presentation of the Sermon on the Mount begins with what have come to be known as the Beatitudes (statements of blessedness). Put yourself in the shoes of someone who is rather poor, under the rule

SOMETHING OLD, SOMETHING NEW

Exodus 16:14-35 ... John 6:22-58

Jesus' listeners were well aware that God, through Moses, had fed the Israelites for 40 years in the wilderness by providing them with daily manna, and they seemed to want Jesus to be more like Moses when it came to supplying them with food. But Jesus quickly pointed out that since the same God who had provided the Old Testament manna had sent Him, it wasn't a matter of Jesus vs. Moses. Rather, God's first provision had been for physical hunger. This time, He was providing a remedy for their spiritual hunger.

IN JESUS' NAME

"THE BREAD OF LIFE" (John 6:35)

As bread is essential for our physical health and survival, so Jesus fulfills that role in a spiritual sense. But like the people in His day, many people continue to be more concerned with their stomachs than with their souls.

OPINION POLL

"Jesus does not give recipes that show the way to God as other teachers of religion do. He himself is the way." —*Karl Barth*

OPINION POLL

"Let us encourage our churches to substitute salt and light for some of the sugar and spice. We need to begin again to know the sort of victory and blessing and humdrum hard work that comes from serving the poor, the widowed, the infirm, the lonely. Jesus Christ often ministered to the people nobody else wanted."—*Peter E. Gillquist*

of the Roman Empire, and feeling somewhat distant from God because of smug religious leaders who try to define God with lists of "Thou shalt" and "Thou shalt not." How would you respond to Jesus' opening statements?

> God blesses those who realize their need for him, for the Kingdom of Heaven is given to them.
>
> God blesses those who mourn, for they will be comforted.
>
> God blesses those who are gentle and lowly, for the whole earth will belong to them.
>
> God blesses those who are hungry and thirsty for justice, for they will receive it in full.
>
> God blesses those who are merciful, for they will be shown mercy.
>
> God blesses those whose hearts are pure, for they will see God.
>
> God blesses those who work for peace, for they will be called the children of God.
>
> God blesses those who are persecuted because they live for God, for the Kingdom of Heaven is theirs.

Wow! These were promises that would have hit home for a lot of people. And Jesus continued to explain that insults and persecution had been a way of life for all God's true prophets, so "join the club" and don't get too discouraged when the same things happen to you. God's people are called to be "the salt of the earth" and "the light of the world." It's up to them to provide good taste, illumination, and spiritual preservation in a world that is all too often dark and rotting.

True Obedience

But Jesus made it clear He wasn't trying to negate Old Testament teachings. Rather, His purpose was to fulfill rather than abolish them. Indeed, He stated clearly that "unless you obey God better than the teachers of religious law and the Pharisees do, you can't enter the Kingdom of Heaven at all!"

First Jesus taps into the prevailing feelings of the people and then immediately places a seemingly impossible condition on them. For all their faults, the Pharisees knew Scripture and modeled righteousness—at least, their definition of it.

As Jesus went on to explain what He meant, watch closely. It's not that He came and gave us a looser definition of what God expected of us. Just the opposite. Jesus *narrowed* those definitions. He taught a much more conservative interpretation of Scripture than even the religious leaders did.

He taught that unbridled anger and demeaning thoughts about others were on the same level as literal murder. Lust for another person was as serious to God as literal adultery. Divorce and swearing were being tolerated much more than they ought to be. And while the eye-for-an-eye mentality had been the prevailing standard for centuries, Jesus began to promote forgiveness . . . lack of retaliation . . . giving beyond what is demanded . . . and even love for one's enemies.

Guarding against Hypocrisy

As His teaching turned toward spiritual disciplines, Jesus knocked the wind out of the puffed-up Pharisees. They enjoyed all the formalities and public displays of religion, since they considered themselves upper echelon participants. But Jesus taught that practices such as giving, prayer, fasting, and so forth should be *private* displays of one's love for God. Since God sees everything, and since God is the source of rewards, there's no need to make a public spectacle of one's practice of religion.

Fasting was an issue between the faster and God—no need to intentionally try to look miserable to muster sympathy from others and build false pride. Prayer was not a matter of how many words you use or how often you repeat them, but rather your humility and honesty. In fact, the model of prayer presented by Jesus was quite short and to the point:

> Our Father in heaven, may your name be honored.
> May your kingdom come soon.
> May your will be done here on earth, just as it is in heaven.

IN JESUS' NAME
"THE LIGHT FROM HEAVEN"
(Luke 1:78)
"THE TRUE LIGHT"
(John 1:9)
"A GREAT LIGHT"
(Isaiah 9:2)
"EVERLASTING LIGHT"
(Isaiah 60:20)

These and other names of Jesus reflect His ability to dispel spiritual darkness. Followers of Jesus are "the light of the world" not on their own merits but in their willingness to reflect His great, true, everlasting light.

Exodus 20:13 . . . Matthew 5:21-22
Exodus 20:14 . . . Matthew 5:27-30
Deuteronomy 24:1 . . . Matthew 5:31-32
Exodus 21:23-25 . . . Matthew 5:38-42

In these and other places in the Sermon on the Mount, Jesus shows a broad knowledge of the Old Testament. And while He explains that certain actions had been allowed in the past, they were no longer the most desirable responses. He was here to teach (and demonstrate) a better way to respond to offenses and impure thoughts.

OPINION POLL

"Christ appeared not as a philosopher or wordy doctor, or noisy disputer, or even as a wise and learned scribe, but he talked with people in complete sincerity, showing them the way of truth in the way he lived, his goodness and his miracles." —Angela of Foligno

Give us our food today, and forgive us our sins, just as we have forgiven those who have sinned against us.

And don't let us yield to temptation, but deliver us from the evil one.

Note again the emphasis on forgiveness. This will be a major recurring theme in the teachings of Jesus. We are no longer to take God's forgiveness for granted. As we come to see how He repeatedly forgives us, we are to apply those same standards to those who offend us.

Words to Remember

The Sermon on the Mount has provided some classic quotations and proverbs to live by that continue to stand the test of time:

> "Just say a simple, 'Yes, I will,' or 'No, I won't.' Your word is enough." (Matthew 5:37).
> "If you are slapped on the right cheek, turn the other, too" (5:39).
> "No one can serve two masters. . . . You cannot serve both God and money" (6:24).
> "Stop judging others, and you will not be judged" (7:1).
> "Get rid of the log from your own eye; then perhaps you will see well enough to deal with the speck in your friend's eye" (7:5).
> "Don't give pearls to swine" (7:6).
> "Ask and it will be given to you; seek and you will find; knock and the door will be opened to you" (7:7, NIV).
> "Do for others what you would like them to do for you" (7:12).
> "Anyone who listens to my teaching and obeys me is wise, like a person who builds a house on solid rock" (7:24).

Simplicity. Illuminating symbols and imagery. Fresh meaning to old, traditional Scriptures. No wonder the crowds were dazzled by Jesus' teaching style, even as they were amazed at the authority in His teaching!

First Things First?

Let's consider that forgiveness theme again. Both in the Sermon on the Mount (Matthew 5:23-24) and in other places (Matthew 18:15-20), Jesus connects one's spiritual life with the grudges he or she may be holding toward other people. He makes it clear that God isn't eager to receive our gifts and offerings if we are harboring resentment (or worse) toward fellow human beings.

We're not supposed to make a big deal out of our disagreements, but we're supposed to settle them if at all possible. And if fellow believers won't come to terms on a mutually satisfactory arrangement, we have the right (and obligation) to enlist assistance from other people and even church leadership. Unresolved conflicts are harmful not only to the people directly involved, but others around them as well.

Jesus made clear that His teaching came from God the Father (John 7:14-19). We will later discover that one of His roles is that of High Priest, serving to connect sinful people with a holy God. While the Pharisees had essentially separated religion from "real life," Jesus' teaching frequently interwove the two to the point where they could not be untangled. Therefore, an offering to God was deemed useless if an interpersonal relationship was out of sync.

Similarly, when asked what was the number one commandment in all of Scripture, Jesus answered, "'You must love the Lord your God with all your heart, all your soul, and all your mind.' This is the first and greatest commandment. A second is equally important: 'Love your neighbor as yourself.' All the other commandments and all the demands of the prophets are based on these two commandments" (Matthew 22:37-40).

It would have been easy enough to leave the focus on loving God, but Jesus made equally important the command to love our neighbors. Indeed, it is by showing love to one another that we exemplify genuine love for God (1 John 2:9). Trying to love others without experiencing the deep, abiding love of God is frustrating and incomplete. And claiming to love God without demonstrating love for others is hypocrisy.

SOMETHING OLD,
SOMETHING NEW

Leviticus 19:18; Deuteronomy 6:4-5 ... Matthew 22:37-40

The two passages that comprise "the greatest commandment" are tucked into lengthy passages in the Old Testament books of law, but Jesus pinpointed them to provide clear direction as to what is most important in life.

It's not easy to focus only on the teachings of Jesus, because He integrated His lessons with everything He did: healing, conversations, miracles, and personal examples. Everything Jesus did or said was a lesson in one way or another. But just to get a feel of what He was trying to communicate, let's take a look at a sampling of His basic teachings in the next chapter.

Questions to Ponder and/or Discuss

1. Which three of the following groups of people best describes you at this point in your life?

- Those who realize their need for God
- Those who mourn
- Those who are gentle and lowly
- Those who are hungry and thirsty for justice
- Those who are merciful
- Those whose hearts are pure
- Those who work for peace
- Those who are persecuted because they live for God

Which group doesn't yet describe you but might become a goal in the future?

2. If you're supposed to be "the light of the world," what kind of candlepower would you say you're currently producing?

- A key-chain penlight
- A Coleman® lantern
- A 60-watt bulb
- A roaring campfire
- The citywide spotlights used to promote new stores and special events
- Other: _____

3. Jesus' philosophy of forgiveness was, "Love your enemies! Pray for those who persecute you!" (Matthew 5:44). If other people were closely watching your life and actions, what would they think *your* philosophy of forgiveness is?

CHAPTER SEVEN

"FOR THE FIFTH TIME, WHICH WORD IS *NOT* A VERB?"

Yes, This *Will* Be on the Final Exam

JESUS THE TEACHER, PART 2

As we continue our examination of Jesus the teacher, think back to teachers you have had in the past. All of them were probably much alike in ways—disseminating knowledge, giving tests, evaluating your regular progress, and so forth. Yet a few of them probably stood out in one way or another. Some may have gone above and beyond the written curriculum, attempting to teach lessons about life, relationships, morality, or other topics that might have seemed more pressing than ancient history or diagramming sentences. In some cases, you might have thought you had a teacher completely figured out until he or she unexpectedly revealed a much deeper understanding of the topic than you had ever imagined.

We saw in the previous chapter that Jesus the teacher was certainly a standout in terms of His authority and presentation. He revealed deep truths about God and made bold promises to those who would learn and apply the things He was teaching—and those were just the basic lessons.

SOME THINGS YOU'LL DISCOVER IN THIS CHAPTER

1. Personal relationships should never be an excuse to postpone our first commitment to God.

2. The end of the world will be frightening for those who aren't prepared.

3. Hell is a real place, but it can be avoided.

SOMETHING OLD,
SOMETHING NEW
Micah 7:6 ... Matthew 10:34-36

In a parallel to the Luke 12:51-53 passage, Matthew quotes Jesus referring to an Old Testament passage describing how "your enemies will be right in your own household." For a time, this was true even in Jesus' own home (John 7:5).

In this chapter we want to move on to some of His "advanced placement" courses. It is one thing to believe that when we mourn, God will comfort us, and that we should be like light and salt in a dark and rotting world. Those are introductory teachings about the Kingdom of God. But Jesus quickly built on those foundations to teach other, deeper things to challenge and motivate His more faithful disciples.

If you don't completely comprehend all the following things on first reading, don't feel bad—neither did Jesus' followers at the time. Yet these are important insights into the bigger picture of life. God sees things we don't, and it's in our best interest to try to see things from His perspective. As we begin to glimpse a few of the truths beyond the basic teachings of Jesus, we find ourselves grappling with some of the concepts that make the Kingdom of God so mysterious.

Rocking the Boat on Relationships

According to Jesus' teachings, strong personal relationships are just as crucial to spiritual growth as a strong relationship with God. Yet Jesus also made it clear that certain relationships might be rocked to the core by one's commitment to spiritual truth. At one point, potential disciples asked for a bit of time to tend to their aging parents and to say goodbye to their family members before following Jesus. In response, Jesus replied, "Anyone who puts a hand to the plow and then looks back is not fit for the Kingdom of God" (Luke 9:57-62). In other words, while our commitment to God is to be demonstrated in the context of personal relationships, our personal relationships should never be used as an excuse to postpone our commitment to God.

Another time Jesus was interrupted while teaching and was told that His mother and brothers wanted to see Him. He motioned to His disciples and said, "These are my mother and my brothers. Anyone who does the will of my Father in heaven is my brother and sister and mother!" (Matthew 12:46-50)

Relationships would either be strengthened as people realized the potential of what God's love could do, or they would be ruined because one person would pursue the life of a disciple while the other refused to do so. Jesus made no attempt to hide this truth: "Do you think I have come to bring peace to the earth? No, I have come to bring strife and division! From now on families will be split apart, three in favor of me and two against—or the other way around. There will be a division between father and son, mother and daughter, mother-in-law and daughter-in-law" (Luke 12:51-53).

As we read through the New Testament, we discover that the Old Testament emphasis on family is supplemented and amended with images that broaden the scope of the unity of believers. Among other things, the followers of Jesus are referred to as a "body" where Jesus is the head (1 Corinthians 12:12), living stones in a holy temple where Jesus is the cornerstone (1 Peter 2:4-6), and so forth. If believers lose support of their immediate family members because of their faith, they are assured that the love of Jesus pulls them together into a new family, His church. God instituted the family and never disputes the importance of it, yet Jesus teaches that the time may come when people opt to put God ahead of their own family members.

Kid Stuff

Adults can make those decisions to follow or not to follow Jesus, to stay with one's family or leave. Children, however, are at the mercy of their parents and other adults, so Jesus had some harsh words for anyone who misrepresented their authority over children.

One day the disciples asked who would be the greatest in the kingdom of heaven. Jesus called up a little child as an example of humility and said, "Unless you turn from your sins and become as little children, you will never get into the Kingdom of Heaven" (Matthew 18:3). But He didn't stop there. He went on to say: "Anyone who welcomes a little child like this on my behalf is welcoming me.

OPINION POLL

"Concern for the child, even before birth, from the very moment of conception and then throughout the years of infancy and youth, is the primary and fundamental test of the relationship of one human being to another."—*Pope John Paul II*

Jesus was a busy guy, usually from morning till night. In the midst of some of His key teachings, parents started bringing their kids to have Him touch them. The disciples rebuked them, but what did Jesus do? He took the kids in His arms and blessed them. And he made it clear: "Let the children come to me. Don't stop them! For the Kingdom of God belongs to such as these. I assure you, anyone who doesn't have their kind of faith will never get into the Kingdom of God" (Mark 10:13-16).

SOMETHING OLD, SOMETHING NEW

Isaiah 13:9-10 ... Matthew 24:29

Isaiah predicted that "the day of the Lord is coming—the terrible day of his fury and fierce anger." It will be a time when "the land will be destroyed and all the sinners with it. The heavens will be black above them. No light will shine from stars or sun or moon." Jesus made a similar prediction of that day, still in the future.

But if anyone causes one of these little ones who trusts in me to lose faith, it would be better for that person to be thrown into the sea with a large millstone tied around the neck. . . . Beware that you don't despise a single one of these little ones. For I tell you that in heaven their angels are always in the presence of my heavenly Father" (Matthew 18:5-6, 10).

Jesus had much to say about the "Kingdom of God," and we'll look at some of those teachings more closely in the next two chapters about His parables. And the more He said, the clearer it became that choosing to pursue the Kingdom of God was no casual choice. Certainly there was much to be gained. (Review the beatitudes if you need to.) And although we've looked at some of the costs of discipleship, we are about to see that occasionally there is much to be lost.

Countdown!

As the time of Jesus' death drew closer, He began to teach more about the future. He said many others would claim to be the Messiah and warned His followers not to be deceived. Then He added: "Wars will break out near and far, but don't panic. Yes, these things must come, but the end won't follow immediately. The nations and kingdoms will proclaim war against each other, and there will be famines and earthquakes in many parts of the world. But all this will be only the beginning of the horrors to come" (Matthew 24:6-8).

Jesus foretold hatred toward His followers, sometimes resulting in persecution and even death. False prophets would arise and some of His followers would forsake their beliefs. But He also said that "The Good News about the kingdom will be preached throughout the whole world, so that all nations will hear it; and then, finally, the end will come" (Matthew 24:14).

But lest His followers lose heart, Jesus also foretold what would happen beyond those terrible days:

"And then at last, the sign of the coming of the Son of Man will appear in the heavens, and there will be deep mourning among all the nations of the earth. And they will see the Son of Man arrive on the clouds of heaven with power and great glory. And he will send forth his angels with the sound of a mighty trumpet blast, and they will gather together his chosen ones from the farthest ends of the earth and heaven. . . . Heaven and earth will disappear, but my words will remain forever." (Matthew 24:30-31, 35)

Yet to the consternation of many people, Jesus made it clear that no one knows the day or hour these events will take place. God the Father knew the plan, yet had not revealed His timing to the angels or even to Jesus while He was on earth (Matthew 24:36). Actually, it makes sense not to go into too much detail. After all, if we could schedule the events of the end times on our calendars, a lot of us would neglect our spiritual lives until the week before and then cram for the final, so to speak. Some people find it quite exciting to live *each* day as if it could be the "day of the Lord."

Of course, certain people still struggle to hack their way into God's timetable, and a few even claim success from time to time. According to one group of self-proclaimed prophets, Jesus was scheduled to return at the end of the first millennium. A New Englander named William Miller was quite sure he could predict the second coming to the year, day, and minute—but his date was in the mid 1800s. Another guy sold a lot of books that gave 88 reasons why the return of Jesus would occur in 1988. A large Korean cult prepared to beam up on October 28, 1992. And as our clocks ticked down to the final seconds of 1999, several groups of people were nervously casting their eyes heavenward. Either a lot of people are wrong about all their speculation, or the rest of us have missed something.

W.D.J.D.?

When teaching a crowd, it's tempting to want your audience to like you, even if that means watering down the message a bit. Many speakers (including preachers) attempt to downplay anything negative or potentially threatening. But what did Jesus do? He spoke clearly of all God's positive promises, yet He also made critical observations and passed along spiritual warnings. Complete truth was more important to Him than being liked.

Hell? . . . Yes!

Jesus' teachings about the last days are connected to His teachings regarding hell. Most of what we know about the topic comes from what Jesus said about it. Many people today prefer to downplay this sensitive subject or to view it as allegory rather than fact. Let's see

Isaiah 66:24 ... Mark 9:48

Jesus teaches that even amputating one's offending limbs or poking out errant eyes is preferable to winding up in hell. Most people consider this passage hyperbole—extreme exaggeration—used to emphasize His point. (After all, even a blind person can lust.) Yet to further emphasize that hell is a bad, bad place, Jesus quotes from the closing passage of Isaiah which reminds His listeners that in hell "the worm never dies and the fire never goes out."

what Jesus taught about it, and you can come to your own conclusions.

In discussing His eventual return to earth, Jesus says He will separate the people of all nations into two groups: "sheep" and "goats." The "sheep" will be blessed and rewarded for their faithful service to Him (which is strongly tied to how they treated other people). The "goats," who have rejected spiritual truth and ignored the needs of those all around them, will be condemned to "the eternal fire prepared for the Devil and his demons" (Matthew 25:31-46, especially v. 41). "And they will go away into eternal punishment, but the righteous will go into eternal life" (v. 46).

So hell was created not for human beings but for the Devil and his angels. Yet people who refuse to follow the loving leadership of Jesus suffer the same end as those angels who rebelled against God before the earth was created. In addition, Jesus says this will be an eternal punishment.

Another time Jesus warned of a place outside of God's Kingdom, in "outer darkness, where there will be weeping and gnashing of teeth" (Matthew 8:12). And of all the things we might fear in life, winding up in hell should be at the top of the list: "Don't be afraid of those who want to kill you. They can only kill your body; they cannot touch your soul. Fear only God, who can destroy both soul and body in hell" (Matthew 10:28). Jesus spoke with assurance and anticipation about heaven, but He was equally firm about its counterpart—hell.

Prose and Context

As we have seen, many of Jesus' teachings were bold and perhaps even frightening. Families torn apart? Earthquakes and famine? Eternity in hell? What kind of teacher is this, anyway?

Clearly, if Jesus hadn't been so positive and optimistic in the majority of His teachings, these unpleasant topics would have driven *everyone* away, not just a few people. But when all His teachings were taken in context, Jesus was a teacher with much to offer.

For example, in the same breath that He told people to "Fear God, who can destroy both soul and body in hell," He continued to say, "Not even a sparrow, worth only half a penny, can fall to the ground without your Father knowing it. And the very hairs on your head are numbered. So don't be afraid; you are more valuable to him than a whole flock of sparrows" (Matthew 10:29-31).

The fear of God that Jesus taught wasn't a kind of quaking terror. Rather, "fear of the Lord" is intended to be a deep reverence, a willingness to place Him at the top of our priority lists. When pressed to make a hard decision, we would be wise to remember that God casts the deciding vote in eternal life or death, heaven or hell, reward or rebuke. We would do well to "fear" Him to the extent that we choose what He has said is best for our lives.

Jesus predicted that opportunities to make such hard decisions would come. He said, "If anyone acknowledges me publicly here on earth, I will openly acknowledge that person before my Father in heaven. But if anyone denies me here on earth, I will deny that person before my Father in heaven" (Matthew 10:32).

Is this some form of spiritual blackmail? Not really. It's merely the final consequence of the biblical maxim that we reap what we sow (Galatians 6:7). We also need to remember that most of these no-holds-barred teachings of Jesus were originally directed to His disciples, not to society at large. Jesus' inner circle would have had the complete picture of Jesus' love and compassion for others.

It's easy for skeptics to isolate a few of Jesus' statements, create a controversy, and cause a lot of confusion. But genuine seekers will sit down with Scripture and read straight through a Gospel or two (Matthew, Mark, Luke, or John). Each Gospel account presents a broad spectrum from the life of Jesus—obviously much more than this book can cover in a single chapter. And when we pay close attention to whom Jesus was addressing, to the point He was trying to make, and to how that point fits into His ministry as a whole, in most cases the statements aren't nearly as controversial as they might sound when taken out of context.

OPINION POLL

"It is highly convenient to believe in the infinite mercy of God when you feel the need of mercy, but remember also his infinite justice."—*B. R. Haydon*

IN JESUS' NAME

"GOOD TEACHER" (Mark 10:17)

Jesus was without dispute a popular and effective teacher. Yet in Mark 10:17-22, the very man who addressed Jesus as "good teacher" refused to follow Him. Not much has changed in 2,000 years.

You may have seen that many of the previous difficult teachings were pulled from Matthew 10. But if you turn the page of your Bible to Matthew 11 and read verse 19, you'll see that the public image of Jesus wasn't one of gloom and doom. He feasted and drank with all kinds of people—so much that He was accused of being "a friend of the worst sort of sinners!" He didn't deny the charge then. He still doesn't.

The next two chapters continue with the teachings of Jesus, focusing on His parables. But before we continue to examine what kind of teacher He was, it might be good to pause for a moment and consider an even more important question: "What kind of student am I?"

Questions to Ponder and/or Discuss

1. Place an X on the following scale to indicate where you are at your current level of spiritual development:

Most of what Jesus taught is still a mystery to me.

I have a certain degree of understanding about Jesus' teachings (even the hard ones).

2. Which of the teachings of Jesus are the most difficult for you to understand and/or believe?

3. What questions have you been asked about Jesus that you were unable to answer to your satisfaction? Where might you go for a more complete answer? (Consider people, books, conferences, and other potential resources.)

"WHY YES, WE DO HAVE A RESERVATION!"

Once upon a Time There Was a Kingdom...

JESUS THE TEACHER, PART 3

If you are planning an extended visit to another country or culture, it is likely that you'll devote some serious time in preparation to discover what you're getting yourself into. Some of your common words or gestures might turn out to be very offensive to your hosts. You want to know something of the etiquette of the new culture so you don't do anything to create undue embarrassment. If you move blindly into your new environment without any prior consideration of what is expected of you, you might find yourself married, cooked, or run out of town before you know what's happening.

In the previous two chapters, we looked at several of Jesus' basic teachings. In the next two, we want to continue by focusing specifically on a number of His parables. The focus of this chapter will be the parables that referred to another culture—the Kingdom of God.

Cracking the Parable Code

Sometimes we tend to think Jesus used parables much the same way we use stories and anecdotes in speeches—to lighten things up

SOME THINGS YOU'LL DISCOVER IN THIS CHAPTER

1. Parables are like a spiritual "code" that can be deciphered only by those seeking God.

2. God determines who will enter His kingdom and what rewards they will receive.

3. We always need to be prepared and waiting for Jesus to return for His people.

**SOMETHING OLD,
SOMETHING NEW**
Isaiah 6:9-10 . . . Matthew 13:14-15
Psalm 78:2 . . . Matthew 13:35

Both Jesus and Matthew verify that Jesus' use of parables fulfilled Old Testament prophecy. Parables would reveal "mysteries hidden since the creation of the world," yet they would not be understood by everyone.

and make the topic easier to understand. But actually, it was just the opposite. When His disciples asked why He spoke in parables, He told them:

> "You have been permitted to understand the secrets of the Kingdom of Heaven, but others have not. To those who are open to my teaching, more understanding will be given, and they will have an abundance of knowledge. But to those who are not listening, even what they have will be taken away from them. That is why I tell these stories, because people see what I do, but they don't really see. They hear what I say, but they don't really hear, and they don't understand" (Matthew 13:11-13).

In other words, parables served as sort of a "code" which spiritually enlightened people could figure out. They were mini-mysteries which required a bit of thought to unravel. But don't feel too bad if they don't all make sense to you at first. Even Jesus' disciples are shown pulling Him aside and asking what in the world He was talking about. In certain cases He patiently explained the symbolism and deeper meaning. In other places the meaning is explained within the parable itself.

To Kingdom Come

According to Jesus, the Kingdom of Heaven was not some strange, mystical realm way off in the distance or the future. Rather, both Jesus and John the Baptist repeatedly taught that "the Kingdom of Heaven is near" (Matthew 3:2; 4:17). And Jesus had much more to say about this heavenly Kingdom:

> The Kingdom of Heaven is like a mustard seed (Matthew 13:31-32)—the smallest seed known to first-century planters, yet capable of reaching a height of perhaps 15 feet in a single season. It may not appear significant at first, but in the long run it will become most impressive.

The Kingdom of Heaven is like yeast (Matthew 13:33). Its potency is without question, requiring only a small quantity to permeate and influence a much larger amount.

The Kingdom of Heaven is like hidden treasure in a field (Matthew 13:44) or a single pearl of great value (Matthew 13:45-46). When someone has an opportunity to attain it, he or she would be wise to sell everything else in order to do so. It's definitely a trade *up*.

The Kingdom of God is like a germinated seed (Mark 4:26-29). Now that the seed has been planted, it's growing whether you're awake or asleep, watching or not. When the grain becomes ripe, the owner will see fit to harvest it.

The Kingdom of Heaven is like a fisherman's net (Matthew 13:47-50). The net brings in all sorts of sea creatures. Those of value will be kept, but the worthless ones will be separated from the others and destroyed.

Similarly, the Kingdom of Heaven is like a field where the owner has planted wheat, but an enemy has sneaked in at night and sown weeds among the good seed (Matthew 13:24-30). When the servants discovered the weeds growing, they asked the owner what to do. Rather than pull the weeds prematurely and risk uprooting valuable wheat as well, the owner determined to wait until harvest. At that time the weeds would be collected first and burned. Then the wheat would be gathered into the barn.

Jesus' disciples claimed to be catching on to everything Jesus was saying (Matthew 13:51). But Jesus was like the owner of a storehouse who could pull out new teachings (or "treasures") as well as old ones (v. 52). Consequently, the disciples needed occasional help to truly understand the symbolism of His parables. One such case was in the previous parable of the wheat and the weeds. But thanks to their confusion, the parable is broken down for us as well (Matthew 13:36-43):

W.D.J.D.?

Jesus hoped His disciples were spiritually astute and able to comprehend His teachings, but sometimes they weren't. So what did He do? In most cases He patiently went into further detail and explanation. Similarly, He doesn't berate us for ignorance of Scripture or spiritual things—not if we're seeking deeper truths. Perhaps the disciples remembered what Jesus said in the Sermon on the Mount about asking, seeking, and knocking. Asking questions and seeking clarification is part of everyone's spiritual growth. A far greater offense is to willfully continue in ignorance, attempting to hide one's spiritual immaturity.

71

"THE SON OF MAN" (Matthew 13:37)

Jesus referred to Himself by this name more than any other—about 80 times in the Gospels. This was a messianic title that seemed to focus on the incarnation—the "becoming flesh"—of Jesus. His willingness to live and associate with the human race was an extended act of humility not to be overlooked.

"THE FARMER WHO PLANTS THE GOOD SEED" OR "THE SOWER" (Matthew 13:37)

Farmers work hard to sow seeds, but the anticipation of the harvest makes it worth the effort. In this case the seed represents people; in a later parable it will represent God's Word going forth into various soils. But in both cases, Jesus is a conscientious sower who initiates and oversees the harvest. He is saddened by failed or stunted growth and is elated to see fruit produced in His "plants."

The sower of good seed is Jesus (the "Son of Man").
The field is the world.
The good seeds are "people of the Kingdom."
The weeds are "people who belong to the evil one."
The enemy who sows the weeds is the Devil.
The harvest is the end of the age.
The harvesters are angels.

The parable of the wheat and the weeds (and others we will see) bears out Jesus' teachings about the last days. Jesus explained:

> "Just as the weeds are separated out and burned, so it will be at the end of the world. I, the Son of Man, will send my angels, and they will remove from my Kingdom everything that causes sin and all who do evil, and they will throw them into the furnace and burn them. There will be weeping and gnashing of teeth. Then the godly will shine like the sun in their Father's Kingdom" (Matthew 13:40-43).

So while the crowds around Jesus were hearing little stories about seeds and weeds, pearls, nets, and such, Jesus' disciples were getting a behind-the-scenes earful about what these stories really meant.

The Plot Thickens

Most of the previous parables were quite short, if not sweet. Others, as we will see next, were longer and a bit more complex. Yet each of the following parables was also told to somehow symbolize the Kingdom of Heaven.

Vineyard Workers ((Matthew 20:1-16)

A landowner went out early one morning to hire workers. They agreed on a price—a standard day's wage—and he put them to work in his vineyard. He went back for more laborers at 9 A.M., and more signed on when the landowner promised to "pay them whatever was right at the end of the day." He went back again at noon and at 3 P.M., each time enlisting more people to work for him. Even at 5

P.M. he found people standing with nothing to do, and they too were willing to work for him.

At the end of the day when he went to pay everyone, he started with those who had begun work at 5 P.M., giving each of them a full day's pay. Of course, the early arrivers expected to get more, but they didn't. So they began to grumble and accuse the landowner of being unfair. But by his standards, he was treating them absolutely fairly because that's what they had agreed to. He challenged them, "Friend, I haven't been unfair! Didn't you agree to work all day for the usual wage? Take it and go. I wanted to pay this last worker the same as you. Is it against the law for me to do what I want with my money? Should you be angry because I am kind?" (Matthew 20:13-15)

Many interpretations have been offered for this parable. One of the more obvious ones, however, is that the religious leaders and people like them had come to expect special favors from God. And while God would certainly be fair to them, He also has every right to reach out to other people in grace and mercy. The Gentiles would be invited into the Kingdom later than the Jews but would still be welcomed with equal rights and privileges. And on a more individual level, someone who lives a life of sin may choose to repent on his or her deathbed, and God has every right to forgive and welcome the person as His child—just as He does for those who choose to live their entire lives for Him. Should we be angry because He is kind?

OPINION POLL

"What Christ had to say was too simple to be grasped, too truthful to be believed."—*Malcolm Muggeridge*

A Poorly Attended Wedding Banquet (Matthew 22:1-14)

A king planned a big wedding feast for his son, inviting many people. But when the servants went out to tell the people the banquet was ready, they refused to attend. He sent other servants with more details, but the invited guests insisted on going about their regular business. Some even seized and killed the servants who brought the message.

In response, the enraged king sent an army to destroy the murderers. In their place, the king's servants recruited people from off the streets—both good and bad—to fill the wedding hall. It would have been the custom of the host to provide appropriate garments for his guests. And while any number of attenders might have felt

unworthy to be there, one in particular had refused to wear the proper attire available to him. As a result, the king told his servants to, "Bind him hand and foot and throw him out into the outer darkness, where there is weeping and gnashing of teeth."

The moral of this story comes at the end: "Many are called, but few are chosen." Apparently people can miss out on the Kingdom of Heaven by spurning the invitation altogether, or by refusing to dress in the appropriate party clothing available only from God.

The "Talent" Show (Matthew 25:14-30)

A man was planning a journey, so he gathered his three servants before he left. To one he gave five talents, to the second he gave two talents, and to the third he gave one talent. (Each "talent" was a quantity of gold or silver between 58 and 80 pounds.) The servant with five talents put his money to work and earned five more. The servant with two talents also doubled his money. But the third servant hid his talent in a hole in the ground.

Some people speculate this guy thought the master might not return. If not, the third servant would have himself a big chunk of change with no financial records to tie the money to the estate, like the other two servants.

But the master did indeed return. The first two servants gave an account of themselves and received the master's praise. The third guy claimed he was afraid of the master and didn't want to risk losing his money. The master saw through his weak defense: "You wicked and lazy servant! . . . You should at least have put my money into the bank so I could have some interest."

The talent was taken away from the third servant and given to the servant who had ten talents. Then the master gave the order (as had the one in the previous parable) to "Throw this useless servant into outer darkness, where there will be weeping and gnashing of teeth."

The New Living Translation substitutes "bags of gold" for "talents." But the lesson applies to nonmonetary talents as well. Other Bible passages encourage us to use our gifts and skills for God. We don't all have a lot of discretionary income, but we do have other "talents."

Did Jesus really teach that "the rich get richer while the poor get poorer"—a philosophy often attributed to the Bible? If you assume the talents in this story to be nothing more than monetary units, you might think so. However, if you believe that in the symbolism of this parable they represent spiritual bestowments that we are expected to cultivate and multiply, you reach a different conclusion. A consistent biblical principle is that faithfulness to little (spiritual) things results in bigger (spiritual) things. To apply the same principle to financial matters requires more of a stretch of interpretation.

The Unforgiving Debtor (Matthew 18:21-35)

When asked to what extent people should be expected to forgive others, Jesus told this story of a servant who had amassed an enormous debt to a king. The king was preparing to sell the servant, his family, and his possessions. Although the debt was the equivalent of millions of dollars, the desperate servant promised to pay it back—even though he certainly couldn't have done so. The king took pity on the servant and canceled his entire debt.

The relieved servant was set free and came upon another servant who owed *him* money—a paltry sum in comparison to the debt the king had canceled. But the first servant physically and verbally threatened the second one, who begged for time and promised to pay. The first servant even had him thrown into prison.

When other servants saw what had happened, they were so distressed they went and told the king. He was angry and pointed out an obvious fact—the servant should have had mercy on his peer since he had received such great mercy from the king. The king revoked his parole of the first servant and "sent the man to prison until he had paid every penny."

And lest we miss the point, Jesus added: "That's what my heavenly Father will do to you if you refuse to forgive your brothers and sisters in your heart."

Ten Bridesmaids (Matthew 25:1-13)

This is another parable based around a wedding celebration, this time with 10 virgin bridesmaids planning to attend the festivities

and welcome the bridegroom when he arrived. All of them had lamps, but only five of the young women were "wise" and had brought along extra oil. It was midnight before the cry went up that the bridegroom was approaching. The women had fallen asleep and awoke to discover their lamps needed oil. The five who hadn't prepared for this possibility ran to buy some, and the bridegroom arrived while they were gone. By the time these five "foolish" bridesmaids returned, the wedding celebration was taking place behind closed doors, and they were denied entrance.

Jesus' point for this parable was to warn His listeners to "stay awake and be prepared, because you do not know the day or hour of my return." That hour will come suddenly, and then it will be too late to run down to the store to get whatever we lack.

What's in It for Me?

If you're not looking too closely, you might miss the significance of these parables. The morals of these stories don't refer to mass murderers, rapists, megalomaniacs, and others we consider to be the worst offenders on the scales of justice and injustice. Rather, Jesus comes down pretty hard on people who don't apply their God-given talents, those who refuse to forgive small debts, those who want to keep their own time sheets rather than letting God reward as He sees fit, and others like ourselves.

We've gotten pretty comfortable with our own set of rules, as had the Pharisees in the first century. But these stories reveal quite a different set of standards for God's kingdom. If we write them off as cute little stories, Jesus' parables go skimming over our heads with little of their intended effect. But if we see them for what they are—calls to action—we will change our attitudes and behavior accordingly. If we don't see ourselves in the parables, we just aren't trying hard enough to see.

The next chapter will continue with other parables Jesus told. We'll get some more practice at cracking the code and discovering some of the hidden nuggets of truth God has in store for those who are willing to go beyond a casual reading.

Questions to Ponder and/or Discuss

1. What do you think about Jesus' parables? Do you appreciate the story formats, or would you have preferred a more straightforward explanation of the kingdom of heaven?

2. How would you say Jesus' parables are similar to Aesop's fables? How are they different?

3. Most of Jesus' parables use situations and activities familiar to the Middle East culture of the first century (planting, laboring, fishing, vineyard pruning, etc.). If Jesus set these stories in your current culture, how do you think He might describe the kingdom of heaven? What contemporary analogies might He use?

CHAPTER NINE

More Incomparable Parables

JESUS THE TEACHER, PART 4

"I think I can. I think I can."

"This porridge is too hot."

"Fe-Fi-Fo-Fum!"

"Mighty Casey has struck out!"

"Curiouser and curiouser!"

All it takes is a phrase or two to bring to mind some of our favorite stories. We've heard them so many times we can usually take it from there and recount the whole plot line.

Some of Jesus' parables have achieved the same degree of familiarity. The house on the rock is as common to many of us as the sword in the stone. The Prodigal Son and the Good Samaritan have become archetypes in modern literature.

Other parables will be less familiar or possibly brand new to you. This chapter will provide a broad spectrum of Jesus' parables. As you read what follows, reexamine the classic parables for fresh insights. There's a reason they are so well-known. We need to examine them as if for the first time, and we need to spend some time examining the lesser known parables as well. Who knows

SOME THINGS YOU'LL DISCOVER IN THIS CHAPTER

1. God will lift up the humble but humble the proud.

2. Jesus said we should keep praying and not get discouraged, because God will answer.

3. How we treat others will have eternal consequences.

OPINION POLL

"There is no discovery of the truth of Christ's teaching, no unanswerable inward endorsement of it, without committing oneself to his way of life."
—J. B. Phillips

which story will strike a chord with where you are in your spiritual journey right now?

Big Differences

Several of Jesus' parables involve contrasting people or figures. The last parable in the previous chapter is a good example. The five wise bridesmaids stood in stark contrast to the five foolish ones. Below are some additional parables where an obvious contrast is made.

Two Homebuilders ((Matthew 7:24-27)

At the end of Jesus' Sermon on the Mount is a short parable, familiar to most people. A wise person builds his house upon rock. A foolish one builds his house on sand. When storms hit both homes, the house on the rock will stand firm while the house on sand is certain to "fall with a mighty crash." The implication is that many of the foundations we build on (money, status, power, etc.) fail to support us when a big "storm" hits.

New vs. Old (Matthew 9:16-17)

If a piece of new, unwashed cloth is used as a patch on an older garment, it is likely to shrink and create a worse tear than before. If new wine is placed into old wineskins, the already expanded and brittle skins will burst and the owner will be left with nothing but a wine-stained floor. Likely explanation: Jesus' teachings were so new and potent, it was more than a matter of tacking them onto already established religious traditions. People would need to take a completely new approach to seeking God's truth.

Two Sons (Matthew 21:28-32)

A man asked his two sons to work in the vineyard. One said he wouldn't, but relented and went. The other said he would, but didn't. Jesus wanted to know which son did what the father had asked. Jesus was addressing the chief priests and religious elders, and He made His point clearly. When they responded that the first son had done as the father asked, He told them: "I assure you, corrupt tax collectors and prostitutes will get into the Kingdom of God before you do." (That had to sting!)

Two Kinds of Servants (Matthew 24:45-51)

In a discourse about the last days and His second coming, Jesus contrasts two kinds of servants. A faithful servant will do his job even when the master is away. When the master returns, such a servant will be praised and promoted. A wicked servant, in comparison, sees opportunity for mischief when the master is gone. He "begins oppressing the other servants, partying, and getting drunk." But when the master returns unexpectedly and sees what is going on, the master "will tear the servant apart and banish him with the hypocrites. In that place there will be weeping and gnashing of teeth."

Sheep and Goats (Matthew 25:31-46)

A shepherd would be accustomed to letting sheep and goats graze in the same pastures. But the time would eventually come to separate them. Jesus used this image to depict how judgment would take place at a future time. He would put the "sheep" on His right, destined for eternal rewards in God's kingdom. The "goats" on the left would be sentenced to "eternal punishment." (Are you beginning to see a recurring ending to many of Jesus' parables?)

A Rich Man and Lazarus (Luke 16:19-31)

This story contains perhaps the greatest contrast between two people. Jesus describes first an unnamed rich man who dressed in purple and fine linen, and who ate well. At this man's gate sat a beggar named Lazarus (not the same guy Jesus had raised from the dead). Lazarus was covered with sores, which the dogs would lick as he sat longing for the crumbs that fell beneath the rich man's table.

Both men eventually died. When Lazarus died, he "was carried by the angels to be with Abraham." The rich man, on the other hand, found himself in hell, where he was in torment.

Far in the distance the rich man could see Abraham with Lazarus by his side. He called out, "Father Abraham, have some pity! Send Lazarus over here to dip the tip of his finger in water and cool my tongue, because I am in anguish in these flames." But Abraham replied that a deep chasm lay between them, keeping the two areas

SOMETHING OLD,
SOMETHING NEW

Genesis 12—22 ... Luke 16:19-31

Abraham was a key figure of the Old Testament and a revered hero of the Jewish people. Jesus' listeners would have understood that someone in Abraham's presence in the afterlife (sometimes referred to as "Abraham's bosom" or "Abraham's side") would have been in a place of special bliss reserved for the souls of righteous people after death prior to their final resurrection. (However, this concept is not explained in Old Testament Scripture.)

OPINION POLL

"Jesus Christ's teaching never beats about the bush."—*Oswald Chambers*

permanently separated. Besides, he said, both the rich man and Lazarus were receiving what was due them based on the decisions they had made in life.

The rich man then begged Abraham to send Lazarus back to the land of the living long enough to warn his five brothers so they would avoid coming to "this place of torment." But Abraham explained, "Moses and the prophets have warned them. Your brothers can read their writings anytime they want to. . . . If they won't listen to Moses and the prophets, they won't listen even if someone rises from the dead."

This is a harsh parable, if indeed it *is* a parable. Some people point out that in no other parable did Jesus refer to a person by name, and they suggest that this might be an actual account related by Jesus. On the other hand, the name "Lazarus" is the Greek form of a Hebrew name that means "God, the Helper." Perhaps Jesus used this name for the purposes of a parable. We don't know for sure.

But either way, Jesus' point is well taken. The teachings of Scripture are clear about how we are to treat others. If we choose to ignore those instructions and focus only on ourselves, we are in danger of the same end as the rich man. In the ultimate contrast, a life of righteousness, even if beset by poverty and disease, will have eternal payoffs.

Parables to Make Us More Prayer-Able

A few of Jesus' parables specifically addressed the topic of prayer and the way to live out our faith. Some of the analogies He used are quite thought-provoking.

The Pharisee and the Tax Collector (Luke 18:9-14)

Since we've been looking at contrasting parables, let's start with one that compares two men. The Bible says Jesus told this particular parable because He was around some people "who had great self-confidence and scorned everybody else."

A Pharisee (a revered, educated religious leader) and a tax collector (hated by many people for being a greedy and dishonest pawn of the Roman Empire) both went to the temple to pray. The Pharisee

stood and prayed: "I thank you, God, that I am not a sinner like everyone else, especially like that tax collector over there! For I never cheat, I don't sin, I don't commit adultery. I fast twice a week, and I give you a tenth of my income."

But the tax collector stood at a distance and beat his chest, not even looking up to heaven. His prayer was simple and to the point: "O God, be merciful to me, for I am a sinner."

Jesus made it clear that, as far as God was concerned, the tax collector went home justified before God. The Pharisee didn't. "For the proud will be humbled, but the humble will be honored."

A Pesky Friend (Luke 11:5-13)

This parable was told by Jesus in the context of teaching His disciples the Lord's Prayer. Suppose you have a friend who shows up at your house unexpectedly and late at night. He's hungry and needs food for a long journey, but you have nothing to offer him. What do you do? (Remember, this is a culture with no 24-hour convenience stores and where you're expected to be a good host.)

You might go to another friend of yours, wake him up, and see if he could do something. That person's first instinct might be to yell, "Don't bother me. The door is locked for the night, and we are all in bed. I can't help you this time." Yet even though he might not want to help you as a friend, because you have boldly knocked on his door in the middle of the night, he will get up and help you out.

The Widow and the Judge (Luke 18:1-8)

Once upon a time, taught Jesus, there was a judge "who was a godless man with great contempt for everyone." A widow brought a legal matter before him concerning someone who had cheated her. The judge didn't respond as she had hoped. But she kept coming back to him and appealing for him to settle the matter. After a while the judge finally concluded, "I fear neither God nor man, but this woman is driving me crazy. I'm going to see that she gets justice, because she is wearing me out with her constant requests!"

Jesus isn't teaching that God is like an apathetic judge. Rather, He wants His disciples to see the principle of persistence at work. Jesus concluded: "Learn a lesson from this evil judge. Even he

SOMETHING OLD,
SOMETHING NEW

Genesis 22:14 ... Luke 11:5-13

Jesus didn't make a direct connection here, but one of the names of God the Father was "Yahweh Yir'eh" (meaning "The Lord will provide"). On the grandest of scales, God had provided a sacrificial ram so that Abraham didn't have to go through with his sacrifice of Isaac. But here Jesus is teaching that the same God is equally concerned with providing the basic daily needs of His children.

OPINION POLL

"I believe in God the Father Almighty because wherever I have looked, through all that I see around me, I see the trace of an intelligent mind, and because in natural laws, and especially in the laws which govern the social relations of men, I see, not merely the proofs of intelligence, but the proofs of beneficence."
—Henry George

rendered a just decision in the end, so don't you think God will surely give justice to his chosen people who plead with him day and night? Will he keep putting them off? I tell you, he will grant justice to them quickly!"

Jesus wanted His disciples to know that God encouraged boldness and persistence in our prayers. If we tend to think we're bothering Him with our needs, that thought should be dismissed as we realize He is a loving friend. In addition, He is a heavenly Father. In yet another contrast, Jesus compared human fatherhood with that of God the Father: "You fathers—if your children ask for a fish, do you give them a snake instead? Or if they ask for an egg, do you give them a scorpion? Of course not! If you sinful people know how to give good gifts to your children, how much more will your heavenly Father give the Holy Spirit to those who ask him."

The Lost-and-Found Trilogy

While some of Jesus' parables dealt with unpleasant topics like death, hell, and judgment, we have seen that others focus entirely on God's concern and compassion for humanity. Perhaps nowhere does this theme come shining through brighter than in Luke 15. Jesus tells a series of three parables about lost things, concluding with perhaps the best-known parable of all—the Prodigal Son. Each parable illustrates essentially the same point, which makes the imagery of the final parable even more emphatic. Jesus told this series of parables after overhearing the religious authorities in His audience mutter that He was associating with—and even eating with—despicable people.

The Lost Sheep (Luke 15:3-7)

Jesus asked: If a shepherd with 100 sheep does a count and discovers one of them missing, won't he leave the 99 in a safe place and go looking for the lost one? Of course! And when he finds it, he joyfully carries it home. Then he calls his friends and neighbors together and throws a party to celebrate. The point of the parable:

"In the same way, heaven will be happier over one lost sinner who returns to God than over ninety-nine others who are righteous and haven't strayed away."

The Lost Coin (Luke 15:8-10)

Jesus continued: Suppose a woman has 10 silver coins and loses one. In a time without electricity and most likely dirt floors, wouldn't she light a lamp, sweep the floor, and search carefully? When she finds her missing coin, she too will call her friends and neighbors together to rejoice. Jesus' point this time: "In the same way, there is joy in the presence of God's angels when even one sinner repents."

The Lost Son (Luke 15:11-32)

A father had two sons. The younger son asked Dad to cash out his share of what he planned to inherit—a presumptuous request, to be sure, but one the father granted. The young son soon left home and traveled to a distant country where he "wasted all his money on wild living." Just about the time his bankroll ran out, a famine hit the area. He hired himself out as a servant to feed pigs for someone else—an obvious act of desperation for someone with a Jewish background. Yet in his first experience with poverty, even what the pigs were being fed looked good to him.

It struck the young man one day that if he was going to be a servant, he was working for the wrong master. He realized his father's servants had decent food and were better treated. So he rehearsed a speech that would convince his father to take him back as a hired laborer.

It must have been a tension-filled journey home, not knowing what to expect when he would eventually confront his father, hat in hand. But his father saw him coming down the road "while he was still a long distance away." (How many times a day do you suppose Dad looked down that road?)

The father ran to his son, filled with compassion. The son began his prepared speech, but the father never let him finish. He would hear nothing of his son being a servant. Instead, he ordered a big

IN JESUS' NAME

"THE GOOD SHEPHERD" (John 10:11)

In this parable, Jesus describes the actions of a good shepherd. In John, Jesus identifies Himself as "the Good Shepherd" who does much more for His flock than knowing and caring for them. He even "lays down his life" for them.

SOMETHING OLD,
SOMETHING NEW

Leviticus 11 ... Luke 15:15-16

The Old Testament was quite specific about which foods were "unclean" and prohibited. Pigs were high on the list of no-no's (Leviticus 11:7-8).

party and feast. The son was given a robe, ring, and sandals. Why? "For this son of mine was dead and has now returned to life. He was lost, but now he is found."

Meanwhile, the older brother was out in the field (perhaps working and drenched with sweat?) when he heard the hubbub. He asked a servant what was going on and got the whole scoop. He wasn't at all enthusiastic about the return of little brother. He was angry and stubbornly refused to join the celebration. So the father went out to him, pleading with him to come in. But the older brother was emphatic: "All these years I've worked hard for you and never once refused to do a single thing you told me to. And in all that time you never gave me even one young goat for a feast with my friends. Yet when this son of yours comes back after squandering your money on prostitutes, you celebrate by killing the finest calf we have."

The father replied, "Look, dear son, you and I are very close, and everything I have is yours. We had to celebrate this happy day. For your brother was dead and has come back to life! He was lost, but now he is found!"

Jesus ended the story there, with no further explanation or resolution. We don't know if the family ever worked out their differences. But we can bet that many of His listeners were relating more with the feelings of the older brother than with the younger one. (After all, don't we tend to do the same?)

Yet in the context of the previous parables, Jesus is driving home a point. The shepherd lost one percent of his property, but we understand his desire to celebrate the return of the wayward sheep. The woman lost ten percent of her savings, and we are even more glad when she gets it back. The father lost fifty percent of what was most precious to him—his children. Yet, in this case, we kind of want to see a presumptuous and arrogant youngster get what's coming to him, especially when he blew off a loving parent to pursue a self-centered life of ease and pleasure.

But God—the ultimate example of what a father should be—didn't heap on the guilt and shame before magnanimously accepting back his prodigal (wasteful) son. When the son was serious about coming home again, bygones were bygones. Forgiveness was total and complete. The repentance and renewal of the younger son was more important in the big picture than the feelings and understanding of the older one. The father loved them both, though neither one could fully comprehend the depth of his love.

A Few Final Favorites

With about 40 parables in Jesus' repertoire (that we know of), we won't detail all of them in this chapter. But before wrapping up, let's take a look at a few more—some of the better known or more unusual ones.

This Little Light of Mine (Matthew 5:14-16)

Young Sunday school students are taught to sing, "This little light of mine, I'm gonna let it shine." But Jesus' command was originally to adults, reminding us that, as "the light of the world," it is our job to be beacons for the kingdom of God. He pointed out that people don't light oil lamps and then place them beneath bowls. (In addition to keeping the room in the dark, you risk either snuffing the flame or burning down your house.)

A Dirt-y Parable (Mark 4:1-20)

Once upon a time a farmer went out to plant seed, scattering it by hand. Some fell along the hard path where the birds came and ate it. Some fell in rocky places where it germinated quickly. But without enough soil to take root and draw water, those young plants quickly scorched and withered. Some seed fell among thorns which eventually choked out the good plants. But some seed fell in the good soil where it produced a crop up to one hundred times the size of what was planted. The end.

Parables like this one even stumped the disciples. When the crowds had dispersed, the disciples pulled Jesus aside to get some clarification. Like He had done for the parable of the weeds (chapter 8), Jesus broke down the symbolism for them:

The farmer is the one who brings God's message to others. The seed that fell on the hard path represents those who hear the message, but then Satan comes at once and takes it away from them.

OPINION POLL

"God pardons like a mother, who kisses the offense into everlasting forgiveness."
—Henry Ward Beecher

W.D.J.D.?

Though Jesus possessed unlimited knowledge, power, and authority, He didn't usually take a "because I said so" stand when teaching people the truth about God's kingdom. He often taught by asking good questions. In this case, he asked the expert: "What is written in the Law? How do you read it?" As the man answered, he came up with a question of his own: "Who is my neighbor?" Jesus had created a teachable moment, and His response, in the form of the parable of the Good Samaritan, has become classic literature—much more effective than verbally bashing the guy over the head with doctrine.

The rocky soil represents those who hear the message and receive it with joy. But like young plants in such soil, their roots don't go very deep. At first they get along fine, but they wilt as soon as they have problems or are persecuted because they believe the word. The thorny ground represents those who hear and accept the Good News, but all too quickly the message is crowded out by the cares of this life, the lure of wealth, and the desire for nice things, so no crop is produced. But the good soil represents those who hear and accept God's message and produce a huge harvest—30, 60, or even 100 times as much as had been planted.

In other words, the seed of God's Word is there for everyone, but the extent to which it influences us depends on the soil—the inner environment we create to allow it to flourish. You probably know people in each of the categories Jesus describes. And from time to time, most of us find ourselves in "dirt" where we aren't exactly producing a bumper crop.

The Good Samaritan (Luke 10:25-37)

Next to the Prodigal Son, this is perhaps the best known of Jesus' parables. It was told as part of a conversation Jesus was having with an expert in the law who had asked about what he must do to inherit eternal life. Part of the expectation was to love one's neighbor as oneself, which gave rise to the question, "Who is my neighbor?"

In response, Jesus told a story about a man on a journey who was surprised by a group of men who robbed him, stripped him, beat him, and left him for dead. A priest went by, but crossed to the other side of the road to avoid helping him. Then another very religious person walked by and did the same. But eventually a Samaritan came by. (Most Jewish people despised Samaritans.) This particular Samaritan bandaged the man's wounds, placed him on his own donkey, carried him to an inn, and cared for him. When the Samaritan had to go, he left plenty of money with the innkeeper to provide for the guy, and he promised to return and cover any additional expenses. Jesus' question was simple: "Which of these three men would you say was a neighbor to the man who was attacked by bandits?"

The "expert in religious law" would have gotten more out of this parable than we do. Centuries before Jesus came, the Jewish people had been conquered by the Assyrians. By the time they returned to their homeland, some had intermarried with their enemies, and had merged their religions to some extent. They still claimed to follow the God of Abraham, yet their conception of Him was incomplete (as it is for most of us). But Samaritans were targets of hatred and prejudice for most Jews.

We can't fully appreciate the parable until we see ourselves lying bleeding and dying in the road. Think of the people you most respect and how you would feel if they walked by without helping you. Then think of the ethnic/religious figure that creates most discomfort or distrust, and imagine how you would feel if *that* person stopped to help. The power of the parable depends on the hearer's honesty in admitting his or her own fears and prejudices.

So now we've spent four chapters looking at the teachings of Jesus, and we've left out a lot more than we've covered. But it's a beginning! As you come back to the Gospels time and time again, you can keep building on what you learned all the times before. And no matter how well you think you know the material, it seems that each reading reveals something new. It's not that the words change, but the reader does. Wherever you are on your spiritual journey, you should be able to find something to encourage you, to enlighten you as to who God really is, and to challenge you as you continue.

Questions to Ponder and/or Discuss

1. If you had been present when Jesus was telling His contrasting parables, where would you have placed yourself on the following scales:

House on a rock   House on sand

OPINION POLL

"The discrepancy between the depth, sincerity and, may I say, shrewdness of Christ's moral teaching and the rampant megalomania which must lie behind his theological teaching unless he is indeed God, has never been got over."
—*C. S. Lewis*

OPINION POLL

"We do not know one-millionth of one percent about anything."—*Thomas Edison*

Stated commitment but little action	No verbal commitment but positive action
Good servant	Wicked servant
Goat	Sheep
Rich man	Lazarus

2. How would you summarize Jesus' prayer parables in 25 words or less?

3. With whom do you most closely relate in the Parable of the Prodigal Son? Why?

- The father
- The younger child
- The older child
- The fattened calf

CHAPTER TEN

What Were You Expecting?

JESUS THE UNEXPECTED

So do you think you're getting Jesus all figured out? So far, the things we've covered have been pretty basic. He was a servant, to be sure. He did some incredible healing miracles, but we already knew that. His teachings were interesting enough, both His parables and His straightforward proclamations. Some of His accomplishments might have been new to you, but they still conform to the image our society has of Jesus.

But like His disciples and parents, just when we think we're getting a clear understanding of the man who was Jesus, He up and does something to knock the blocks out from under us and cause us to start again from the ground up.

What's the Word on This Baby?

For example, we looked at the Christmas story as recorded by Matthew and Luke. We get a healthy reminder of this story every December. But now let's look at John's account of the "Christmas story," which has nothing to do with mangers, shepherds, wise men,

SOME THINGS YOU'LL DISCOVER IN THIS CHAPTER

1. Jesus expressed a whole range of emotions, from compassion to anger.

2. Jesus treated both men and women with respect—regardless of their reputations.

3. Jesus expects His followers to put Him first in their lives.

IN JESUS' NAME
"THE WORD" (John 1:1)

Prior to Jesus' birth, God's Word was *printed* in the Old Testament Scriptures, where it was largely ignored by many people. God's Word had been *spoken* by numerous prophets, who were routinely rejected and even persecuted. But with the birth of a very special baby in Bethlehem, God's Word "became human and lived here on earth among us." When God's Word became flesh and blood and skin and bones, we weren't limited to reading or hearing what God was like. We could see for ourselves and even interact with Him.

or even babies for that matter. But keep in mind the context of the traditional Christmas account as you add the following insight about Jesus.

> In the beginning the Word already existed. He was with God, and he was God. He was in the beginning with God. He created everything there is. Nothing exists that he didn't make. Life itself was in him, and this life gives light to everyone. The light shines through the darkness, and the darkness can never extinguish it.
>
> God sent John the Baptist to tell everyone about the light so that everyone might believe because of his testimony. John himself was not the light; he was only a witness to the light. The one who is the true light, who gives light to everyone, was going to come into the world.
>
> But although the world was made through him, the world didn't recognize him when he came. Even in his own land and among his own people, he was not accepted. But to all who believed him and accepted him, he gave the right to become children of God. They are reborn! This is not a physical birth resulting from human passion or plan—this rebirth comes from God.
>
> So the Word became human and lived here on earth among us. He was full of unfailing love and faithfulness. And we have seen his glory, the glory of the only Son of the Father.
>
> No one has ever seen God. But his only Son, who is himself God, is near to the Father's heart; he has told us about him. (John 1:1-14, 18)

According to John (the disciple), the birth of Jesus was nothing less than the Word of God, which has always existed, *being made human.* The ultimate standard of life and light was leaving His Father's side to come to earth to surround Himself with darkness and death. Representing God as Father, Creator, and Friend, He was not recognized by those He came to deliver. Yet by choice He "lived here on earth among us." When we pair this behind-the-scenes view of Jesus' birth with the more traditional one, the baby in the manger draws His first breath with a plan and purpose that few if any of His human peers would ever expect. A handful of people realized He was special, but did they really know *how* special?

Yet Another Miracle: An Obedient Teenager

We know little about Jesus' infancy and childhood. Yet the one account we do have shows behavior by a young teen that most of us probably wouldn't expect of our own children.

Each year Jesus' parents traveled from Nazareth to Jerusalem to celebrate the Feast of the Passover. They likely traveled in large groups of family and friends, and one year while on the way home, they discovered Jesus wasn't with them. Eventually they turned around and went back to the city. After three days, they found him in the temple. (Is that the first place *you* would look for an errant 12 year old?) Jesus was sitting among the teachers, listening to them and asking questions. The people in attendance were amazed at Jesus' answers and depth of understanding.

When His parents scolded Him a bit, He said, "But why did you need to search? You should have known that I would be in my Father's house" (Luke 2:49). They didn't really comprehend what He meant. But in another surprising act for a recently chastised 12 year old, Jesus "returned to Nazareth with [his parents] and was obedient to them." Even at 12 it seems His priorities were different than those of most people.

Not Your Normal Minister

Before Jesus, people thought they knew what to expect from religious leaders. The Pharisees were serious and somber. Their spiritual commitment was very public. Jesus didn't downplay the importance of spiritual actions, but He repeatedly pointed out the problems of pride and hypocrisy that frequently accompanied such actions.

Let's take a look at some of the aspects of Jesus' ministry that people found new, different, and/or unexpected:

OPINION POLL

"Welcome, all wonders in one sight! Eternity shut in a span!

Summer in Winter, Day in Night! Heaven on earth, and God in man!

Great little One! whose all-embracing birth

Lifts Earth to Heaven, stoops Heaven to Earth."—*Richard Crashaw*

W.D.J.D.?

Even as a youngster, Jesus had an above-average passion for spiritual development and enlightenment. So what did He do when He came across others who weren't up to His level of knowledge or concern? In this case, He submitted to the authority of His parents. At other times He would patiently try to raise people's understanding. There is no hint of spiritual arrogance—a common complaint many nonbelievers have against some of today's Christians.

"MASTER OF THE SABBATH"
(Matthew 12:8)

No one gets bent out of shape when preachers work on Sunday. Similarly, everything Jesus did on the Sabbath (or any day) was for God. The Pharisees criticized many of His actions because they were attempting to protect the Sabbath to honor God. Yet Jesus (who, as God, had set apart the Sabbath to begin with) had every right to challenge their restrictive traditions. He demonstrated that people could honor the Sabbath by doing *good* on it, rather than by doing *nothing*.

OPINION POLL

"It is part of the amazing originality of Christ that there is to be found in his teaching no word whatever which suggests a difference in the spiritual ideals, the spheres, or the potentialities of men and women."—*Maude Royden*

Jesus and His disciples didn't fast.

The Pharisees called Jesus on this point, and so did the disciples of John the Baptist (Matthew 9:14-15; 11:16-19). Jesus explained that fasting was a sign of mourning, which would take place when He was no longer with His friends. But as long as He was with them, it was a time to celebrate.

Jesus' interpretation of "keeping the Sabbath holy" was less restrictive than normal.

Jesus performed numerous miracles on the Sabbath, as we have seen (which would have been classified as "work" by the Pharisees). He and the disciples picked and ate grain. And when pressed by the authorities, Jesus explained that it was perfectly normal and acceptable to do good on the Sabbath. He even cited some Old Testament case law to back up His actions (Matthew 12:1-14).

Jesus' ministry had a large female following.

Jesus had cured many women of evil spirits and diseases, and some of those women were quite well to do (Luke 8:1-3). Some traveled with the disciples from place to place, and others provided financial support. This would have been very unusual—and perhaps quite scandalous—in this male-oriented culture.

Jesus redefined what it meant to be "clean."

It didn't take much under Old Testament Law to cause a period of "uncleanness," preventing the person from participating in certain worship activities and social contacts. Anything from touching a dead body, to a menstrual period, to leprosy or other serious diseases could limit a person's acceptance by the community at large. The Pharisees made a big point of ceremonial washing to demonstrate their cleanliness. But Jesus didn't always wash up before dinner (Luke 11:37-54). And He justified His actions by explaining that what made a person "unclean" wasn't what touched his body from the outside, but rather what came out of his heart (Mark 7:1-23, especially v. 15). While the religious leaders went about cleansing cups, plates, and hands, Jesus' mission was to cleanse people from the inside out.

Jesus' language and emotions were often surprising.

Jesus called Herod a fox (Luke 13:31-33). He called the Pharisees hypocrites, blind fools, sons of hell, snakes, sons of vipers, white-washed tombs, and more (Matthew 23). Once when people tried to prevent Him from helping a physically challenged man on the Sabbath, He "looked around at them angrily, because he was deeply disturbed by their hard hearts" (Mark 3:5). And at least once (perhaps twice, depending on one's interpretation of the Scriptures) Jesus ran moneychangers out of the temple, scattering coins across the floor, and even crafted a whip out of cords to herd out the animals (Matthew 21:12-17; John 2:12-17).

Jesus seems to have had a sense of humor.

Did Jesus' listeners laugh (or at least snicker a little) when He spoke of someone with a plank in his eye trying to remove a speck of saw-dust from someone else's eye (Matthew 7:3-5)? Was there a twinkle in His own eye when He described puffy Pharisees carefully straining drinking water to remove any "unclean" gnats, only to swallow entire camels (Matthew 23:24)? He is making valid points, to be sure, but perhaps He intentionally used ludicrous images to make those serious teachings more memorable.

Unexpected Power

We have already examined many of Jesus' healing miracles—even three resurrections from the dead—which seemed to reflect great power from God. Yet the disciples witnessed additional acts by Jesus that most people missed out on. We mentioned in chapter 5 that after Jesus publicly fed a crowd of over 5,000 people with a few small loaves and a couple of fish, He then walked on the water out to a boat where the disciples were gathered. Actions such as these astounded (and frightened) even the disciples—the people who best understood His power. And there were other examples we don't want to overlook.

A Couple of Fish Stories (Luke 5:4-11; John 21:1-11)

One of the earliest contacts Jesus had with His disciples involved fishing. So did one of the final ones. In the first case, Simon Peter

SOMETHING OLD,
SOMETHING NEW
Isaiah 29:13 ... Mark 7:6-7

Both Isaiah and Jesus speak for God: "These people honor me with their lips, but their hearts are far away. Their worship is a farce, for they replace God's commands with their own man-made teachings." Apparently the Pharisees' example of "cleanliness" wasn't next to godliness—it was nowhere close!

SOMETHING OLD,
SOMETHING NEW
Psalm 69:9 ... John 2:17

Jesus' actions in the temple sparked the disciples' recollection of Old Testament Scripture. David had expressed a powerful "passion for [God's] house," but Jesus' bold actions reflected the sentiment even more strongly.

95

OPINION POLL

"Beware of the attitudes which try to
make God smaller than the God who has
revealed himself to us in Jesus."
—*Arthur Michael Ramsey*

(though he wasn't called Peter yet) was washing his nets after a long and frustrating night of catching nothing. Jesus stood by the lake, teaching, and a large crowd assembled. He asked to borrow Peter's boat so he could sit just offshore and let people gather around to hear. Peter agreed.

When Jesus finished speaking, He told Peter to sail on out into the deeper water and let down his nets. Peter tried to explain that he had already tried that, and was very tired. Still, Jesus had a way of convincing people that He knew what was best for them. When Peter did as Jesus instructed, his nets snared so many fish that they began to break. He quickly called out to his partners in another boat, and the haul of fish was so enormous that both boats began to sink from the weight.

Peter didn't blow off this unexpected catch as a coincidence. He fell at Jesus' feet and said, "Oh, Lord, please leave me—I'm too much of a sinner to be around you." Jesus replied, "Don't be afraid! From now on you'll be fishing for people!" This was a deciding factor in convincing Peter and his fishing buddies to leave behind their nets and follow Jesus.

For three years Peter and the others "discipled" for a living. But after Jesus' crucifixion, they were at a loss as to what to do with their lives. So Peter went back to what came naturally—fishing. Having established himself as something of a leader for the group of disciples, several others went with them. They fished all night, but couldn't catch anything.

Early the next morning, a figure from shore called out to ask how they were doing. They told him not so good. Then he told them to throw the net over the other side of the boat. When they did, they were unable to retract the nets because of the great number of fish. Peter realized the figure on shore had to be Jesus, and couldn't even wait to row the boat to shore. He jumped into the water and swam while the others followed in the boat, dragging their nets behind them. A later inventory revealed a rather miraculous catch of 153 fish—yet this time without even tearing the net.

(Another good fish story is found in Matthew 17:24-27.)

Who Says Nobody Ever Does Anything about the Weather? (Mark 4:35-41)

Certainly, the miracles Jesus performed were all spectacular. But perhaps one of the most emphatic ones took place as He and the disciples were sailing from one side of the Sea of Galilee to the other. Having concluded a long day of teaching, Jesus was fast asleep. But a sudden storm blew up and powerful waves began crashing into the boat, nearly swamping it. Many of the disciples were experienced fishermen, yet they were all afraid for their lives. Finally, they woke Jesus and said, "Teacher, don't you even care that we are going to drown?"

Jesus got up and spoke to the wind and waves, saying, "Quiet down!" At once the sea became completely calm. Jesus chided the disciples a bit for their lack of faith, but they were dumbfounded. Perhaps they were more scared *after* seeing what happened than they had been during the storm. Even after the time they had spent with Him, they were still asking each another, "Who is this man, that even the wind and waves obey him?"

Who knows what they had in mind when they woke Jesus up and asked for help. But it's clear from their reaction that His command over nature was entirely unexpected.

Unexpected Relationships

Jesus displayed knowledge that people didn't expect. He demonstrated power that people didn't expect. He was regularly surprising people in one way or another. But perhaps the most unconventional attribute of Jesus was the way he built relationships. His teaching, healing, and service were all based on the importance and value of other people. And He showed this in magnificent ways in His one-on-one confrontations with others.

The Newlyweds (John 2:1-11)

Many people can tell you that Jesus' first miracle was turning water to wine. But how many people can tell you why?

Jesus and His disciples had been invited to a wedding, as had His mother. During the festivities, Jesus' mother made a simple

OPINION POLL

"Christ's character was more wonderful than the greatest miracle."—*Alfred Tennyson*

IN JESUS' NAME

"PRINCE OF PEACE" (Isaiah 9:6)

By instantly stilling a raging meteorological storm, Jesus demonstrated His power as Prince of Peace. Some people attest that His power is just as effective when the storms they face are emotional, financial, spiritual, and so forth.

statement: "They have no more wine." Jesus knew she was looking to Him to do something, and told her, "My time has not yet come." Yet His mother instructed the servants to do whatever Jesus told them.

Jesus had them fill six large jars with water—each jar with a capacity of between 20 and 30 gallons. Then He simply told them to take a sample to the master of ceremonies. They did as He said, and the "instant" wine was proclaimed to be superior than anything that had been served so far.

But the question remains: Why did Jesus perform this particular miracle? It's not like anyone would have died of thirst if they had to drink water instead of wine. No lives were in danger. No one was in pain.

However, failure to provide for their guests would have been a major faux pas for this newly married couple. In addition, it was more difficult for them to plan weddings than for most of us. In their culture, the party might last as long as a week as revelers celebrated the new marriage. A group of party-happy people could go through a lot of wine in a week, and to run out would cause embarrassment or shame for the hosting newlyweds.

Is this why Jesus acted when His mother told Him of the problem? We can only speculate as to His motives. We could spiritualize the results and see how Jesus can take something plain and ordinary (like water or people) and transform it into something spectacular and praiseworthy. But we have to consider that the primary reason Jesus performed this miracle was because He cared about the newlyweds.

Rather than allowing the most memorable day of this couple's lives to be marred with painful recollections, Jesus unexpectedly stepped in and circumvented a social blunder. It wouldn't become a habit; He wouldn't make His living from doing party tricks and bar bets. But in this case He surprised a lot of people—both with the miracle itself, and perhaps more so with His very willingness to do it.

Mary and Martha (Luke 10:38-42)

Another time Jesus was visiting with Mary and Martha, two sisters whose brother, Lazarus, Jesus would later raise from the dead. On this earlier visit, Martha was determined to be a good hostess. She was fussing in the kitchen and fretting about all the preparations that needed to be made. Mary, on the other hand, sat at Jesus' feet and was soaking up everything He had to say.

Finally Martha had had enough. She asked Jesus to tell Mary to get off the floor and get to work. But Jesus gently told Martha that Mary had her priorities straight. Jesus was talking about spiritual things, and Martha was missing out because she was "upset over all these details!" Only one thing was essential, and Mary was on the right track. Jesus turned water to wine because hospitality was an important thing. But He corrected Martha because it wasn't the *most* important thing.

A Man Up a Tree (Luke 19:1-10)

When Jesus came to town, all sorts of people turned out to see Him. One day in Jericho, a filthy rich tax collector named Zacchaeus was desperate to sneak a peek. The trouble was that Zacchaeus was short and couldn't get a decent view through all the crowds. He ran ahead to a place where Jesus would pass, and he climbed a tree to be sure to see Him.

When Jesus got to the tree, He did something unexpected. He stopped the procession, spoke above the clamor of the crowd, called Zacchaeus by name, and invited Himself to the tax collector's house. Zacchaeus was thrilled, though the crowds wondered why Jesus would single out a "notorious sinner" to spend time with. But after their meeting, Jesus declared that salvation had come to Zacchaeus, and explained that *that* was precisely His purpose for coming to earth. Zacchaeus was immediately a changed person, promising to give half his possessions to the poor and to pay back anyone he had cheated four times as much as he had taken. Great things happened because Jesus unexpectedly stopped His stroll down the road and called a short guy down out of a tree.

The Woman at the Well (John 4:1-42)

Many of Jesus' relationships were unusual not so much because of what He did, but because of whom He chose to hang around with in the first place. The religious leaders made a big point of separating

W.D.J.D.?

If Jesus had simply acknowledged Zacchaeus up in the tree, it would have thrilled the little guy. But what did Jesus do? He walked away from His own public acclaim to spend some one-on-one time with a spiritually hungry person who needed a friend. Sometimes wisdom deems an individual more significant than a crowd.

"PHYSICIAN" (Luke 4:23)
"DOCTOR" (Luke 5:31-32)

Luke was a physician, so he must have taken special interest when Jesus made a couple of passing references to Himself as a doctor. Clearly, Jesus was making a spiritual analogy. Just as we seek out an oncologist to help rid our bodies of potentially fatal cancer, Jesus was the only specialist capable of dealing with the consequences of sin. Yet in light of His physical miracles and power over diseases of all kinds, it is not unusual to hear Him referred to as "The Great Physician."

OPINION POLL

"Christ was the only rabbi who did not discriminate against women in his time."
—*Grace Eneme*

100

themselves from "sinners" like Zacchaeus. They felt threatened by even the taint of sin that might be associated with contact with such people. But Jesus made it clear that "Healthy people don't need a doctor—sick people do" (Matthew 9:12). He had come to help those who confessed sins and realized their need for forgiveness and salvation. The Pharisees who felt themselves to be in the peak of spiritual health were not ready for anything Jesus had to offer.

Jesus crossed "sin barriers" to associate with people. But He also crossed gender and ethnic barriers as well. Perhaps the best example of this was while He was resting at a well one day while the disciples had gone to get food. A Samaritan woman came for water, and Jesus broke all the rules of expected social etiquette by asking her for a drink. She was taken aback for several reasons. He was a Jew and she was a Samaritan. That was strike one. He was male and she was female. Strike two. And in the course of the conversation, Jesus told her He knew she was living with a man she wasn't married to after already having five husbands. Strike three!

For most people, the differences would have been far too great to allow bonds of friendship to develop. Yet as Jesus confronted this sexually promiscuous Samaritan woman, their conversation focused on spiritual things—living water, spiritual forefathers, eternal life, prophets, worship habits, and the eventual revelation that Jesus was the Messiah everyone was expecting.

As a result of the conversation, the woman left her water at the well, ran back to town, and brought out a Samaritan delegation who invited Jesus to stay with them. Two days later, many of them were convinced that Jesus was the Savior of the world. It's not what was expected from most encounters between Jews and Samaritans.

One of "That Kind" of Women (Luke 7:36-50))

Jesus had another encounter with a woman of questionable reputation. This time it was at a dinner party thrown for Him by a Pharisee named Simon. People reclined at low tables in order to eat, and Jesus was still at the table when the woman approached Him. She is identified only as "a certain immoral woman." She stood behind Jesus and began crying, her tears falling on His feet. She dried His feet with her hair, then kissed them, and finally anointed them with expensive perfume, poured from a beautiful jar.

As all this was going on, Simon was thinking that if Jesus really had any kind of prophetic insight, He would know what kind of woman this was. So Jesus told a parable—one that we skipped in the last chapter. He said: "A man loaned money to two people—five hundred pieces of silver to one and fifty pieces to the other. But neither of them could repay him, so he kindly forgave them both, canceling their debts. Who do you suppose loved him more after that?"

Simon guessed that the one who had the larger debt canceled would be more grateful. Jesus agreed, and then pointed out that Simon had not washed Jesus' feet or provided the opportunity to do so (which should have been done by the host). He had shown no customary signs of affection for Jesus (a greeting kiss, anointing His head, etc.). But the woman, somehow realizing who Jesus was and what He could do for her, wasn't going to miss this opportunity—as public as it was—to attend to Him.

So Jesus told the woman, "Your sins are forgiven," and told her to go in peace. The party guests were amazed that someone claimed to forgive sins. But perhaps equally impressive was the fact that no other male in the community could have handled that situation with as much grace and aplomb as Jesus.

(Another classic example of Jesus' tact and grace with women of questionable character is described in John 8:1-11.)

A Gentile Woman with a Demon-Possessed Daughter (Matthew 15:21-28)

When it came to relationships, one of the unexpected aspects of Jesus' ministry was that He didn't coerce people to follow or believe in Him if they didn't want to. Sometimes it seemed that He intentionally challenged people as a test of their faith. In one case, for example, a Gentile (non-Jewish) woman came to Him because her daughter was possessed by an evil spirit. The woman wouldn't stop crying out for Jesus to remove the demon.

Jesus ignored her at first, but finally the disciples asked Him to do something because she wouldn't stop shouting. Jesus explained that He was sent to "the people of Israel—God's lost sheep" (the

W.D.J.D.?

If we look to Jesus as a model for evangelism, we see a vastly different strategy from what a lot of churches seem to practice. Personal contact and interaction meant more to Jesus than accumulating names on a list, or merely getting people saved. He spelled out the facts and let people make their own decisions. He called them into deeper relationships or no relationship at all. Some, like the Gentile woman, were insistent on getting involved. Others, like the rich young man, decided to take a pass on the opportunity. Jesus always seemed to allow and encourage personal choice, whether He agreed with it or not.

Jews). Still she pleaded for help. He told her, "It isn't right to take food from the children and throw it to the dogs." Someone else might have taken offense and walked away, but the woman was sharp and would not be denied. She shot back: "Yes, Lord, but even dogs are permitted to eat crumbs that fall beneath their master's table."

Jesus publicly acknowledged the woman's great faith and granted her request. Her daughter was healed immediately.

Such behavior seems rather peculiar coming from Jesus, yet He knew the woman's heart. She not only received what she asked for, but became an example of faith recorded in Scripture to challenge readers throughout the centuries.

The One Who Got Away (Mark 10:17-25)

Another time Jesus was pursued by a wealthy young man who asked how to inherit eternal life. Jesus reminded him of the Old Testament commandments, which the young man said he had followed all his life. Then Jesus added: "You lack only one thing. Go and sell all you have and give the money to the poor, and you will have treasure in heaven. Then come, follow me."

To our knowledge, Jesus never asked anyone else to sell all he or she had before becoming His follower. But again, He seemed to know what was on this guy's heart and mind. The young man had convinced himself he was putting God above everything else, when in reality he had more faith in his wealth. It is noted in the text that "Jesus felt genuine love for this man as he looked at him." It is also clear that the young man had the highest regard for Jesus. And Jesus could certainly have recruited him as a new disciple and *then* taught him how to place love for God above love for money. But instead Jesus let him walk away. It's not what many of us would expect.

Now for Something Completely Different

Have you been surprised by anything in this chapter? Many of the things Jesus did simply don't fit the preconceptions we have formed about Him. He certainly wasn't someone the religious leaders of His time could figure out—which eventually put Him on their hit list. But even the church of the 21st century has trouble comprehending some of the statements and actions of Jesus. Just when we begin to get a little too comfortable, we come across one of His comments, challenges, or questions that remind us we don't understand Him as well as we thought we did.

Yet any confusion or questions that remain in our minds about the motivations and declarations of Jesus are usually insignificant compared to what we *can* be sure about. Yes, Jesus did some things that people didn't expect. He still does. But we must not make the erroneous assumption that He is inconsistent or untrustworthy. We are told in the Bible that Jesus is "the same yesterday, today, and forever" (Hebrews 13:8).

In the next couple of chapters we will take a closer look at some of the things He has done to convince us we can trust Him.

Questions to Ponder and/or Discuss

1. Of all these stories—and other biblical accounts you might know about—which of Jesus' actions seems the most unexpected? Why?

2. Has God ever done anything unexpected in *your* life? If so, what did you learn from the experience?

3. When you see something unexpected done in the name of God, how do you normally tend to react?

- "Warning! Warning! Run away!"
- "My, that's interesting. I think I'll investigate more closely."
- "Cool! Bring it on! The weirder, the better."
- Other: _____

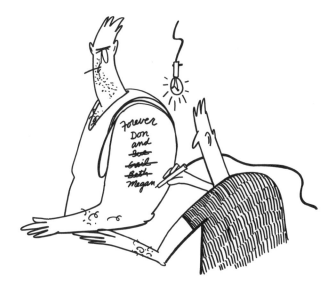

CHAPTER ELEVEN

Bold Claims

JESUS THE SAVIOR

Around the turn of the eighteenth century, an English woman had a visitor from the Royal Society of London. During the course of their conversation, she started talking about her neighbor, a "poor crazy gentleman." It seems that in the heat of the day, when most people sought relief indoors, he would sit in the sun, dip a clay pipe into soapsuds, and blow bubbles for hours. The woman's visitor peered out her window, saw the man, and said, "The person you suppose to be a poor lunatic is none other than the great Sir Isaac Newton, studying the refraction of light upon thin plates—a phenomenon which is beautifully exhibited upon the surface of common soap bubbles."

The woman, from every indication and to the best of her knowledge, saw a demented lunatic. Her visitor, who had a small bit of additional knowledge and a different perspective, saw one of the world's greatest scientific minds at work.

Savior Self

When you look at Jesus, what do you see? When many people witness His behavior, His relationships, and His quizzical statements,

SOME THINGS YOU'LL DISCOVER IN THIS CHAPTER

1. Jesus made great claims about Himself that forced His listeners to make tough decisions.

2. Jesus underwent a magnificent transfiguration in front of some of His disciples.

3. Jesus foretold details about His death before it happened.

they see a nice guy, perhaps, yet one who must surely be deluded. Others see the savior of the world.

When it comes to Jesus, most people agree on a lot of the basics. As we have seen so far in this book, His life was committed to service toward humanity. He was an interesting teacher, and He seems to have had quite a special ability to heal the sick and cure people of various afflictions such as blindness, deafness, possession by evil spirits, and so forth. He seems to have fulfilled a number of Old Testament prophecies concerning the coming Messiah. And in light of His unique personality and uncharacteristic behavior, you might even have come to expect the unexpected from Him.

Jesus was most definitely an interesting and challenging individual. But a major dividing line will be drawn in this chapter. In addition to all these other functions Jesus performed, was He also the Savior of the world? Ah, there's the rub! Was He indeed the Messiah who had been foretold? Was He the Son of God—barely recognizable in a grotesque, awkward, flesh-and-blood version of deity? Was His mission on earth not primarily to teach and heal, but more specifically to die for the sins of everyone alive, who had ever lived, and who would ever live? And if so, how are we to juxtapose the images of the suffering servant who was Jesus with those we expect from the Lord of the universe?

A major factor in determining on which side of the dividing line you will stand is your interpretation of the Bible. Some people *think* they know what Scripture has to say but haven't done a lot of personal examination. This chapter will encourage you to take a look at what the Bible really says about Jesus, and then you can make your own determinations.

Can I Get a Witness?

Previous chapters have covered teachings and events that have pointed to Jesus in His capacity as Savior. Let's start by reviewing a few of them:

- Joseph was told by an angel not to divorce Mary because of her unexpected pregnancy. Instead, he was to name the child

OPINION POLL

"You must make your choice. Either this man [Jesus] was, and is, the Son of God: or else a madman or something worse. You can shut Him up for a fool, you can spit at Him and kill him as a demon; or you can fall at His feet and call Him Lord and God. But let us not come with any patronising nonsense about His being a great human teacher. He has not left that open to us. He did not intend to."
—C. S. Lewis

Jesus ("Savior") because "he will save his people from their sins" (Matthew 1:20-21).

- Mary was told by the angel Gabriel that her son "will be very great and will be called the Son of the Most High. And the Lord God will give him the throne of his ancestor David. And he will reign over Israel forever; his Kingdom will never end!" (Luke 1:30-33)

- John the Baptist was such a dynamic speaker and figure that some people were guessing *he* might be the Messiah. But he spoke of one greater and more powerful to follow. Later John the Baptist encouraged some of his own disciples to follow Jesus instead. Andrew came back from his first encounter saying, "We have found the Messiah." Another early follower, Nathanael, immediately proclaimed Jesus to be "the Son of God" and "the King of Israel." Jesus didn't deny any of these titles (John 1:35-51).

- At Jesus' baptism, a voice from heaven spoke and said, "You are my beloved Son, and I am fully pleased with you" (Mark 1:11).

- In Jesus' conversation with the woman at the well, she had said she knew the Messiah (Christ) was coming. Jesus told her, "I am the Messiah!" (John 4:25-26)

- Just before He brought Lazarus back to life, Jesus told Martha: "I am the resurrection and the life. Those who believe in me, even though they die like everyone else, will live again. They are given eternal life for believing in me and will never perish" (John 11:25-26).

So both Jesus and other people were making claims to His deity. In addition to these events we have already covered in previous chapters, let's take a look at a few additional statements:

- Within a longer discourse directed toward people who were persecuting Him, Jesus said, "I assure you, those who listen to my message and believe in God who sent me have eternal life. They will never be condemned for their sins, but they have already passed from death into life" (John 5:24).

IN JESUS' NAME
"SON OF GOD" (John 1:49)
"KING OF ISRAEL" (John 1:49)

The relationship of Jesus to His heavenly Father is emphasized in the title Son of God. His relationship with human beings comes through in his King of Israel title.

SOMETHING OLD,
SOMETHING NEW
2 Samuel 7:16; Isaiah 11:1-2 ... John 1:49

God had made a promise to King David: "Your dynasty and your kingdom will continue for all time before me, and your throne will be secure forever" (2 Samuel 7:16). But a lot of rotten kings followed David, and they allowed the glory of Israel to be destroyed. Isaiah described David's kingdom as a mighty tree that had been cut down, leaving only a stump. Yet someday, he predicted, a fresh fruit-bearing shoot would arise from that stump. Jesus would step into His role as "King of Israel." God's promise of an eternal reign from the line of David would be fulfilled.

Exodus 17:5-7 ... John 7:37-38

As the Israelites leaving Egypt grew thirsty (and desperate) in the wilderness, more than once God miraculously provided water from solid rock. Similarly, in a time of spiritual thirst and need, Jesus proclaimed Himself a source of "living water."

IN JESUS' NAME

"I AM" (JOHN 8:58)

As God was speaking to Moses from the burning bush, Moses asked what he should tell the Israelites if they wanted to know God's name. God replied, "I AM WHO I AM. This is what you are to say to the Israelites: 'I AM has sent me to you'" (Exodus 3:14, NIV). In other words, God is not limited to human definitions or comprehension. Jesus used this same name for Himself. The religious leaders knew exactly what He meant, because they tried to stone Him on the spot (John 8:59).

- At one point people were in a public debate as to whether or not Jesus was indeed the Messiah. Jesus proclaimed at that point, "If you are thirsty, come to me! If you believe in me, come and drink! For the Scriptures declare that rivers of living water will flow out from within" (John 7:37-38).

- When the Jewish leaders spoke of how they revered Abraham, Jesus told them, "I tell you the truth, before Abraham was born, I am!" (John 8:58, NIV)

- Jesus called Himself "the good shepherd" who "lays down his life for the sheep." He added, "The Father loves me because I lay down my life that I may have it back again. No one can take my life from me. I lay down my life voluntarily. For I have the right to lay it down when I want to and also the power to take it again. For my Father has given me this command" (John 10:11, 17-18).

In addition to making it clear that He was sent from God, was given authority from God, and was indeed the Son of God, Jesus also said that He was the *only* way to God. Again, this is not a widely appreciated viewpoint outside the Christian church, nor did it make Jesus popular with the religious leaders of His own time. But He made such statements nevertheless. Here are some examples:

- "I assure you, anyone who sneaks over the wall of a sheepfold, rather than going through the gate, must surely be a thief and a robber! . . . I am the gate for the sheep. All others who came before me were thieves and robbers. But the true sheep did not listen to them. Yes, I am the gate. Those who come in through me will be saved. Wherever they go, they will find green pastures" (John 10:1, 7-9).

- "I am the way, the truth, and the life. No one can come to the Father except through me" (John 14:6).

- "Yes, I am the vine; you are the branches. Those who remain in me, and I in them, will produce much fruit. For apart from me you can do nothing. Anyone who parts from me is thrown away like a useless branch and withers. Such branches are gathered into a pile to be burned" (John 15:5-6).

Teachings like these forced crucial decisions from the people who heard them. As a result, Jesus faced a lot of rejection in His lifetime. The people of Nazareth, where He had grown up, wanted to toss Him over a cliff after they heard Him speak but never got to act on their intentions (Luke 4:14-30). Jesus' own brothers humored Him, but they didn't believe in Him—at least, not to begin with (John 7:1-5). And as we have seen, the Jewish leaders tended to oppose Jesus publicly at every opportunity. Meanwhile, they were secretly looking for the right time and place to arrest and/or kill Him. However, there are a couple of notable exceptions to this attitude.

A Pharisee More Fair, I See

One man on the ruling council of the Pharisees was named Nicodemus. He came to see Jesus at night, which suggests that he may not have wished to be seen with this unorthodox teacher or perhaps that he wanted an opportunity to talk without all the interruptions Jesus would have in a normal day. Nicodemus began the conversation by acknowledging that Jesus must be sent from God—otherwise there was no explanation for His miracles. Jesus replied, "I assure you, unless you are born again, you can never see the Kingdom of God."

While the phrase "born again" is used with much regularity by certain denominations within the Christian church, it is found only in a couple of places in the Bible. Nicodemus picked up right away that Jesus wasn't referring to physical birth, yet when Jesus spoke further about "the Spirit," Nicodemus had trouble following His train of thought. But rather than nod as if he knew what Jesus was talking about (as many of us might be prone to do), he interrupted and asked for further clarification. Because he did, Jesus kept talking and spoke the words that have become perhaps best known of any in Scripture: "For God so loved the world that he gave his only Son, so that everyone who believes in him will not perish but have eternal life."

SOMETHING OLD, SOMETHING NEW

Isaiah 53:6; Ezekiel 34 . . . John 10:11-18

In a prophetic passage, Isaiah had written, "All of us have strayed away like sheep. We have left God's paths to follow our own" (Isaiah 53:6). In this regard, Jesus came as a Good Shepherd to show us the way back to the fold (see John 10). Similarly, Ezekiel had contrasted all the "bad shepherds" of the world with Christ, the Good Shepherd.

OPINION POLL

"Follow me; I am the way, the truth, and the life. Without the way there is no going. Without the truth there is no knowing. Without the life there is no living."—*Thomas à Kempis*

W.D.J.D.?

In one case of point-blank rejection, an entire Samaritan village refused to welcome Jesus (Luke 9:51-56). Some of the disciples suggested calling down fire from heaven to flambé the stubborn Samaritans. What did Jesus do? He simply moved on to another town. Why waste a lot of energy butting heads with people who didn't want to listen when so many others *did* want to hear what He had to say?

In fact, the words are so familiar we may neglect to place them in context of what comes immediately before and after them. Jesus had just spoken about coming from heaven to earth and the difficulty of helping people understand heavenly things when they couldn't even comprehend the earth-based symbolism He used. He also referred to an Old Testament story that symbolized the death He would eventually face.

The passage that immediately follows John 3:16 is equally important: "God did not send his Son into the world to condemn it, but to save it. There is no judgment awaiting those who trust him. But those who do not trust him have already been judged for not believing in the only Son of God" (John 3:17-18).

This "one way to God" issue is troublesome to many people. And it's hard to explain to people of other faiths or those who have not yet seen the need to put faith in someone other than themselves. On one hand, it is clear that Jesus' main purpose is salvation and redemption rather than condemnation. He calls people to God and is grieved when they reject Him. He seeks a relationship with His followers and wants only the best for them. But on the other hand, a rejection of Jesus (according to Scripture) leaves no other option for the person. It's not our good deeds that God is (primarily) interested in. It's not church attendance nor community service. While these are fine and worthwhile activities in themselves, they are not a valid substitute for faith in Jesus. We will look more closely at the theology behind this thinking in later chapters.

Two Good Questions

Even Jesus' inner circle of disciples was continuing to make new discoveries about Him. One day Jesus asked His disciples a couple of key questions. First He asked, "Who do people say I am?" (Luke 9:18)

The disciples responded that some people thought He was a reincarnated John the Baptist. (Herod, the presiding Roman ruler of the area, was in this group even though he had been the one who had given the order for John the Baptist to be beheaded. Herod had liked

John. He also feared him because he realized John was "a good and holy man." But after being manipulated and publicly put on the spot, Herod reluctantly had him killed [Mark 6:14-29].)

But there were other opinions about Jesus. Some people thought He was the Old Testament prophet Elijah. Others speculated He was Jeremiah or another one of the prophets. The disciples reported these theories to Jesus (Matthew 16:13-14).

Then Jesus asked the second, more important question: "Who do *you* say I am?" The disciples had spent a couple of years with Jesus at this point. But that was long enough for Peter, who spoke up: "You are the Messiah, the Son of the living God" (Matthew 16:16). Jesus was impressed with Peter's answer and pointed out that the insight had to have come from God the Father. But with about another year of ministry ahead of Him, Jesus warned His group of disciples not to tell anyone that He was the Messiah.

But Peter's acknowledgement of Jesus as the Messiah seems to have been a turning point. We are told that "From then on Jesus began to tell his disciples plainly that he had to go to Jerusalem, and he told them what would happen to him there. He would suffer at the hands of the leaders and the leading priests and the teachers of religious law. He would be killed, and he would be raised on the third day" (Matthew 16:21).

The disciples couldn't understand this kind of talk, much less condone it. Peter pulled Jesus aside one day and was going to straighten Him out. Peter said, "Heaven forbid, Lord. This will never happen to you!" (Matthew 16:22) But Jesus quite firmly explained that Peter's opinion didn't much matter since it was God's will for these events to take place. Jesus also promised that some of His disciples would "not die before you see me, the Son of Man, coming in my Kingdom" (Matthew 16:28). It was a strange statement, but the following story in the Bible explains what Jesus meant.

A Booth for Three?

Jesus and His "inner circle" of disciples—Peter, James, and John—went high on a mountain where Jesus was "transfigured." Through

SOMETHING OLD, SOMETHING NEW
Numbers 21:4-9 ... John 3:14-15

A story tucked into the Old Testament describes a time when, after a lengthy period of whining and complaining by the Israelites, God sent poisonous snakes into their camp. Many who were bitten died immediately, causing instant repentance from the others and a plea to Moses to appeal to God. In response, God had Moses sculpt a snake and place it high on a pole. Anyone in the camp who was bitten could look at the serpent and live. Jesus used this story to indicate to Nicodemus that in a similar way, He too would be lifted up as a remedy for death. While people would still feel the bite of sin, Jesus would provide the antidote to prevent eternally fatal consequences.

SOMETHING OLD,
SOMETHING NEW
Malachi 4:5-6... Matthew 17:10-13

The final promise of the Old Testament was that God would send the prophet Elijah prior to "the great and dreadful day of the Lord." It's not surprising that people would be looking for Elijah and might assume Jesus was the fulfillment of the prophecy. But Jesus made it clear that the prophecy in Malachi referred to John the Baptist.

metamorphosis a tadpole becomes a frog and a caterpillar becomes a butterfly. But the transfiguration of Jesus was more than a stage He was going through. It was an unveiling . . . a revealing . . . an opportunity for some of His disciples to see Him closer to His true form, without the cumbersome costume of humanity that had been shielding the glory of God within.

As His disciples looked on, Jesus' face "shone like the sun" (Matthew 17:2). His clothing "became dazzling white, far whiter than any earthly process could ever make it" (Mark 9:3). And as if that weren't enough for the stunned disciples, Moses and Elijah appeared and began to converse with Jesus.

Not quite knowing how to respond to these amazing sights, Peter suggested the disciples erect "three shrines"—one for Jesus and one for each of His visitors. No doubt Peter's intentions were good, but he was probably hoping to hasten the onset of the kingdom of God on earth. Jesus had been trying to prepare His disciples for His suffering and death, but little of that part of His teaching seemed to be soaking in.

Peter was still speaking when he was interrupted. A brilliant cloud appeared and a voice spoke from it: "This is my beloved Son, and I am fully pleased with him. Listen to him" (Matthew 17:5). At this, the disciples hit the ground in fear. Jesus told them to get up and not be afraid. As He helped them to their feet, they saw that He was again alone with them. Jesus told them not to reveal what had happened "until I, the Son of Man, have been raised from the dead" (Matthew 17:9).

Death Talk and Deaf Ears

All this talk about the kingdom of God approaching seemed to bring out the competitive spirits of the disciples, who started jockeying for positions of prestige in the coming kingdom. There seemed to be an ongoing debate among them about who was the greatest (Luke 9:46-48; 22:24-30). One time one of the mothers even got involved, trying to convince Jesus to have her two good boys positioned on either side of Him once the kingdom was established (Matthew 20:20-28).

Her efforts were in vain. Jesus explained that God the Father was in charge of seating arrangements and future entitlements in the kingdom. All Mom did was cause the other ten disciples to become "indignant" with her sons, James and John. Jesus attempted to diffuse the conflict by teaching them all (yet again) of the importance of humility. In God's kingdom, He noted, greatness would be based on humble service to others. He was no exception Himself, as He reminded them: "For even I, the Son of Man, came here not to be served but to serve others, and to give my life as a ransom for many" (Matthew 20:28).

Jesus was beginning to do a lot of talking about His death, but very little seemed to be sinking into the hearts or minds of the disciples. Sometimes He spoke quite directly. Other times He tried to help people understand by using familiar stories and symbols.

For example, when some of the Pharisees and religious teachers asked Jesus directly for a miraculous sign, He refused. (It's not like they couldn't see what He was doing among the people every day.) Instead He replied, "Only an evil, faithless generation would ask for a miraculous sign; but the only sign I will give them is the sign of the prophet Jonah. For as Jonah was in the belly of the great fish for three days and three nights, so I, the Son of Man, will be in the heart of the earth for three days and three nights" (Matthew 12:39-40).

Jesus went on to point out that the wicked Ninevites had repented, while the Pharisees continued to reject the clear message (and messenger) of God.

Jesus wasn't changing His message; He simply continued to clarify it as the time of His death grew closer. He had earlier stood outside the temple and said, "Destroy this temple, and in three days I will raise it up" (John 2:19). The people who heard Him were amazed and confused, because the construction of Herod's temple had taken 46 years. But the "temple" Jesus referred to was His body. Only in retrospect, after His death, did the disciples really figure out what Jesus had meant (John 2:22).

Who can blame the disciples for being slow to comprehend when Jesus' symbolism was so obscure? But as His crucifixion approached,

SOMETHING OLD,
SOMETHING NEW

Leviticus 23:33-43 ... Matthew 17:4

The Feast of Tabernacles (or Festival of Shelters) was an annual Jewish celebration where people would build booths and camp out for a week as a reminder of how their ancestors had lived while coming out of Egypt and traveling to the Promised Land. Perhaps Peter was suggesting something like this for Jesus, Moses, and Elijah. Or perhaps his intentions were even more ambitious—to reinstitute something like the Old Testament "Tent of Meeting" where Moses had communicated with God on behalf of the people (Exodus 40:34-38). Either way, he was getting ahead of himself. Jesus was giving His friends a *preview* of the Kingdom of God, not yet establishing it on earth.

1 Kings 10:1-10 . . . Matthew 12:39-42

In addition to the Old Testament reference to Jonah, Jesus also referred to the Queen of Sheba's visit with King Solomon. The foreign, non-Jewish queen traveled far to hear God's wisdom through the mouth of Solomon and then bestowed him with gifts. The extremely wicked people of Nineveh had changed their evil ways when they heard God's message through the mouth of Jonah. Yet the supposedly enlightened Jewish religious leaders continued to reject God's teaching through the mouth of Jesus. This was no small spiritual shortcoming on their part.

OPINION POLL

"Cowards die many times before their deaths; the valiant never taste of death but once."—*William Shakespeare*

He couldn't get much clearer. He pulled His disciples aside and told them: "When we get to Jerusalem, the Son of Man will be betrayed to the leading priests and the teachers of religious law. They will sentence him to die. Then they will hand him over to the Romans to be mocked, whipped, and crucified. But on the third day he will be raised from the dead" (Matthew 20:17-19).

Notice that Jesus has identified where and how His death will take place. He has foretold His betrayal. He knows He will be tried and found guilty. He is aware of the pain, humiliation, and other extenuating circumstances surrounding His death. He tells His disciples how long He will be dead and promises a return to life afterward.

The extent of detail Jesus provides is important for a couple of reasons. First, it should have better prepared His followers for what was about to take place. Maybe if they hadn't been so concerned about being first to the table in the kingdom of God, they could have been more supportive of what Jesus was about to do.

But even more importantly, Jesus' foreknowledge of the events to come are evidence that what He did, He did willingly. It's not that Judas's betrayal was a sneak attack. Jesus saw it coming. The clock had kept ticking and the time had finally come. He was about to be "lifted up" on a cross.

Could It Be True?

Consider the question we asked previously: What do you see when you look at Jesus? Perhaps you recall the craze a few years back when everyone seemed to have books and posters of computer-generated three-dimensional art. The two-dimensional picture would be a not-very-attractive repeated pattern. Newcomers to this type of art would wonder what the big deal was. But if you gazed at the pattern long enough and allowed your eyes to focus in just the right manner, a rich and textured three-dimensional image would seem to arise out of the jumbled patterns.

Some people just can't see the Savior of the world when they look at Jesus. He remains something of a two-dimensional character creating little if any curiosity. But others are amazed that, if they look at Jesus the right way, out of His deceptively plain and simple life appears a character of indescribable depth, mystery, and wonder.

Perhaps you still don't see Him as a savior, but Scripture is clear that Jesus saw Himself in that role. Some people would suggest that means He was delusional, but if so, He had certainly fooled large crowds of people with His charm, insight, intelligence, compassion, and power.

Because of the beliefs of the New Testament writers, we will need to continue to pursue the assumption that Jesus did indeed come as Savior of the world. Otherwise, the rest of the Bible won't make much sense. If you're not in agreement, please bear with us for the sake of argument.

Besides, we haven't seen Him under pressure yet. How will He handle Himself as His own leaders and the weight of the Roman Empire come down on Him simultaneously? That's what we'll see in the next chapter.

Questions to Ponder and/or Discuss

1. If, like Nicodemus, you had the opportunity to talk with Jesus alone and uninterrupted, what would be the first thing you would ask Him?

2. How do you think your life would be affected if you knew ahead of time how and when you were going to die?

3. On a scale of 1 (least) to 10 (most), rate how strongly you believe that Jesus fulfills each of the following roles:

Teacher	1 2 3 4 5 6 7 8 9 10
Prophet	1 2 3 4 5 6 7 8 9 10
Healer	1 2 3 4 5 6 7 8 9 10
Good Shepherd	1 2 3 4 5 6 7 8 9 10
Son of God	1 2 3 4 5 6 7 8 9 10
King of Israel	1 2 3 4 5 6 7 8 9 10
Savior	1 2 3 4 5 6 7 8 9 10

W.D.J.D.?

Since Jesus was aware everything would take place in Jerusalem, He could have simply gone the opposite direction. But He didn't. Jesus knew of His impending death and walked right into it. It's what He had come to do. As unpleasant as the ordeal would be, He was going to see it through to the end.

OPINION POLL

"As Man alone, Jesus could not have saved us; as God alone, he would not; Incarnate, he could and did."—*Malcolm Muggeridge*

CHAPTER TWELVE

"BOBBY, NOT EATING YOUR BROCCOLI HARDLY CONSTITUTES MAKING A PERSONAL SACRIFICE. I DOUBT THAT'S WHAT THE PASTOR HAD IN MIND."

A Seed Is Planted

JESUS THE SACRIFICE

Most people these days have a limited and shallow understanding of the concept of sacrifice. We bemoan having to "sacrifice" a few hours of leisure time to do something with the kids, or to "sacrifice" a Saturday to put in some overtime at work. We play baseball and "sacrifice" our at-bat to lay down a bunt or pop a long fly to advance a runner.

And blood sacrifices? Fuhgeddaboudit! These days—aside from a few farmers, slaughterhouse workers, and animal-rights activists—people hardly think about death and sacrifice in regard to their food. We grocery shop and unthinkingly toss packets of neatly shrink-wrapped meat into our carts. We go into restaurants, point to items on a menu, and the food automatically appears before us.

Yet a century or two ago, it was still common for people to kill and clean what they ate. And a few millennia ago, blood sacrifice was a big part of religion for a lot of people—including the Old Testament Jews. God had given very specific instructions for what He expected in their offerings and ceremonies. A common theme runs through the Bible: "Without the shedding of blood, there is no forgiveness of sins" (Hebrews 9:22).

SOME THINGS YOU'LL DISCOVER IN THIS CHAPTER

1. On one of Jesus' final trips to Jerusalem, He was treated like a king.

2. Jesus modeled servanthood by wrapping a towel around His waist and washing the feet of His own disciples.

3. Jesus died a horrible death but continued all the while to think of others.

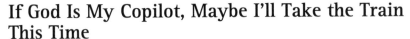
If God Is My Copilot, Maybe I'll Take the Train This Time

One group of people who truly understood the nature of complete and total sacrifice were the Japanese kamikaze pilots of World War II. These were highly regarded men of honor who found no greater purpose than to sacrifice their own lives for the people and country they loved. They would load their planes with explosives and fly them into ships and other key targets. When it came to dealing with the enemy, they acted with great certainty and finality, dying in the process.

If we believe Jesus was a Savior, we must consider the nasty corollary that He was also a human sacrifice. Many New Testament books will come back to this theme, but in this chapter we want to see exactly what He did, what He was thinking, and what it meant for Jesus to voluntarily give up His life.

In spite of what we might have been led to believe, Jesus' enemy was not Judas or Pontius Pilate. His enemies were not the Pharisees or others who rejected Him. The only enemy He came to destroy was sin, and He had come with the determination of a kamikaze pilot to obliterate that enemy regardless of the cost. He was at the controls. He knew what the outcome would be. He realized His act of sacrifice would have painful consequences. It would require the highest possible cost—His very life. Yet He didn't let anything deter Him. And when He had completed His mission, the enemy would be incapacitated and ultimately defeated.

In Previous Episodes . . .

We want to take a look at Jesus' sacrificial death, but let's put it into context. The previous chapters have set the scene. After Jesus' baptism and temptation, He had a public ministry for about three years. While He did a bit of teaching in the synagogues (as any teacher of His day would be invited to do), most of His ministry was unstructured and informal. He would go from place to place, instructing those who would listen and healing masses of people who came to

OPINION POLL

"Death is the supreme festival on the road to freedom."—*Dietrich Bonhoeffer*

OPINION POLL

"He never errs who sacrifices self."
—*Bulwer-Lytton*

Him for help. At first He tried to downplay His miracles, but human nature being what it is, no one seemed able to keep a secret.

As He attracted more public attention, He also faced intensified opposition from the traditional religious leaders. They eventually stopped trying to hide their disdain for Him and engaged in an ongoing plot to silence Jesus one way or another.

All along the way, Jesus made references to indicate that He was on a timetable. More than once He commented that "My time has not yet come." No one else had much of an inkling what He meant. But after about three years, with His support growing among the crowds and His critics getting more and more vocal, His time had come at last. So let's take a look at the last few days of Jesus' life to see exactly what led up to His final sacrificial act.

Sunday Morning Coming Down (to Jerusalem)

It was approaching time to celebrate Passover. While the holiday itself was a solemn religious observance commemorating the departure of the Israelites from Egypt centuries ago (Exodus 12), it was followed by a week of feasting. Jerusalem at Passover was like New Orleans at Mardi Gras. The usual population of 50,000 was multiplied several times over. And this year, many of the people in the crowd were looking specifically for Jesus to show up (John 11:55-56). The Pharisees and priests were looking for Him too, but they planned to arrest Him (John 11:57).

A Jesus sighting took place on Sunday, and the crowds left the city to go out and meet Him. Along the way they gathered palm branches, which were used in victory celebrations. The people lined the highway as Jesus rode into Jerusalem on a young donkey.

The people spread their palm branches, as well as their coats, on the ground before Jesus in sort of a "green carpet treatment" as He neared the city. They were also yelling and cheering for Him, shouting hosannas ("Hosanna" means "Save now") and quoting from the psalms: "Bless the one who comes in the name of the Lord" (Psalm 118:26).

SOMETHING OLD, SOMETHING NEW
Zechariah 9:9 ... Matthew 21:1-5

Conquering heroes were known to ride into large cities on horses. Jesus' choice, a donkey's colt, was a less flashy symbol of peace. His choice also confirmed a prophecy that foretold a king approaching Jerusalem who "is righteous and victorious, yet he is humble." This king would be riding the colt of a donkey, and would bring peace to the land.

IN JESUS' NAME
"HEIR TO DAVID'S THRONE" (Isaiah 11:10)

The cheering crowd addressed Jesus as "Son of David," a title which would have been especially relevant at this time. Jerusalem had been David's capital city, but it had been centuries since the golden years when King David had set foot in the city. According to prophecy, the Messiah would not only be a descendant of David, but "heir to David's throne" as well.

W.D.J.D.?

With less than a week to live, it seems Jesus was undergoing a wide range of emotions. He had just been weeping over the future of Jerusalem, and He was about to conduct a zealous rampage to purify the temple. He must have certainly been dwelling on the ordeal He was about to endure. And yet in the midst of His own personal crises, He continued to tenderly and patiently teach those closest to Him. He never used "I was just in a bad mood" as an excuse for not dealing with other people as He should.

Some of the watching Pharisees were alarmed by all the attention focused on Jesus. They even asked Him to scold the people for saying such things. But Jesus replied, "If they kept quiet, the stones along the road would burst into cheers!" (Luke 19:40)

Yet while the frenzied crowds were ecstatic, this was a somber moment for Jesus. When Jerusalem came into sight, He began to cry and said, "I wish that even today you would find the way of peace. But now it is too late, and peace is hidden from you. Before long your enemies will build ramparts against your walls and encircle you and close in on you. They will crush you to the ground, and your children with you. Your enemies will not leave a single stone in place, because you have rejected the opportunity God offered you" (Luke 19:42-44). (Jesus was an accurate prophet. In A.D. 70 the Romans would do exactly as He predicted.)

Visitors to Jerusalem were amazed at all the attention directed toward Jesus. In less than a week, some of them were bound to wonder how that same popular figure could be hanging on a cross.

Call It Stormy Monday

Jesus was staying not in Jerusalem, but in the nearby town of Bethany. He had arrived too late to do much on Sunday, so He returned to the city early Monday. On the way He saw a fig tree in the distance and approached it, although it wasn't the season for figs. The tree was leafy, which meant it should have had fruit—but this one didn't. Jesus said, "May no one ever eat your fruit again!" (Mark 11:12-14). The next morning when the disciples passed the same tree, they found it withered. Peter was amazed, and Jesus told Him, "Have faith in God. I assure you that you can say to this mountain, 'May God lift you up and throw you into the sea,' and your command will be obeyed. All that's required is that you really believe and do not doubt in your heart. You can pray for anything, and if you believe, you will have it" (Mark 11:22-24).

When Jesus and the disciples arrived in Jerusalem, they went to the temple, which was filled with money changers and merchants

selling animals. People needed animals to offer as sacrifices, and since Jerusalem was such an important city, currency exchange was an ongoing need—and a terrific opportunity to make a profit. Yet Jesus saw that such common things had taken center stage in a place where God was supposed to be the primary focus. In addition, some people suggest the whole point of sacrifice required that the death of the animal mean something to the person. Yet it was possible to breeze into Jerusalem, buy a sacrificial animal, and offer it on the spot with very little thought about the animal—or even about God.

But *Jesus* was thinking about what it meant to be a sacrifice. He started knocking over tables and animal stalls, and running out the merchants and their customers. Most people think this was the second time He had purged the temple of "robbers," the first time being near the beginning of His public ministry.

SOMETHING OLD,
SOMETHING NEW

Isaiah 56:7; Jeremiah 7:11 ... Matthew 21:13

As Jesus was driving out the animals and money changers from the temple, He said, "The Scriptures declare, 'My Temple will be called a place of prayer,' but you have turned it into a den of thieves!" Again, He knew His Old Testament well enough to reference two different passages and make a relevant connection.

Busy Tuesday

Tuesday was a relatively normal day for Jesus. He spent it teaching, healing, and debating the religious leaders—both in the temple and on the Mount of Olives overlooking the city. And since He was in Jerusalem during this festive time of year, He was probably under more public scrutiny than usual. The first thing the chief priests and other leaders wanted to know was who had given Jesus the authority to presume to drive out the merchants from the temple. In reply, Jesus said, "Let me ask you a question first. Did [John the Baptist's] baptism come from heaven, or was it merely human?" (Luke 20:3-4)

The religious leaders huddled and considered their response. They realized if they said it was of God, then Jesus would want to know why they didn't respond to John. And if they said it wasn't of God, the people were likely to stone them because John was a very popular figure. So they said, essentially, "No comment." And since they wouldn't answer Jesus' question, He refused to answer theirs.

The religious leaders left but later sent some "secret agents pretending to be honest men" with a new question: "Teacher, we know that you speak and teach what is right and are not influenced by

W.D.J.D.?

In regard to the widow's offering, Jesus (1) saw what this widow did; (2) knew the extent of the sacrifice it was to her; and (3) commented to His disciples about her complete devotion to God. What we *don't* see Him doing is saying anything to the widow herself. While believers may not always get a big verbal affirmation or spiritual pat on the back for the good things they do in Jesus' name, they can be confident that He always notices.

what others think. You sincerely teach the ways of God. Now tell us—is it right to pay taxes to the Roman government or not?" (Luke 20:20-22) The religious leaders were doing their best to get Jesus to say something that would get Him arrested by the Romans.

But Jesus wasn't fooled. He had someone hold up a coin and identify the picture on it, which was Caesar's. Then He said, "Well then, give to Caesar what belongs to him. But everything that belongs to God must be given to God" (Luke 20:25). The people listening were amazed at the wisdom of His statements.

Tuesday was the day Jesus told several parables concerning His eventual return (which we've already seen). Many of these stories weren't very flattering to the established Jewish religious leaders. And later He came right out with direct accusations, warning people not to be fooled by hypocritical religious behavior. He told them to follow what the Pharisees *taught* about Scripture but not to be deceived by their actions, "for they don't practice what they teach" (Matthew 23:1-36).

Jesus also drilled His disciples on what it would mean for Him to be a sacrifice. His imagery is clear and encouraging: "The time has come for the Son of Man to enter into his glory. The truth is, a kernel of wheat must be planted in the soil. Unless it dies it will be alone—a single seed. But its death will produce many new kernels—a plentiful harvest of new lives" (John 12:23-24). The lesson from nature was that death was necessary to bring about new life. From Jesus' perspective, the same principle would apply on a spiritual level.

While Jesus was in the temple teaching His disciples and debating the religious leaders, He happened to see a widow approach the area where people would give money. Many rich people had passed by and dropped large sums into one of the thirteen collection boxes. The woman, in contrast, dropped in two coins worth only a fraction of a penny. Jesus witnessed this offering and said to His disciples: "I assure you, this poor widow has given more than all the others have given. For they gave a tiny part of their surplus, but she, poor as she is, has given everything she has" (Mark 12:41-44). To others, the woman's offering was essentially worthless. To her, it was 100 percent. Knowing what lay ahead of Him this weekend, Jesus could probably relate quite strongly to this sacrificial act.

When Jesus returned to Bethany that night, a party was thrown in His honor by a man known as Simon the Leper (perhaps someone Jesus had healed). As a prostitute had anointed Jesus' feet at a previous gathering in Galilee, this time Mary (the sister of Martha and Lazarus) did the same thing. She brought in an alabaster jar containing "pure nard," a valuable fragrance from India. She broke the jar, apparently poured the expensive perfume on Jesus' head and feet, and dried His feet with her hair. As the sweet aroma filled the room, the attitudes of some of the disciples weren't so pleasant. Judas Iscariot spoke for the dissenters: "That perfume was worth a small fortune. It should have been sold and the money given to the poor."

His point might have been well taken except for a couple of facts. First, Judas' vocal concern for the poor was a cover-up. He was the one designated to keep up with the disciples' money, and he was a thief who would help himself from time to time. Second, Jesus interpreted Mary's sacrificial action as preparation for His death. She probably didn't intend it as such, but it served the purpose. In His words, "Leave her alone. She did it in preparation for my burial. You will always have the poor among you, but I will not be here with you much longer."

(Some of the specifics of this event vary among the different Gospel writers, though the significance of the story is not disputed. You can check it out for yourself in Matthew 26:1-13, Mark 14:1-9, and John 12:1-8).

SOMETHING OLD, SOMETHING NEW

Exodus 12:1-30 . . . Matthew 26:17-19

The Passover preparation, and the food itself, was a reminder of how the Israelites under Moses had prevented the death of their firstborn sons by placing lamb's blood on the top and sides of their doors. Then they had eaten the lamb as a final meal in the place where they had lived as slaves of an Egyptian pharaoh. (Some people suggest that the marks of blood on the doors would have roughly formed the outline of a cross.)

Quiet Wednesday

Nothing is written about the last Wednesday in Jesus' life. Perhaps it was "more of the same" for Jesus. On the other hand, maybe He tried to carve out a little quiet time for Himself. Thursday was going to be emotionally draining, and Friday would be even worse. Maybe Jesus was preparing for what He knew was coming.

W.D.J.D.?

Even with the knowledge that these were His final hours of freedom, Jesus was ever the servant. He not only taught humility but also modeled it. He made it clear that this was something He wanted his followers to imitate (John 13:14-15). Yet even this relatively simple action was somewhat embarrassing for the disciples. The next day He would die for them. What would they think then?

We do know that the religious leaders were active during this time. It was shortly after Mary's anointing of Jesus that "Satan entered into Judas Iscariot, . . . and he went over to the leading priests and captains of the Temple guard to discuss the best way to betray Jesus to them" (Luke 22:3). The religious leaders were delighted to have a "mole" so close to Jesus and rewarded Judas with 30 silver coins. From that point on, it was only a matter of determining the right time and place so they could arrest Jesus without getting a lot of interference from a crowd of His supporters.

Black Thursday

A Supper to Remember

If you knew the police had a warrant for your arrest and would serve it within 24 hours, how would you spend that time? Jesus didn't seem to do anything out of the ordinary. This was the first day of the Feast of Unleavened Bread and the day when everyone got ready for Passover. As the disciples prepared for just another meal, Jesus prepared for the Last Supper.

Jesus had previously sent two disciples ahead and told them to look for a man carrying a jar of water. He told them that when they explained their need for lodging to this man, he would provide them with a guest room. Everything happened just as Jesus said it would, and a large upstairs room had been made available to them (Luke 22:7-13).

That evening Jesus wrapped a towel around His waist, took a basin of water, and went around washing His disciples' feet, drying them with the towel. When He got to Peter, the ever-impetuous disciple wouldn't hear of letting Jesus wash his feet. Jesus explained: "But if I don't wash you, you won't belong to me." So Peter said, "Then wash my hands and head as well, Lord, not just my feet!" Jesus replied that most of the disciples—but not all—were pretty much clean. Jesus' cryptic comment was a clue that He could see into the heart of Judas Iscariot and knew He was about to be betrayed (John 13:1-11).

During the meal, Jesus announced that He had looked forward to celebrating this Passover meal with His disciples, yet this would be His last supper "until it comes to fulfillment in the Kingdom of God" (Luke 22:15-16). He also announced that one of the group would betray Him. The disciples could only stare at one another and wonder what He meant. Each began to ask if he would be the guilty party. And when Judas asked, Jesus made it clear that He knew exactly what was going on (Matthew 26:25). He even told Judas to go ahead and "do it now." At that point "Satan entered into [Judas]" and he went out into the night to betray Jesus (John 13:26-30).

Jesus then broke bread and gave it to His disciples and passed around a cup of wine for all of them to drink from. He explained that the bread represented His body, and the wine symbolized His blood, "poured out for many" (Mark 14:24).

Jesus had just washed their feet. Judas was at this very moment arranging to have Him arrested. Jesus was trying to help them understand what a sacrifice He was about to make. Yet the disciples, even here, even now, began another argument about which of them was greatest. So once again Jesus had to remind them that in the kingdom of God, greatness would be equated with sacrifice and service (Luke 22:24-30).

With Judas gone, Jesus attempted to warn the other disciples what they would be in for during the next 24 hours. He told them, "Tonight all of you will desert me. . . . But after I have been raised from the dead, I will go ahead of you to Galilee and meet you there" (Matthew 26:31-32).

None of the disciples would hear of anything bad happening to Jesus and boldly promised to die with Him if necessary. Peter, as usual, was the most vocal of them all. In response, Jesus told him: "Peter, the truth is, this very night, before the rooster crows, you will deny me three times" (Matthew 26:34). Peter and the others didn't believe Him, of course.

But rather than dwell on the conflict, Jesus began to comfort his disciples. He explained that He was leaving them, but He would be preparing a place for them "in my Father's home" (John 14:1). He

SOMETHING OLD,
SOMETHING NEW
Zechariah 13:7 ... Matthew 26:31

In attempting to prepare His disciples for the bad news of His certain death, Jesus referred to a passage in Zechariah and reminded His friends: "God will strike the Shepherd, and the sheep of the flock will be scattered."

SOMETHING OLD,
SOMETHING NEW

Psalm 115–118 ... Matthew 26:30

After the Last Supper, Jesus and the disciples sang a hymn and then went out to the Mount of Olives. The traditional "hymn" sung after Passover is taken from Psalms 115 through 118. Consider some of the lyrics:

> "Death had its hands around my throat; the terrors of the grave overtook me. I saw only trouble and sorrow. Then I called on the name of the Lord: 'Please, Lord, save me!'... He has saved me from death, my eyes from tears, my feet from stumbling" (Psalm 116:3-4, 8).

> "In my distress I prayed to the Lord, and the Lord answered me and rescued me. The Lord is for me, so I will not be afraid. What can mere mortals do to me?... I will look in triumph at those who hate me.... Though hostile nations surrounded me, I destroyed them all in the name of the Lord" (Psalm 118:5-7, 10).

It seems that Jesus had appropriate music as He left the upper room to head for the cross.

also promised that in His absence, He would send "another Counselor, who will never leave you. He is the Holy Spirit, who leads into all truth" (John 14:16-17). Although Jesus was going away, He wasn't abandoning them. He would live again, and so would they. Jesus realized they weren't soaking in everything He was telling them but explained, "I have told you these things before they happen so that you will believe when they do happen" (John 14:29).

Retiring to the Garden

From their upper room, Jesus and the disciples went to an olive grove known as Gethsemane ("oil press"), a place they had been many times. Jesus reviewed many of His important teachings with His disciples and then spent much of the evening in prayer. He prayed for Himself, for His disciples, and for everyone who would believe on Him in the future (John 17). Then He wanted to spend some time alone, but He recruited Peter, James, and John to cluster and support Him in prayer as He prayed.

Jesus was intent on using this opportunity to pray. His years on earth had dwindled to hours. He wasn't any more eager to experience the pain and fear of death than anyone else. He prayed with great fervency. We are told that "He was in such agony of spirit that his sweat fell to the ground like great drops of blood" (Luke 22:44). Three times that night He checked on the disciples He had asked to support Him. Each of the three times He found them asleep. The third time, He told them to get up because His betrayer was here. And as He was speaking, Judas arrived with a "mob" of priests and armed men.

Judas walked right up and kissed Jesus—the signal that Jesus was indeed the man they should arrest. Coming out of a fog of sleep, Peter was alarmed at what was happening and whipped out a sword, cutting off the right ear of a servant named Malchus. Jesus told Peter to put away the sword, explaining that He could summon thousands of angels if He wished. Jesus agreed to go with the crowd, but He asked, "Am I some dangerous criminal, that you have come armed with swords and clubs to arrest me? Why didn't you

arrest me in the Temple? I was there teaching every day" (Matthew 26:56).

Jesus asked that His disciples be released (John 18:8). Apparently, they didn't need coaxing because "at that point, all the disciples deserted him and fled" (Matthew 26:56). But a young man was seen lurking around, wearing only a linen nightshirt. The crowd tried to seize him but only got his nightshirt. He escaped naked. (Since this person is only mentioned in the book of Mark, and since Mark would have been young at this time, it is often presumed that he was the man described.)

Jesus was taken before Caiaphas, the high priest. (Additional references are made to Annas, father-in-law of Caiaphas and a former high priest who apparently still had a lot of influence). Apparently, after much of the turmoil had died down, some of Jesus' disciples began to try to find out what was going on. Peter, for one, got as close as he dared, warming himself at a fire in the courtyard of the high priest.

Friday Morning (Who Called This Good Friday?!)

We don't know exactly when, in this account, the late hours of Thursday night turned into the wee hours of Friday morning. But assuming a rooster tends to crow sometime around daybreak, it was probably after midnight when a servant girl saw Peter in the high priest's courtyard and asked if he wasn't one of the disciples of Jesus. He denied it and walked away. After a while he returned to get warm again, and a second servant girl echoed the sentiments of the first: "This man was with Jesus of Nazareth." This time Peter took an oath to declare that he didn't even know Jesus. About an hour later, other bystanders suggested Peter must be associated with Jesus because he had a distinctive Galilean accent. Peter replied, "I swear by God, I don't know the man." Immediately a rooster crowed. The sound must have pierced Peter's soul, causing Him to instantly recall Jesus' words. To make things worse, "At that moment the Lord turned and looked at Peter" (Luke 22:61). All Peter's bravado and promises of loyalty had lasted less than 12 hours. He left crying bitterly (Matthew 26:69-75).

OPINION POLL

"Sorrow is like a precious treasure, shown only to friends."—*African proverb*

W.D.J.D.?

Jesus knew why He had come to earth. He had already told the disciples everything that was going to happen to Him. Still, in His final prayers in Gethsemane He prayed, "My Father! If it is possible, let this cup of suffering be taken away from me. Yet I want your will, not mine" (Matthew 26:39). Jesus showed that one's faith may not completely eliminate fear, uncertainty, and reluctance. He also demonstrated that honest expression of one's feelings is never inappropriate in prayer. However, such honesty should be accompanied by submission to God. In spite of everything Jesus was feeling, He readily acknowledged that God knew what was best. Ultimately, that's what Jesus prayed for.

SOMETHING OLD,
SOMETHING NEW

Zechariah 11:12-13 ... Matthew 27:1-10

Centuries before, Zechariah had written, "I took the thirty coins and threw them to the potters in the Temple of the Lord." This incident with Judas is remarkably similar. (Matthew's reference to the prophet Jeremiah might be in regard to Jeremiah 19 or Jeremiah 32:6-12 and would have been inclusive of the minor prophet Zechariah as well.)

Meanwhile, Jesus was getting the third degree by the equivalent of the Jewish Supreme Court—a body known as the Sanhedrin. A number of false witnesses came forward to speak against Jesus, but their statements didn't agree, which was a requirement to obtain a conviction. Jesus remained silent much of the time. Finally they pressed Him to say whether or not He thought He was the Messiah and the Son of God. He replied, "Yes, it is as you say. And in the future you will see me, the Son of Man, sitting at God's right hand in the place of power and coming back on the clouds of heaven" (Matthew 26:64).

That's all they needed to convict Him of blasphemy. But their resentment toward Jesus had been building for years. They wanted more than a guilty sentence. Now He was at their mercy. This was the highest legal/religious court, yet some of the members began to spit in His face. Others blindfolded Him, punched Him with their fists, and taunted Him: "Prophesy to us, you Messiah! Who hit you that time?" (Matthew 26:67-68) Even the people assigned to guard Jesus began mocking and beating Him, "and they threw all sorts of terrible insults at him" (Luke 22:63-65). At daybreak they passed a death sentence on Jesus, bound Him, and handed him over to Pontius Pilate, the Roman governor.

Meanwhile, Judas was experiencing seller's remorse. When he saw what was happening, he returned to the chief priests and elders, attempting to return the 30 silver coins and convince them that "I have betrayed an innocent man" (Matthew 27:4). When they couldn't be swayed to change their minds, Judas threw the money on the floor and stormed out. The dilemma of the priests is telling: "We can't put it in the Temple treasury since it's against the law to accept money paid for murder" (Matthew 27:6). So they used the money to purchase a "potter's field" which they converted into a cemetery for foreigners. It quickly came to be known as the "Field of Blood."

When Judas left, he went out and "hanged himself." Further details from Acts 1:18 tell us that "he burst open, spilling out his intestines." The simplest explanation is that he hanged himself first, and the unfortunate "bursting" occurred when he was cut down (or fell), perhaps after a period of decay. Another possibility is that sometimes when the Bible speaks of "hanging," the concept is more like being impaled than the images of hangings we have from movie westerns. But either way, Judas couldn't live with his actions and met a rather messy end.

Jesus was brought before Pilate, but after interviewing Him, Pilate couldn't understand what the big deal was. The Jews had no power to execute criminals; the authority had to come from Rome. So Jesus' accusers lied: "This man has been leading our people to ruin by telling them not to pay their taxes to the Roman government and by claiming he is the Messiah, a king." Jesus even acknowledged being the King of the Jews. But since the Jews were all under Roman authority, Pilate still didn't see that anything Jesus had done was a capital offense. The Jewish leaders wouldn't give up: "But he is causing riots everywhere he goes, all over Judea, from Galilee to Jerusalem" (Luke 23:1-5).

As soon as the religious authorities mentioned Galilee, Pilate thought he had found a loophole. Galilee was under the jurisdiction of Herod, the ruler who had put John the Baptist to death. Pilate had Jesus transferred to Herod.

Pilate and Herod had an adversarial relationship prior to this, but afterward became friends. Herod had heard a lot about Jesus and was glad to see Him, hoping to witness a miracle firsthand. But he was disappointed. He asked a long series of questions, but Jesus remained silent. Jesus' accusers weren't silent, however. As they continued to shout accusations, the soldiers began to ridicule Jesus, even placing a royal robe on Him in mockery. And when they got tired of their fun, Herod returned Jesus to Pilate. (Apparently Herod wasn't willing to pass sentence on Jesus, either.)

Pilate seemed desperate to placate the crowd without actually killing Jesus. He kept explaining that he could find no basis for putting Jesus to death. First, he offered to have Jesus flogged and released, but the people wouldn't hear of it. Next, Pilate tried a different political maneuver. Each year at the Feast of the Passover,

OPINION POLL

"The deeper the sorrow, the less the tongue has to say."—The *Talmud*

IN JESUS' NAME
"MAN OF SORROWS" (Isaiah 53:3)

Jesus never exactly had it easy during His time on earth. But in these final hours of His life, He truly lived up to this title revealed by the prophet Isaiah.

the governor traditionally pardoned a convicted criminal. Pilate assumed the crowd would choose to release Jesus, but instead they voted to free a man named Barabbas—a murderer and insurrectionist. When Pilate asked what they wanted to happen to Jesus, their shouts got louder and louder: "Crucify him! Crucify him!" To make things worse for Pilate, his wife had told him about a dream she had had about Jesus, and she warned her husband to "leave that innocent man alone" (Matthew 27:19).

Pilate released Barabbas and had Jesus flogged—beaten with a whip embedded with lead pieces to more effectively rip open the victim's flesh. His soldiers fashioned a "crown" of long, sharp thorns and jammed it onto Jesus' head. They dressed Him in the purple robe. Pilate stood Jesus before the people so they could see the abuse He had already endured. Then he told them once more that he could find no reason for having Him put to death, but the crowd would not be silenced. Finally, they suggested that unless Pilate had Jesus killed, he would appear to be an enemy of Caesar (John 19:1-16).

In a final act of opposition, Pilate had a basin of water brought out and washed his hands in the presence of the crowd, saying, "I am innocent of the blood of this man. The responsibility is yours!" (Matthew 27:24) Fine with them! The crowd continued to mock and beat Jesus until they grew tired and finally led Him away to be crucified.

Friday Evening: The Worst That Could Happen

It was customary for criminals to carry their own crosses (or at least the crossbeam) to the execution site. But after all Jesus had been through, apparently He was in no shape to bear such a weight. A man named Simon from Cyrene, an African city, was enlisted to carry Jesus' cross for Him. Meanwhile, crowds of people lined the streets to witness this procession. Many women were weeping, and Jesus told them not to cry for Him but for themselves and future generations. If Jesus was here in person and being rejected, what would the future hold for them when He was gone?

The place of crucifixion was called *Golgotha* in Aramaic, or *Calvary* in Latin, which both translate to "The Place of the Skull." Perhaps the site was so named because of what took place there, or maybe because the geographic features of the hill resembled a skull. Crucifixion was an intentionally cruel punishment that the Roman Empire adapted from the Phoenicians, Carthaginians, and Egyptians. It was reserved for slaves and the worst of criminals; Roman citizens were exempt.

Spikes were driven through the wrists and heel bones to attach the convicted person to the cross, and when the cross was placed upright, the whole weight of the body hung by those spikes. Any movement would cause excruciating pain. Within minutes, as blood sank into the lower portions of the body, the pulse would double as blood pressure dropped to half the normal rate. Breathing became more and more difficult. But since none of the injuries were fatal in themselves, death usually took two or three days before the heart just gave out or the person suffocated in his own body fluids.

Jesus was one of three people being crucified this day. He was placed between two thieves. His clothes were all He possessed, so they had been removed and the soldiers gambled to see who would get them. Jesus was offered a drink of wine mixed with gall (or myrrh), a bitter substance. Some suggest this was simply to add to the cruelty of the event. Others believe it was a narcotic concoction prepared by the women of Jerusalem to help alleviate the pain of prisoners. Either way, Jesus refused to drink it.

The people in attendance were taunting Jesus, suggesting that if He had come to save the world, maybe He ought to try to save Himself. In addition to the jeers and sneers of the crowd below, the two crucified thieves were insulting Jesus as well. However, as time passed, apparently one of them had a change of heart. He asked that Jesus remember Him when He came into His kingdom. Jesus promised that the thief's repentance would soon be rewarded.

Meanwhile, Pilate arranged for a sign to be placed above Jesus' cross, declaring in three languages that Jesus was "The King of the Jews." The chief priests quickly tried to edit it to read that Jesus *said*

SOMETHING OLD,
SOMETHING NEW
Hosea 10:8 . . . Luke 23:26-31

Looking ahead to times of turmoil on earth, as Jesus was on the way to the cross He quoted Hosea's prediction of a time when things would be so bad that people "will beg the mountains to bury them and the hills to fall on them."

SOMETHING OLD,
SOMETHING NEW
Psalm 22:16-18 . . . John 19:23-25

David the psalmist, while describing a time of personal turmoil, was also quite prophetic about what would happen to his descendant, Jesus. He wrote, "My enemies surround me like a pack of dogs; an evil gang closes in on me. They have pierced my hands and feet. I can count every bone in my body. My enemies stare at me and gloat. They divide my clothes among themselves and throw dice for my garments."

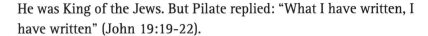

IN JESUS' NAME
"KING OF THE JEWS" (Mark 15:2)

We tend to speak rather glibly about servant leadership. Jesus was a true servant leader who acknowledged this regal title only hours before going to the Cross to die for His people—as well as the rest of the world. It wasn't a job fit for a king, but He was willing to do it anyway.

OPINION POLL

"One drop of Christ's blood is worth more than heaven and earth."—*Martin Luther*

He was King of the Jews. But Pilate replied: "What I have written, I have written" (John 19:19-22).

At one point Jesus saw His mother standing next to John. He asked John to take care of Mary, which the disciple did from that point on. This was one of seven statements recorded that Jesus spoke from the cross:

> "Father, forgive these people because they don't know what they are doing" (Luke 23:34).

> (To the repentant thief) "I assure you, today you will be with me in paradise" (Luke 23:43).

> (To Mary) "Woman, he is your son." (And to John) "She is your mother" (John 19:26-27).

> "My God, my God, why have you forsaken me?" (Matthew 27:46)

> "I am thirsty" (John 19:28).

> "It is finished" (John 19:30).

> "Father, I entrust my spirit into your hands!" (Luke 23:46).

From noon until three an eerie darkness fell on the land as Jesus hung on the cross. And although it frequently took days for crucifixion victims to die, His ordeal was over in a matter of hours. Theologians like to point out that Jesus voluntarily "bowed his head and gave up his spirit" (John 19:30). Though He may have seemed to be at the mercy of these events, He was there willingly.

But the moment Jesus declared that it was finished, strange things started happening. The earth shook and rocks split apart. Tombs opened, and the bodies of people long dead were raised to life, appearing to many people. And the veil in the temple that separated the forbidden Most Holy Place mysteriously ripped in half, from the top to the bottom. People might not have known *what* was happening, but they knew *something* was. And the Roman soldiers at ground zero, Jesus' cross, exclaimed, "Truly, this was the Son of

God!" (Theirs was not necessarily a Christian confession [Matthew 27:54] but was a clear acknowledgment that they believed Jesus to be someone special.)

Since the next day was the Sabbath, the Jews wanted to hasten the deaths of the crucifixion victims. (Touching a dead body would have made them unclean and unable to participate in all the Passover ceremonies.) The legs of both thieves were broken because that made it impossible to push themselves up to breathe—effectively suffocating them. But since Jesus was already dead, one of the soldiers rammed a spear into His side just to be sure. As a result, blood and water flowed out, suggesting that the pericardial sac around the heart was pierced.

The bodies of Jesus and the criminals were taken down and buried before sundown. Jesus was placed in a borrowed tomb, as we will see in the next chapter.

But His mission had been accomplished! The divine kamikaze had hit his target head on. With His sacrificial death on the cross on Calvary, His enemy had been destroyed. Sin had been effectively and eternally dealt with. Or had it?

Our opinions about that dilemma depend on another crucial bit of information. If Jesus died on the cross and stayed dead, that would be the end of the story. Things should have quieted down after a couple of weeks and Jesus would be just one more good guy who died too soon because of some controversial teachings. But if He actually rose again to prove that He had conquered death . . . well, that would be another story. Either way, it's going to be another chapter.

Questions to Ponder and/or Discuss

1. What would you say is the biggest sacrifice you've made on behalf of another person or persons?

2. Between Palm Sunday (Jesus' triumphal entry into Jerusalem) and Good Friday (His crucifixion), the attitude of the crowds toward Him seemed to change dramatically. Can you

SOMETHING OLD, SOMETHING NEW

Exodus 26:31-33 . . . Matthew 27:51

The Most Holy Place, which held the ark of the covenant, symbolized God's throne room. With the exception of the high priest, who entered the Most Holy Place once a year to make an offering on the ark of the covenant, anyone who stepped behind the curtain would die. But the tearing of the veil at Jesus' death symbolized a new and freer access to God's presence by His people.

IN JESUS' NAME

"LAMB OF GOD" (JOHN 1:29)

John the Baptist called Jesus "the Lamb of God who takes away the sin of the world." While hundreds or thousands of other Passover lambs were being slaughtered as a commemoration of a past event, Jesus the Lamb was being sacrificed for sins of the past, present, and future.

think of times in your own life or in the life of someone close to you when an attitude toward God shifted strongly (either positively or negatively)? What were the circumstances? What were the results?

3. Which statement best summarizes your feelings about Jesus as a sacrifice?

- He shouldn't have bothered. I can take care of myself.
- To be honest, I'm bewildered by the whole thing.
- I don't fully understand it, but I'm very grateful.
- I totally get it. Wow, God!
- Other: _____

CHAPTER THIRTEEN

"I GUESS CHARLIE'S TAKING IT WITH HIM AFTER ALL."

A Matter of Life and Death... and Life

JESUS: HIS RESURRECTION

Down, but not out.

This phrase has become a cliché in our vocabulary and media presentations because it's such a recurring theme. We hold our breath a bit with each obstacle Odysseus faces on the way home from Troy, wondering if he will get there before Penelope has to choose a new husband from her slew of suitors. We cheer as Rocky keeps getting up off the mat and back into the fight. We root for the *Star Wars* rebels to keep making against-all-odds progress against the evil Empire. Whether set in the past, present, or future, we relate to those who are oppressed and beaten down yet won't give up. Those people give us hope and inspiration for our own struggles.

But perhaps the world's greatest down-but-not-out story—whether or not you believe it actually happened—is the resurrection of Jesus. Millions of people believe He was completely down in the grave but got back up three days later for the most incredible comeback anyone will ever see. Millions of others disagree. And lots and lots of people remain undecided.

Most of us have wanted to believe in an assortment of fantastic

SOME THINGS YOU'LL DISCOVER IN THIS CHAPTER

1. After Jesus' crucifixion, He was seen by several groups and individuals who attested that He was alive again.

2. There are some alternative explanations as to what happened to Jesus' body, but none seem to convincingly disprove that Jesus was resurrected.

3. Jesus made amends with Peter after Peter's denial.

135

OPINION POLL

"Christianity is in its very essence a resurrection religion. The concept of the resurrection lies at its heart. If you remove it, Christianity is destroyed."
—*John R. Stott*

and wonderful things during our lifetimes—Santa Claus, the Loch Ness monster, leprechauns, life on Mars, or whatever. Some of our beliefs are proven beyond doubt to be nothing but fables. In other cases, no one seems able to provide enough facts for a reasonable mind to believe with any degree of certainty. Is the resurrection of Jesus another item that goes on this list? Does it take a fanatic to believe? Is the only difference between Christians and Trekkers the person they pledge loyalty to? Or is there cause for a logical and reasonable person to consider that the resurrection of Jesus might be a factual event?

Grave Matters

When the body of Jesus was taken off the cross, the disciples still hadn't put together enough pieces to see the big picture of what was going on. They were down *and* out. Later they would remember some of the things Jesus had tried to tell them. He would be lifted up like the bronze serpent in the wilderness so that people could look to Him and live (John 3:14-15). He would be like a seed planted in the earth that had to die before new life could spring forth from it (John 12:23-24). He would be like Jonah who spent three days in the stomach of the great fish but then went back to God's business (Matthew 12:38-41).

But Jesus' usual disciples weren't even around to take care of His body. That task was done by two volunteers who were, of all things, Jewish religious leaders. One was a man named Joseph, from the town of Arimathea, who had been a secret follower of Jesus for a time. The other was Nicodemus, who had spoken with Jesus at night and apparently had a lot of respect for Him. These two men approached Pilate and asked if they could tend to Jesus' body (John 19:39-42).

Pilate was surprised that Jesus was already dead. He called in the officer in charge to verify the fact. When the soldier confirmed it (Mark 15:44-45), Pilate had the body released to Nicodemus and Joseph. Nicodemus brought 75 pounds of embalming spices and ointment to apply to Jesus' body. Joseph provided strips of linen cloth in which they wrapped the body. Joseph also owned a never-used tomb cut out of solid rock, so he arranged to place Jesus there. When they finished, they rolled a large stone against the entrance of the tomb.

Meanwhile, a group of Jesus' women friends were gathering spices and perfumes to anoint His body as well. As an act of love, it was their tradition to pour spices over a corpse to mask the stench of decay. But they were planning to wait until after the Sabbath. (The Jewish Sabbath would have begun at sundown on Friday night and lasted until sundown on Saturday.)

So based on their actions, all Jesus' friends seemed to think He was gone for good. Surprisingly, it was the chief priests and Pharisees who hadn't forgotten that Jesus had said, "After three days I will be raised from the dead" (Matthew 27:63). They wanted to ensure that His body didn't go anywhere. To avoid any likelihood of the disciples stealing the body and perpetrating a hoax, the religious leaders appealed to Pilate to provide a security detail to keep watch at Jesus' tomb. So Pilate told them to "Take guards and secure it as best you can." An official seal was placed on the tomb itself, and Roman guards were posted around it (Matthew 27:65-66).

Saturday was the Sabbath, and it must have been an extremely gloomy one for Jesus' friends and family. The last memory His disciples had of being with Him was the view over their shoulders as they fled the Garden of Gethsemane. Some were present at the crucifixion, certainly, which would have been of no comfort at all. If they could see Jesus, He could see them. After all, it was only Thursday night when they had all pledged to die *with* Him.

Prelude Tomb Mourning

The Sabbath ended at sundown, but then, so did the daylight. So the first good opportunity the women would have to anoint Jesus' body was early Sunday morning. They set off for the tomb before daybreak, but they weren't sure what was going to happen. They didn't

SOMETHING OLD,
SOMETHING NEW
Isaiah 53:9 ... Matthew 27:57-60
Isaiah had written that the Messiah would be "buried like a criminal" and "put in a rich man's grave." An additional irony was that Jesus' tomb was supplied by a Pharisee, of all people.

OPINION POLL

"Our noblest piles and stateliest rooms, are mere out-houses to our tombs; cities, tho' ere so great and brave, but mere warehouses to the grave."
—*Samuel Butler*

W.D.J.D.?

Most of us are especially hurt when those closest to us let us down. Peter's three denials of Jesus were brutal. And Jesus was well aware of how Peter had let Him down (Luke 22:60-62). Even the most forgiving of us tend to want our deniers and betrayers to suffer a bit before we forgive them. But what did Jesus do? He sent advance word to Peter by angelic messenger that everything was going to be all right. There was no hint of stretching out Peter's suffering because "he had it coming." Jesus' forgiveness was complete . . . and immediate.

seem to know about the guard that had been posted or the seal on the tomb, but they did know about the enormous stone and were concerned about whom they might find to roll it away.

Hey, no problem. When they arrived, the stone had been touched by an angel who had rolled it back single-handedly and was using it as a seat. "His face shone like lightning, and his clothing was as white as snow." The Roman guards literally shook and "fell into a dead faint" (Matthew 28:1-4). But the angel told the women not to be afraid. And he said, "I know you are looking for Jesus, who was crucified. He isn't here! He has been raised from the dead, just as he said would happen. Come, see where his body was lying. And now, go quickly and tell his disciples he has been raised from the dead, and he is going ahead of you to Galilee. You will see him there. Remember, I have told you" (Matthew 28:5-7).

Mark's version of this account gives a slightly different message by the angel, who said, "Now go and give this message to his disciples, *including Peter*: Jesus is going ahead of you to Galilee" (Mark 16:7, italics added). Isn't is interesting that Peter, of all people, was singled out to hear the wonderful news of Jesus' resurrection?!

Filled with a strange combination of fear, shock, and joy, the women rushed back to find the disciples. They told them what had happened, "but the story sounded like nonsense, so they didn't believe it" (Luke 24:11). Peter and John, however, thought it was worth checking out. John was faster and got there first but stopped before going into the tomb. Peter was bolder and rushed on in. Burial cloths were lying around, some of them even folded up (John 20:3-10). They could tell something had happened, but the truth was slow to sink in. The empty tomb was a pretty big clue, but some bigger clues were coming.

Meanwhile, the Pharisees had a problem. They had gone to the trouble of securing some professional "muscle" to secure the tomb, but both their hired guards and the body of Jesus had disappeared. The Roman military didn't look kindly upon soldiers who either fell asleep on watch or deserted their post. Such acts could be punishable by death.

Yet the Jewish religious leaders needed a good cover story. They offered a large bribe to have the soldiers say the disciples stole the body while they were sleeping, and they promised the soldiers wouldn't get into any trouble as a result of their story. The guards took the money, told the story, and a lot of people believed it. We'll come back to this theory that the disciples stole the body. But first we want to look at some additional biblical evidence of Jesus' resurrection—His post-crucifixion personal appearances.

OPINION POLL

"The Lord who vacated his tomb has not vacated his throne."
—G. R. Beasley-Murray

Now You See Me, Now You See Me Again

According to Scripture, Jesus didn't just appear once or twice to the same people. His appearances were quite varied. Below is a list of people and circumstances for each of the times He was seen after His crucifixion and burial.

Mary Magdalene

Mary Magdalene (or Mary of Magdala) had been a follower of Jesus since He had cast out seven evil spirits from her body (Luke 8:2). Apparently she had run back to the disciples before the other women and even before hearing the angel's explanation, because when she got there she told them, "They have taken the Lord out of the tomb, and we don't know where they have put him" (John 20:1-2). And it seems that she later returned to the tomb alone. She peered inside and saw two angels where the body of Jesus had been (though she may have thought they were only two men). They asked why she was crying and she replied, "Because they have taken away my Lord and I don't know where they have put him" (John 20:13). Someone behind her asked whom she was looking for. Assuming that he was a gardener, she said, "Sir, if you have taken him away, tell me where you have put him, and I will go and get him."

Mary didn't realize the figure speaking to her was Jesus. But the moment He spoke her name, the truth hit her. And as soon as she identified the speaker, she also was flooded with the reality of His resurrection. The fact that Jesus instructed Mary not to cling to Him

W.D.J.D.?

It has been pointed out that if someone had been making up the resurrection accounts of Jesus, he certainly wouldn't have started with Mary Magdalene—or any woman—as a witness. Yet according to Scripture, Jesus appeared first to her, rather than to the Roman governor (Pilate), the Jewish high priest (Caiaphas), or even one of His disciples. We can only speculate as to why. However, one popular opinion is that Mary had been one of the most faithful followers during His death. She had been at the cross Friday afternoon (John 19:25) and among the first to His tomb on Sunday morning. The same couldn't be said of His disciples. Perhaps it's simply another reminder that faithfulness has its rewards.

raises questions. Some people suggest that Jesus was in a unique physical form, yet He certainly didn't appear to be "untouchable." Others feel His instructions were more symbolic: from that point on, His physical presence would no longer be key to one's spiritual health and growth. Mary—and everyone else—could relate to Him on a whole new level.

The Other Women

The second appearance of Jesus was also to an all-women group. Apparently the other women spent more time at the empty tomb than Mary Magdalene. When they finally left to give the angel's message to the disciples, Jesus met them on the way. He greeted them and repeated what the angel had told them: "Don't be afraid! Go tell my brothers to leave for Galilee, and they will see me there" (Matthew 28:8-10). The women ran to Him, grabbed His feet, and worshiped Him.

Peter

Details are sketchy about this appearance of Jesus, but it is mentioned twice in Scripture. At a later appearance of Jesus, the people are aware that He has already appeared to Peter (Luke 24:34), and Paul refers to this appearance in one of his letters (1 Corinthians 15:5). It's not surprising that little is said of this reunion between Peter and Jesus. Peter probably appreciated some privacy, perhaps to apologize for his desertion and denials of Jesus. It is also encouraging to see that Jesus apparently offered Peter this private audience at a time when he really needed it.

Two Men on the Road to Emmaus

Two of Jesus' followers (one named Cleopas and the other unnamed) were going to a village called Emmaus, about seven miles from Jerusalem. A third man joined them along the way and started talking to them. They told him everything they had witnessed and heard in Jerusalem concerning the crucifixion and death of Jesus. They had heard that the tomb was empty and that angels had said Jesus was alive, yet they were still quite sad.

The third man began to review Old Testament Scripture with

them, explaining that the prophets had foretold awful things happening to the Messiah "before entering his time of glory." They were still talking when they arrived at Emmaus, and the two men insisted their new friend join them for a meal. As he broke the bread, prayed over it, and handed it to them, they suddenly realized it was Jesus. And at that moment, He disappeared! (Luke 24:13-31) They immediately started back toward Jerusalem to spread the word to Jesus' other friends and followers.

Ten Apostles (and Others) in the Upper Room

While the women had been running around town, first to anoint the body of Jesus and then to share the excitement of His resurrection with others, the disciples were behind locked doors in the upper room because they were scared of the Jewish religious leaders (John 20:19). Cleopas and his friend from Emmaus found them there, and they traded stories. The friends and followers of Jesus in the upper room shared the news of His resurrection, and the two other disciples started telling how Jesus had appeared to them on the road.

But in the middle of their story, Jesus appeared to the whole group. They weren't accustomed to this kind of entrance and were fear-stricken because they thought they were seeing a ghost. Jesus assured them He was real and encouraged them to investigate His hands and feet and to touch Him. Although they were filled with joy and wonder, they were still somewhat doubtful. Jesus asked if they had something to eat. They gave Him a piece of broiled fish, which He ate—something a ghost would be unable to do (Luke 24:32-43). But then, He could pass through locked doors which was something a flesh-and-blood being would have a bit of trouble doing.

For some reason, Thomas wasn't with the rest of the disciples when Jesus appeared to them. And in spite of all the other witnesses who agreed about what had happened, Thomas said, "I won't believe it unless I see the nail wounds in his hands, put my fingers in them, and place my hand into the wound in his side" (John 20:24-25).

Again to the Disciples, This Time with Thomas

Just over a week after Thomas missed seeing Jesus, with the disciples still behind locked doors, Jesus again appeared to them. This

IN JESUS' NAME
"THE RESURRECTION AND THE LIFE" (John 11:25)

Jesus used this name for Himself just prior to raising Lazarus from the dead. His followers had been convinced that He was a resurrect-*or*, but only now were they comprehending what it meant that He was literally the resurrect-*ion* and the life.

OPINION POLL

"Jesus blames no man for wanting to be sure. Jesus did not blame Thomas for his doubts; Jesus knew that once Thomas had fought his way through the wilderness of his doubts he would be the surest man in Christendom."—*William Barclay*

time Thomas was there. Jesus wasted no time addressing him directly: "Put your finger here and see my hands. Put your hand into the wound in my side. Don't be faithless any longer. Believe!"

Scripture doesn't say Thomas needed to do as he was told. Instead, he immediately exclaimed, "My Lord and my God!" (John 20:26-30) Jesus pointed out that for Thomas, seeing was believing. However, "Blessed are those who haven't seen me and believe anyway."

(We tend to prematurely brand Thomas as a weakling and/or a bad example. However, the Bible points out that when Jesus was about to go raise Lazarus from the dead, His life would be in jeopardy. At that point it was Thomas who spoke up and said to the other disciples, "Let's go, too—and die with Jesus" (John 11:16). Thomas had faith and courage, but he wanted to ensure it was based on something substantial.)

A Group of Disciples While Fishing

We jumped the gun on this appearance of Jesus in chapter 10 so we could consider the surprising catch of fish that day. But let's review and look at a few additional details.

Apparently the disciples had grown tired of hiding out in the locked upper room, fearful that at any minute the authorities might show up and drag them away to jail. At some point they had left Jerusalem and returned to Galilee. Imagine the sense of upheaval they must have been feeling. They had dropped everything to follow Jesus three years ago. Now that He was gone—or only popping in to say hello once in a while—what were they to do?

Peter decided to go fishing, perhaps because that was the life he had known prior to meeting Jesus. Six other disciples were there, and they all decided to tag along. But even after the seven of them fished all night, they had caught nothing.

As you may remember, a figure on shore told them to throw their nets on the other side of the boat. When they did, they caught 153 large fish, somehow without tearing their net. Peter realized the person ashore was Jesus, and swam to meet him as the others followed in the boat. Jesus already had some bread and a charcoal fire started on which fish were frying. He served them breakfast this time—their third meeting since His resurrection.

After the meal, Jesus started a conversation with Peter and asked Him three consecutive times: "Do you love me?" Each time Peter said yes, Jesus told him, "Then feed my sheep" (John 21:15-19). By the third time, Peter was pretty upset. Yet many people feel that by allowing Peter to affirm his love three times, Jesus led him to consciously counteract his previous denials.

Jesus went on to tell Peter: "When you are old, you will stretch out your hands, and others will direct you and take you where you don't want to go." The Bible explains that this was a prediction of how Peter would someday die to glorify God. (Tradition says that Peter was crucified, but he requested that he be crucified upside down because he didn't feel worthy to die in the same manner as Jesus.)

IN JESUS' NAME
"THE GREAT SHEPHERD OF THE SHEEP" (Hebrews 13:20)

Jesus is not only a good shepherd. He is *the* Shepherd . . . the *great* Shepherd. He would no longer be physically present with His sheep, but He was still responsible for seeing to their care and feeding.

A Large Crowd, Including the Disciples

John ended his gospel by describing the previous appearance of Jesus. Matthew ended his with a different Jesus sighting. Most people think it's the same one Paul refers to later where he says Jesus was seen by more than 500 of His followers at the same time (1 Corinthians 15:6). On this occasion some of the people in the crowd worshiped Jesus; others still doubted. And this was when Jesus instructed His followers to "go and make disciples of all the nations," teaching and baptizing them. He also promised: "I am with you always, even to the end of the age" (Matthew 28:16-20).

James

Paul also tells us that the resurrected Jesus appeared to James, His half brother (1 Corinthians 15:7). This incident isn't mentioned in the Gospels, but it makes sense with what we read in other places. We know that Jesus' brothers didn't believe in Him at first (John 7:5). Yet not long after Jesus' death, His mother and brothers were meeting regularly with the disciples for prayer (Acts 1:12-14). And James became a prominent leader of the early church (Acts

15:13-21). He is generally accepted as the author of the New Testament book of James as well.

The Disciples—One Final Time

It had been 40 days since Jesus had been crucified. During the time spent with His disciples, He had continued to teach them about the kingdom of God and to prepare them for the coming of the Holy Spirit (Luke 24:44-53; Acts 1:1-11). In retrospect, they started to understand what He had been trying to tell them: "That the Messiah must suffer and die and rise again from the dead on the third day" (Luke 24:46).

He appeared to them once more and had a meal with them, giving them specific instructions: "Do not leave Jerusalem until the Father sends you what he promised. Remember, I have told you about this before. John baptized with water, but in just a few days you will be baptized with the Holy Spirit" (Acts 1:4-5). Jesus promised them that after they received the Holy Spirit, "you will receive power and will tell people about me everywhere—in Jerusalem, throughout Judea, in Samaria, and to the ends of the earth" (Acts 1:8).

Not long after telling them these things, as they all watched, Jesus was taken up into the sky and disappeared into a cloud. Like any of us would do, they stood there staring into the heavens until a couple of angles showed up to say, essentially, "Nothing to see here." But the angels did tell them that someday Jesus would return just as they saw Him leave (Acts 1:9-11).

Reasonable Doubt?

So there we have 10 separate Jesus sightings after His crucifixion. Perhaps there were more, but no less than 10 are mentioned in the Bible. Some were to individuals. Some were before large crowds. What is to be made of these accounts?

Noted Christian author Josh MacDowell has written much about these things, and one of his best-selling books is called *Evidence That Demands a Verdict.* Scripture presents the evidence, and it's up to the reader to determine what to make of it.

Not surprisingly, many people resist any likelihood that Jesus really rose from the dead. It's incredulous, unreasonable, unexpected, unprecedented, and as Mr. Spock might say, illogical. But for other people, that's exactly the point. If Jesus didn't do anything *you* couldn't do, what kind of God would He be? Only doing something so unbelievably incredible would prove that He was who He said He was.

But before you make any hasty decisions, let's take a look at some of the alternative explanations that have popped up during the centuries. Many of them continue to be popularly held beliefs to explain away the Resurrection. Yet because they've been around for so long, true believers have had ample opportunity to rebut them. Consider both sides and see what *you* think.

Possibility #1: The women went to the wrong tomb.

This was a traumatic time for the people close to Jesus. Could it have been that the women simply got confused as to their directions and went to the wrong tomb, finding it open and reaching the erroneous conclusion that Jesus had risen?

For one thing, both Mary Magdalene and another woman from her group were watching "nearby" as Joseph of Arimathea laid the body of Jesus in his tomb (Matthew 27:57-61). It is unlikely both of them would return to the wrong location. Besides, if it wasn't where Jesus had been, then the angels they saw and heard there must have been announcing the resurrection of someone else (Matthew 28:5-7).

Possibility #2: Grave robbers opened the tomb and either they, or someone else, took the body of Jesus.

This seemed to be the fear of Mary Magdalene (John 20:11-13). But anyone who knew anything about Jesus had to know He had nothing worth stealing. All He owned were the clothes on His back, and the Roman soldiers had gambled to see who got those.

And Mary Magdalene didn't realize the tomb had been officially sealed (Matthew 27:62-66). No grave robber in his right mind (if, indeed, anyone who robs graves is completely competent) was going to tangle with "Jerusalem's finest"—a military force that had already conquered the known world.

IN JESUS' NAME
"CHRIST JESUS OUR HOPE"
(1 Timothy 1:1)

If indeed Jesus rose from the dead, He is certainly a source of hope for all who desire to do the same.

Possibility #3: His followers "hallucinated" Jesus, or at least saw what they wanted to see.

The thinking behind this argument is that His friends and family were so desperate and forlorn after losing Jesus that they essentially made up the sightings—either consciously or subconsciously. Maybe Mary Magdalene *did* see a gardener but convinced herself it was Jesus. Maybe the fatigue and fear of the disciples caused them to believe He appeared in the upper room when He actually didn't.

However, the number of times Jesus appeared shoots holes in this argument, as well as His appearance in front of numerous witnesses at the same time. Hallucinations don't work that way, where 500 people (or 10, for that matter) see exactly the same thing. In addition, the Bible makes it clear that Jesus' disciples weren't expecting to see Him. His appearances to them were *in spite of a lack of anticipation*—not because they were hoping for and expecting it.

Possibility #4: Jesus didn't actually die.

Some people speculate that Jesus lived through His crucifixion. He certainly looked dead on the cross, but He revived in the cool of the tomb and escaped.

The physical toll on Jesus is undisputed by Scripture and historians. He was flogged with a whip, which had been known to kill people in itself. He was crucified. A spear was thrust into His side—most likely right up to or into His heart. He was pronounced dead by a qualified official. He had been operating on no sleep, and the tomb would have lacked a minibar where He could get food or water. And more than likely, the stone across the entrance would have overlapped the opening of the tomb, making it much more difficult to roll back from the inside than from without. It seems highly unlikely, even if Jesus *had* been alive, that He could have revived, shaken off the physical weakness and loss of blood, performed a Houdini-like maneuver to extract Himself from 75 pounds of spices and tightly wrapped grave clothes, knocked aside the huge stone, and gotten past the Roman guard. Frankly, rising from the dead would appear to be an easier task.

Possibility #5: The disciples stole the body.

Let's suppose they did. Even though they ran like rabbits from the Jewish leaders in the Garden of Gethsemane, let's say they reconvened and put together a *Mission: Impossible* plan to divert the Roman guard, roll back the enormous stone, remove the body of Jesus (while leaving the grave clothes in the tomb, intact), and escape unnoticed. Then they returned to the upper room to quiver behind locked doors. What then?

It's not like they had anything to gain from such a move—just the opposite. Between what we read in the Bible and what tradition says about Jesus' disciples, 10 of the remaining 11 (since Judas was already gone) were put to death for what they believed. If it was all a sham, wouldn't at least one of them have cracked and confessed before dying for a cover-up? In every police show on TV, it only takes two suspects for the cops to get one to "roll" on the other. With 10 people feeling the heat, surely one would have told the truth to save himself.

Possibility #6: The religious authorities took the body.

Jesus had been a thorn in the side of the Jewish authorities for three years. When He died, maybe they took the body for reasons of their own. They had a close relationship with the Roman authorities and could have arranged something like this if the price were right.

But what we haven't seen in the Gospels so far is what a big deal Jesus would become in Jerusalem and the surrounding area. The stories of His resurrection fueled fires of faith, devotion, and worship. As we will see in the next chapter, while Jesus had been one person to deal with, His death would produce dozens of new teachers and preachers who were just as detested by the traditional religious authorities. If they had Jesus' body, they would certainly have produced it to quash the rapidly growing following that was to become the church.

The Bible Tells Me So

If you weren't convinced of the reality of the Resurrection at the beginning of this chapter, you probably still aren't. But perhaps you

IN JESUS' NAME
"MY WITNESS" (Isaiah 55:4)

This title was first applied to David but is also believed to be applicable to David's descendant, Jesus. And what better way to be a witness for God than to die, come back to life, and replace past sufferings with present and future glory?

IN JESUS' NAME
"ROSE OF SHARON" "LILY OF THE VALLEY"
(Song of Songs 2:1)

These two flowers mentioned in an Old Testament love story have become endearing names for Jesus. Lilies, in particular, remain popular flowers connected with Easter.

OPINION POLL

"Our Lord has written the promise of the resurrection, not in books alone, but in every leaf of springtime."—*Martin Luther*

can see why some people believe as they do. And as we continue through this book, it is important to understand the way of thinking that accepts the resurrection of Jesus as truth. The doctrines and theology that follow are all built on the fact that Jesus conquered death and sin through His death and resurrection.

Some people despise winter when they are forced to contend with cold weather and harsh elements of nature. Others love winter as the snow lays a unique blanket of beauty over the earth and provides numerous opportunities to get out the skis, snowmobiles, ice skates, and other recreational toys. Christmas is usually a highlight of the year, with its seasonal songs, foods, and traditions. But in spite of how much people love or hate the winter season, most will confess to an annual longing for spring to arrive.

The first day each year when you can enjoy the outdoors without a coat is a reminder of exactly how good life can be. God seems closer in spring as nature comes back to life in almost-forgotten sounds, smells, colors, and other physical sensations. And there, right in the middle of this new cycle of life, is Easter.

Similarly, some lives are filled with joy and wonder. Other lives are filled with more than their fair share of pain and suffering. But for those who don't believe death is the end, the resurrection of Jesus provides hope that we too can pass from death into new life—an eternal life without all the hassles we face in this one.

A new cycle of life. That's what Easter is all about. Those plants and trees only *looked* dead. But winter is behind us. Now spring brings them back even stronger than before, beckoning those bright colors and fragrant smells to return. Similarly, resurrection allows us to shed our physical skins for a more impressive spiritual wardrobe. Death has occurred, but it was just the briefest of stops on the way to eternal life.

One significant biblical premise of Jesus' resurrection is that He conquered death and sin. Another is that He led the way for the rest of us to expect the same thing. Now that He has blazed the trail from the depth of the tomb to the heights of heaven, we have an unimpeded expressway where we can follow. In the following chapters, various New Testament writers will build on their belief in the resurrection and provide a "new and improved" outlook on who Jesus was and what we can expect from Him.

Questions to Ponder and/or Discuss

1. Where would you place yourself on this scale of belief in Jesus' bodily resurrection from the grave?

Bah, humbug   Fully convinced

2. How important is the resurrection of Jesus in regard to your concept/definition of Christian faith?

3. If you wanted to try to disprove the Resurrection, what argument(s) would you raise? If you wanted to defend the Resurrection, how might you respond to your own argument(s)?

CHAPTER FOURTEEN

Now What?

JESUS IN ABSENTIA

A line from a Joni Mitchell song states, "Don't it always seem to go that you don't know what you've got till it's gone." That must have been the exact sentiment felt by the disciples and other followers of Jesus. When He had been with them, they took His presence for granted. Now what was life going to be like?

After all, Jesus had done the teaching. Jesus had performed the miracles. Jesus had handled all the squabbles with the religious leaders. Jesus had calmed the storms—both literal and symbolic. The disciples had had a bit of rookie training, but no one seemed ready to step up to the plate and take over.

In fact, it wasn't so very long ago that the disciples had scattered like dandelion seeds at the first big puff of opposition. They had all boldly professed loyalty to Jesus—even to death (Matthew 26:33-35). But when danger presented itself and Jesus wasn't there to bail them out, they quickly forgot their hasty promises.

We have seen that for lack of other options, Peter had returned to fishing, but Jesus put him back on track "feeding sheep" (John 21:15-19). Jesus had also told the disciples to wait in Jerusalem for the gift God promised (Acts 1:4).

SOME THINGS YOU'LL DISCOVER IN THIS CHAPTER

1. The disciples were unexpectedly filled with the Holy Spirit and began to speak in other languages.

2. Stephen was stoned to death, but his martyrdom initiated the spread of the Christian faith.

3. A vision about food prompted Peter to present the gospel to the Gentiles.

Although Jesus knew *He* was the one who was going to die, He did everything possible to prepare His disciples for the events to follow. He kept encouraging them, He promised them the Holy Spirit, and He gave them clear instructions on where to go to receive it. The disciples may have felt alone and adrift during this time, but Jesus was still in charge of things whether they knew it or not.

SOMETHING OLD,
SOMETHING NEW
Joel 2:28-32 ... Acts 2:1-21

In this instance, Peter was the one who realized the (partial) fulfillment of what Joel had foretold. The Holy Spirit was being "poured out" and would continue to be the driving force behind the growth of the early church. Other portions of Joel's prophecy seem to be as yet unfulfilled.

So they hung around the city for a while. After the trauma of witnessing Jesus' crucifixion and the cardiopulmonary strain of His appearances and disappearances over 40 days, they probably needed the rest. They had the support of each other, the comfort of staying in one place without so much traveling, and the opportunity to reflect on the previous three years. They also used this time to select a replacement for Judas (a guy named Matthias, whom we never hear from again), and they spent a lot of time in prayer.

Holy Tongues of Fire!

The 50th day after the Sabbath of Passover week was known as the day of Pentecost, or the Festival of Harvest. This was another major time of celebration as people gathered again in Jerusalem to feast and give thanks for the gathering of their crops. It was on this day that a rather unusual event took place among the disciples. They had gathered in a house with others who believed in Jesus, which at this time was a group of only about 120 people.

With no fanfare, a sound like a violent wind came from heaven and filled the house. Something that appeared to be "tongues of fire" descended onto each of them. They were filled with the Holy Spirit and began to speak in different languages they had not learned. However, the people present in Jerusalem from other lands all heard about "the wonderful things God has done" in their own language.

Jesus had tried to brief His disciples on the importance of this event. Even as He was saying His final farewells prior to His crucifixion, He promised a replacement—"another Counselor, who will never leave you" (John 14:16). True to His word, the Holy Spirit was this new "Counselor." Jesus would be the cornerstone on which the church was built, but the Holy Spirit would be the inner source of energy, insight, and direction for all who believed in Jesus.

Motivated by this visitation of the Holy Spirit, Peter stood and delivered an impromptu sermon. First he had to set the record straight. The unusual circumstances and unusual behavior of Jesus' followers gave certain observers the impression that they must all certainly be drunk. But Peter corrected that misperception. For one thing, he said, it was only nine in the morning. And in addition, the unlearned ability to speak other languages was certainly a work of God.

Then Peter pointed out that the Holy Spirit was only active because of what Jesus had already done. He said that even though Jesus had been "endorsed" by God through His miracles, the people of Israel had still "nailed him to the cross and murdered him" (Acts 2:22-23). It didn't take long before his listeners were asking the disciples, "Brothers, what should we do?" (Acts 2:37). Peter told them, "Each of you must turn from your sins and turn to God, and be baptized in the name of Jesus Christ for the forgiveness of your sins. Then you will receive the gift of the Holy Spirit. This promise is to you and to your children, and even to the Gentiles—all who have been called by the Lord our God" (Acts 2:38-39). Then Peter continued preaching "for a long time."

But on this day, only a week and a half after His ascension into heaven, Jesus is clearly defined as the key figure to effect forgiveness of sin, inclusion of the Gentiles into God's kingdom, and the privilege of having the Holy Spirit in one's life. About 3,000 people responded to Peter's message that day. And Jesus has remained the crucial figure in church growth and unity ever since.

IN JESUS' NAME
"WONDERFUL COUNSELOR"
(Isaiah 9:6)

In John 14:17, Jesus plainly identifies the "replacement" Counselor as the Holy Spirit. Yet Jesus continues to fulfill the role of Wonderful Counselor as well. Whether believers turn to God the Father, God the Son, or God the Holy Spirit, they can find wisdom, truth, and peace.

More Power!

The coming of the Holy Spirit at Pentecost marked a definite change in the followers of Jesus. They took on a whole new boldness and courage, as well as a sense of authority. Jesus had previously given them power and authority (Matthew 10:1), but they had sometimes lacked the faith and conviction to properly apply it (Matthew 17:14-16). Now, however, they found new passion and strength.

First we are told the apostles "performed many miraculous signs and wonders." They shared everything they had with one another

"Nobody worries about Christ as long as he can be kept shut up in churches. He is quite safe inside. But there is always trouble if you try and let him out."
—*Geoffrey A. Studdert-Kennedy*

IN JESUS' NAME

"[GOD'S] SERVANT JESUS" (Acts 3:13)
"THE AUTHOR OF LIFE" (Acts 3:15)

While speaking of the importance of the name of Jesus, Peter used a couple of names for Him. At last, the dichotomy of who Jesus was seemed to be sinking in for Peter. The risen Jesus was and continues to be "the author of life." But His significance lies in the fact that He was also a servant who fulfilled God's will.

154

and met together "constantly" where they worshiped, ate together, and met in one another's homes to celebrate the Lord's Supper—a sacrament established to remember the sacrificial death of Jesus. New people became believers every day (Acts 2:43-47).

The book of Acts provides a story of a beggar, lame since birth, who stopped Peter and John as they were going to the temple. He asked for some spare change, and Peter replied, "I don't have any money for you. But I'll give you what I have. In the name of Jesus Christ of Nazareth, get up and walk!" Then Peter reached down and pulled the man to his feet. The man felt sudden strength in his feet and ankles, and began to walk. Soon he was leaping around and praising God, and for the first time in his life, he was able to walk into the temple under his own power (Acts 3:1-11).

As he had learned to do from Jesus, Peter used this miracle as an object lesson. Now that he had the crowd's attention, he began to speak to them about Jesus. He discounted any notion that the healing power was his, and made it clear that "The name of Jesus has healed this man. . . . Faith in Jesus' name has caused this healing before your very eyes" (Acts 3:16).

And as the crowds had done for Jesus, Peter's listeners quickly divided into two camps—those who believed and those who refused to do so. The essence of Peter's message was that the people had made a big mistake in killing Jesus instead of listening to Him. And even though they had acted in ignorance, they now needed to repent and put their faith in Him. After all, Jesus would be coming back again.

By the time Peter finished, two things had happened. First, the number of believers in Jesus had increased to about 5,000 men, plus women and children. And second, Peter and John had been arrested by the Jewish religious leaders who were alarmed to see that even though Jesus had been crucified almost two months ago, He still seemed to get a lot of "press" in the streets of Jerusalem (Acts 4:1-4).

The next day Peter and John were interrogated. The Jewish leaders demanded to know, "By what power, or in whose name, have you done this?" Peter responded to their question with one of his own: "Are we being questioned because we've done a good deed for a crippled man?" But then he answered their question with great clarity: "Let me clearly state to you and to all the people of Israel that he was healed in the name and power of Jesus Christ from Nazareth, the man you crucified, but whom God raised from the dead. ... There is salvation in no one else! There is no other name in all of heaven for people to call on to save them" (Acts 4:5-12).

Same Disciples, Different Demeanor

The religious leaders could hardly believe these were Jesus' disciples who had previously cowered in fear under the threat of arrest. They were amazed at the newfound boldness of Peter and John. Although the authorities didn't care for the disciples' message, the formerly crippled man was standing right there among them, so there wasn't much they could do. They acted very magnanimous and offered to let Peter and John go with a warning as long as they never again spoke or taught about Jesus. But in a nice way, Peter and John replied, "Fat chance." The council threatened them further but didn't think they could do anything more without risking a riot.

After Peter and John were released, they reported what had happened to the rest of the believers. A prayer meeting followed, where they all asked for great boldness in preaching, for healing power, and for miraculous signs and wonders. After this prayer, the building where they were meeting began to shake as they all felt the strong presence of the Holy Spirit.

This experience of Peter and John would be the first of many similar ones yet to come. The followers of Jesus would take a stand for Him, they would be hassled by the established religious authorities, and they would frequently be jailed as a result. Sometimes those arrests would result in further opportunity to preach the gospel and eventual release. Other arrests would result in physical punishment and/or death.

As far as the established Jewish leaders were concerned, this Jesus following must have seemed as much like a cult as anything we've

SOMETHING OLD,
SOMETHING NEW
Psalm 118:22 ... Acts 4:11

While addressing the religious leaders, Peter interpreted a quotation from Psalms: "The stone rejected by the builders has now become the cornerstone." The Messiah should be the very foundation of their faith—the cornerstone. But those in charge had very clearly rejected Him.

SOMETHING OLD,
SOMETHING NEW
Psalm 2:1-2 ... Acts 4:25-26

David the psalmist had asked, "Why do the nations rage? Why do the people waste their time with futile plans?" Then he answered his own question: "The kings of the earth prepare for battle; the rulers plot together against the Lord and against his anointed one." The early believers in Jerusalem recalled this passage during their prayer meeting. Many would soon have to deal with the "rage" of those who opposed them.

known or seen today. Many believers were vocal to the verge of being fanatic. The miracles that accompanied their teachings were attracting large crowds of interested seekers. No matter what was being promoted—truth or not—the sheer level of enthusiasm must have been threatening for those who were trying to maintain the status quo in the temple and synagogues. And to further complicate things, "many of the Jewish priests were converted, too" (Acts 6:7).

The apostles remained active, holding regular public meetings at the temple. Their miracles quickly became legendary, and crowds came to see and hear the apostles. Both men and women were becoming believers, although many were careful about saying too much in public for fear of what might happen. It got to the point where sick and injured people would position themselves so Peter's shadow would fall on them and they would be healed (Acts 5:12-16).

Just as the name of Jesus brought out the boldness and courage of His followers, it had an equally strong effect on His opponents. After the furor refused to die down, even following another series of imprisonments, many on the Jewish high council were ready to have the apostles killed. But a popular teacher named Gamaliel put a different spin on the matter. He said, "My advice is, leave these men alone. If they are teaching and doing these things merely on their own, it will soon be overthrown. But if it is of God, you will not be able to stop them. You may even find yourselves fighting against God" (Acts 5:33-40). The council accepted his advice, but that didn't stop them from flogging the apostles before releasing them. However, the punishment only motivated the disciples, causing them to rejoice because God counted them worthy to suffer dishonor in Jesus' name.

Let's See Whose Martyr

In spite of Gamaliel's advice, the Jesus debate was far from settled. Too many people were involved for all of them to back off and walk away from the conflict at this point. As the church continued to grow, more people were appointed to assist the apostles with some of the basic and practical aspects of church leadership (such as food distribution and other daily needs of the growing number of believers). One of these men was named Stephen, and is described as "a man full of God's grace and power" who was also gifted in speaking and reasoning (Acts 6:8-10). When certain men started to debate with him but couldn't hold their own against his wisdom, they convinced some other people to lie about his character, which eventually got him arrested.

When the council asked Stephen to defend himself, he launched into a history lesson of the Jewish people that interwove the stories of Abraham, Joseph, Moses, David, and the prophets. He ended with the observation that the Jewish leaders had discounted all these examples—which had pointed to the coming of a Messiah—when they had "betrayed and murdered" Jesus. They were making the same mistakes their people had made throughout history in rejecting special leaders sent by God.

The authorities weren't just a little upset by these accusations; they were "infuriated" and began to shake their fists with rage. But Stephen didn't seem to care. He peered upward and said, "Look, I see the heavens opened and the Son of Man standing in the place of honor at God's right hand" (Acts 7:56).

That was the last straw. The religious leaders clamped their hands over their ears and shouted to drown out Stephen's voice. Then they dragged him outside of the city and began to stone him. As the stones found their target, Stephen prayed, "Lord Jesus, receive my spirit." And his last words were, "Lord, don't charge them with this sin!"

Believers in Jesus had been given a hard time before this. John the Baptist had been beheaded, but his execution was more due to his observations about the sex life of Herod than his personal association with Jesus. And Jesus had been crucified, a drastic action which the leaders hoped would put an end to the hoopla that had been developing among the people. But Stephen is remembered as the first martyr—the first kill—and more were certain to follow.

The notation is made that "A great wave of persecution began

OPINION POLL

"We multiply whenever we are mown down by you; the blood of Christians is seed."—*Tertullian*

IN JESUS' NAME
"THE WAY" (John 14:6)

At one point, Jesus had referred to Himself as "the way." For a time, that was the title adopted by His followers. The term "Christians" would come later.

**SOMETHING OLD,
SOMETHING NEW**
Isaiah 53:7-8 ... Acts 8:26-39

The Ethiopian official was reading about a man who was "led as a sheep to the slaughter. And as a lamb is silent before the shearers, he did not open his mouth. He was humiliated and received no justice." The recent treatment of Jesus in Jerusalem had definitely fulfilled Isaiah's prophecy.

that day, sweeping over the church in Jerusalem, and all the believers except the apostles fled into Judea and Samaria" (Acts 8:1). Sides were forming. People were either for Jesus, or against Him. And their decision might be the difference between life and death.

Another notation is made that, at the stoning of Stephen, a young man was present whose name was Saul (Acts 7:58). He seemed to be in charge of the "cloakroom" that day. But soon he had volunteered to track down and bring to justice (arrest and/or put to death) any people he could find who were "followers of the Way" (Acts 9:1-2).

The persecution of Jesus' followers in Jerusalem has been compared to someone attempting to stamp out a blaze. The intent was to put out the original fire, but the unintended result was scattering the single flame into numerous other smaller fires in the surrounding areas. One of the last things Jesus had said was that His disciples "will tell people about me everywhere—in Jerusalem, throughout Judea, in Samaria, and to the ends of the earth" (Acts 1:8). The persecution quickly moved people out of Jerusalem into those areas.

And remarkable things continued to happen. One case in point is a story about Philip, one of the men who had been chosen with Stephen to help oversee the needs of the church. Philip was directed by the Holy Spirit to go into the desert where he came upon an official from Ethiopia reading aloud from the book of Isaiah. He asked the man if he understood what he was reading, but the man didn't have a clue. Philip explained the connection between the sacrificial Messiah prophesied by Isaiah and Jesus who had recently been crucified. The Ethiopian understood, believed, and was baptized at the first pool of water they found. It is thought that he is the one who carried the gospel to Africa.

Saul, You Need His Love

So even though Jesus was no longer physically around to teach, heal, and minister to the people, His presence was certainly being felt among His followers who stepped in to get the job done for

Him. On one hand were the disciples and their new crop of followers like Stephen and Philip, who were dedicated, devoted, and determined to speak for Jesus. On the other were the hardcore, gung-ho traditionalists like Saul who were beginning to go to great lengths to silence the new voices that had replaced Jesus'. First was the crucifixion of Jesus Himself. Then the stoning of Stephen. And now persecution was intensifying in scope.

Saul had a passion for eliminating any kind of Jesus influence on the world. He was a door-to-door anti-evangelist who "went from house to house, dragging out both men and women to throw them into jail" (Acts 8:3). He was "uttering threats with every breath" (Acts 9:1). He even asked the high priest for letters authorizing him to go to Damascus, a hub of travel and communication, about 150 miles away. He planned to do a little Christian exterminating—rounding up believers and extraditing them back to Jerusalem in chains.

But on the way to Damascus, Saul's best-laid plans had to be changed. A brilliant light from heaven focused on him, and as he fell to the ground he heard a voice say, "Saul! Saul! Why are you persecuting me?" (Acts 9:3-4) When he asked who was speaking, the voice responded, "I am Jesus, the one you are persecuting! Now get up and go into the city, and you will be told what to do."

The men who were with Saul were befuddled. They could hear the sound of a voice, but they couldn't see anyone. And when Saul stood up, he discovered he was blind. His companions had to guide him the rest of the way to Damascus where he went without food or water for three days.

In the meantime, Jesus was making Himself known to a believer named Ananias. In a vision, Jesus told Ananias to connect with Saul and restore his sight. Talk about your tests of faith! Even while Jesus was humbling Saul, He was sending a faithful disciple into a one-on-one confrontation with the person who was Public Enemy Number One as far as believers were concerned. But Ananias was up to the task. He found Saul and explained that Jesus had sent him to restore Saul's sight. At that instant "something like scales" fell from Saul's eyes and his sight was restored. He also was baptized and began to eat again.

W.D.J.D.?

Much was being taught and preached about Jesus during this time after the Holy Spirit had come. Yet Jesus continued to appear in visions from time to time, followed by dramatic changes in the lives of those He appeared to. These appearances both comforted and assured the early believers that they were on the right track in their faith.

"Men reject their prophets and slay them, but they love their martyrs and honor those whom they have slain."—*Fyodor Dostoyevsky*

Even while spending a few days with the believers in Damascus, Saul began to preach that Jesus "is indeed the Son of God" (Acts 9:19-20). Saul had trained under Gamaliel, the wise Sanhedrin member who had diffused the tension for a while between traditional Jews and believers in Jesus. And when Saul began to use his knowledge of Old Testament Scripture with his newfound belief that Jesus was indeed the Messiah, no one could refute his arguments. So guess what? The Jewish leaders in Damascus decided to have *him* killed. But Saul found out about the plot and escaped, eventually returning to Jerusalem. (According to Galatians 1:15-18, Saul made a side trip to Arabia sometime immediately after his conversion.)

In Jerusalem, however, the believers were quite sure he was faking his belief in Jesus just to get them to come out, come out wherever they were. A man named Barnabas acted on his behalf, as Ananias had done in Damascus. And when Saul continued to preach "boldly in the name of the Lord," it wasn't long before the religious leaders in *Jerusalem* were plotting to kill him. This time when the plot was discovered, the believers helped Saul escape to his hometown of Tarsus.

Peter's New Diet (Sounds Like Cajun Food)

Meanwhile, Peter was having visions of his own. He saw something like an enormous sheet drop out of heaven, filled with animals of all kinds—birds, reptiles, wild animals, and so forth. Even though many weren't part of a balanced daily diet according to Old Testament law, a voice from heaven said, "Get up, Peter; kill and eat them." Peter refused, explaining that his food choices were completely kosher. This happened three times, and immediately after the third time a group of men arrived to see him.

Peter's visitors were Gentiles, yet they wanted to "hear the message the Lord has given you" (Acts 10:33). Peter then understood that his vision was God's way of telling him there were going to be some changes made in what was and wasn't acceptable to Him.

Peter explained to his visitors the importance of the life, death, and resurrection of Jesus. And when he finished, the Holy Spirit came upon all who were listening—Jews and Gentiles alike.

As far as dietary standards were concerned, Jesus had already paved the way for changes to be made (Matthew 15:11). But more important than what was for dinner was who could join the newly forming church. When the Jewish believers in attendance saw that the Holy Spirit was clearly as present among the Gentiles as among themselves, they had no problem allowing Peter to baptize their new Gentile friends. The church would struggle later with a more widespread acceptance of Gentile believers, but the oneness and acceptance Jesus had taught was for now being applied to everyday life and relationships.

No Term Limits in the Kingdom of God

A U.S. president who serves a single four-year term isn't usually considered successful. Indeed, much of the first term is frequently devoted to getting reelected for a second term. Similarly, politicians who serve only single terms in the House or Senate hardly get their political feet wet.

Jesus spent only about three years in public ministry, yet He made quite an impression during that time. He came, did what He needed to do, and moved on. But His influence didn't stop there. It is still being felt.

Miraculous things kept happening to the believers in the months and years after His resurrection, and the word about Jesus kept spreading out from Jerusalem in ever-widening circles. In a town called Antioch, the disciples of Jesus began to be called "Christians" (Acts 11:26). It has been suggested that it might have been a derogatory term to begin with. (Depending on whom you talk to, perhaps it still is.)

But suffice it to say that the influence of Jesus was much more widespread and potent now than it had ever been, even when He was walking the earth in Galilee. There were still plenty of doubters

IN JESUS' NAME

"THE LORD JESUS" (Acts 7:59)
"LORD OF ALL" (Acts 10:36)
"THE LORD" (Romans 10:13)
"OUR GLORIOUS LORD"
(1 Corinthians 2:8)

When we see a reference to "the Lord" in the Old Testament, we tend to think of God the Father. But after Jesus' death and resurrection, many mentions of "the Lord" refer clearly to Jesus. "Lord" is a title of respect and position, and it also acknowledges Jesus' inseparable connection to His heavenly Father.

OPINION POLL

"Jesus Christ will be Lord of all or He will not be Lord at all."—*Augustine of Hippo*

and detractors, to be sure. But the news of His resurrection, fueled with the power of God's Holy Spirit, had given momentum to the Jesus movement.

The disciples had picked up the torch, and some of them quickly began to feel the heat. James (the disciple) was soon executed "with a sword" by Herod (Acts 12:1-2). Others were being imprisoned. Yet the persecution only seemed to act as fertilizer for the growing faith of these once-cowardly followers of Jesus. And soon these men would find themselves in the shadow of the new disciple, Saul. He had tried to make life rough for the early believers, but that was nothing compared with all that was about to happen to *him*!

Questions to Ponder and/or Discuss

1. How does it affect your faith to believe in a God you cannot physically see, hear, or touch?

2. If you had been around in the first century, which group do you think you would have been in?

- The traditional religious leaders who wanted to quash the new movement
- Saul prior to his conversion, personally seeking out offenders to arrest or persecute
- Followers of Jesus eager to grow in faith and teach others
- Stephen and other believers ready to die for what they believed
- A secret follower, hoping not to capture the attention of the authorities
- Other: _____

3. Do you think contemporary Christianity includes, with equal attention and respect, everyone who wants to participate? Or do you feel some groups seem to get preferential treatment?

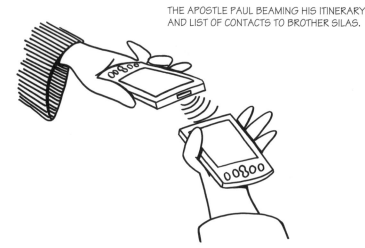

CHAPTER FIFTEEN

THE APOSTLE PAUL BEAMING HIS ITINERARY
AND LIST OF CONTACTS TO BROTHER SILAS.

Brother Paul's Traveling Salvation Show

JESUS AND PAUL

As a young man in the mid-1700s, John Newton was a British slave trader. He would fill his ship with men and women from Africa, bought from tribal chiefs who had captured them during wars or raids. His next stop was the New World, where he would sell them and acquire sugar and molasses for making rum. Then he would return to England, cash in his cargo, and start the cycle over again. But after surviving a particularly violent storm, he sensed God's "great deliverance," became a Christian, and saw his life change dramatically. Today he is little remembered for his slave trading. He is more often acknowledged for his later life as a clergyman and poet. Perhaps you know his work. One of the hundreds of hymns he wrote was "Amazing Grace," which has become perhaps the most universal and best-known standard of the church. When he wrote of God's grace "that saved a wretch like me," he wasn't exaggerating.

Charles Colson was Special Counsel to President Richard Nixon. After the Watergate scandal, he went to prison for seven months when he was found guilty of obstruction of justice charges. He had

SOME THINGS YOU'LL DISCOVER IN THIS CHAPTER

1. Paul faced trials of many kinds as he attempted to take the gospel to the Gentile world.

2. One day our physical bodies will be replaced with new and improved eternal bodies.

3. After Paul's conversion, Jesus became the sole purpose for Paul's life's work.

become a Christian shortly before his prison sentence, and when he got out he became a vocal and intelligent proponent of Christianity. In addition, he formed Prison Fellowship Ministries. His autobiography, *Born Again*, has sold millions of copies since its release in 1976. People are fascinated with his story of spiritual transformation.

Pastors and bumper stickers like to proclaim that Jesus changes lives. Christians by the thousands will attest to wonderful and miraculous inner changes that have occurred after placing their faith in Jesus and committing their lives to Him. Sometimes onlookers are quite skeptical that anything significant has taken place, and perhaps for good reason.

You can probably list a dozen or so celebrities who lived very colorful, earthy lives during the height of their popularity and later surprised the world by declaring themselves Christians. Some of them seem genuinely committed to a different set of morals and values. Others, after a period of time, just as quickly appear to become "unborn again" in a spiritual sense.

But one of the most drastic—and seemingly indisputable—changes on record is that of the apostle Paul.

Then I Heard His Voice, Now I'm a Believer

Paul is the same guy who went by the name of Saul in the last chapter. Perhaps the name change later in life was because he began to devote much of his time to working with the Gentiles and decided to use a more Greek-sounding form of his Jewish name. The switch occurs in Scripture without much ado or explanation.

We don't know that Paul ever met Jesus personally—at least, not while Jesus was alive and walking the earth. But Paul's conversion experience (see last chapter) was certainly dramatic. It is described in Acts 9:1-19, and then he repeats it to various people at least twice more before the book of Acts comes to a close (22:1-21; 26:9-23). And why not? Wouldn't you? It is a gripping story.

In fact, when Paul lists the resurrection appearances of Jesus, he includes his own experience. He says, "Last of all, I saw him, too, long after the others, as though I had been born at the wrong time" (1 Corinthians 15:8). While on the way to arrest and/or kill believers in Jesus, Paul became a believer himself. And while we may tend to suspect that some so-called Christians are faking their faith, Paul could never be accused of doing so.

Paul is an enigma for anyone hoping to promote a gospel of health and prosperity for those who follow Jesus. He didn't particularly like to boast or complain, but he once felt compelled to defend his ministry against people who were badmouthing him. Listen to Paul's "testimony":

> I have worked harder, been put in jail more often, been whipped times without number, and faced death again and again. Five different times the Jews gave me thirty-nine lashes. Three times I was beaten with rods. Once I was stoned. Three times I was shipwrecked. Once I spent a whole night and a day adrift at sea. I have traveled many weary miles. I have faced danger from flooded rivers and from robbers. I have faced danger from my own people, the Jews, as well as from the Gentiles. I have faced danger in the cities, in the deserts, and on the stormy seas. And I have faced danger from men who claim to be Christians but are not. I have lived with weariness and pain and sleepless nights. Often I have been hungry and thirsty and have gone without food. Often I have shivered with cold, without enough clothing to keep me warm. Then, besides all this, I have the daily burden of how the churches are getting along. (2 Corinthians 11:23-28)

As the old joke goes, "Other than that, Mrs. Lincoln, how was the play?"

We might think that no amount of positive experiences could offset the tremendous trials of the apostle Paul. Yet Paul never wavers from his commitment to Jesus in spite of all these things. Does this sound as if Paul was "faking it"? From every appearance,

OPINION POLL

"Jesus could have written books, but he chose not to. He could have had his disciples memorize a fixed message word for word, but we have no convincing evidence that he ever did. Instead, he worked by exposing people to the good news, letting it do its work on them, and then sending them out to expose others."—*William Countryman*

it seems his encounter with the unseen Jesus was real and life-changing. So, in this chapter, we want to take a look at what Paul had to say about the Jesus he served.

On the Road Again

Since the apostles seemed to have things covered in Jerusalem, Paul was designated by the Holy Spirit and commissioned by the church to conduct a number of "missionary journeys." He took the news about Jesus to many cities surrounding Jerusalem, speaking in the synagogues and establishing new churches. The book of Acts (chapters 13–28) provides a pretty good overview of these road trips conducted by Paul, and we get further insight from the epistles he wrote to the churches as follow-ups to his visits. Occasionally he would spend a couple of years in one place, but usually he stayed on the move. And it wasn't at all unusual for him to get run out of town by people who didn't care at all for him or his message.

Paul was a mystery to the traditional Jews because his own credentials surpassed most of theirs. At one point he said:

> We boast about what Christ Jesus has done for us. Yet I could have confidence in myself if anyone could. If others have reason for confidence in their own efforts, I have even more! For I was circumcised when I was eight days old, having been born into a pure-blooded Jewish family that is a branch of the tribe of Benjamin. So I am a real Jew if there ever was one! What's more, I was a member of the Pharisees, who demand the strictest obedience to the Jewish law. And zealous? Yes, in fact, I harshly persecuted the church. And I obeyed the Jewish law so carefully that I was never accused of any fault. I once thought all these things were so very important, but now I consider them worthless because of what Christ has done. Yes, everything else is worthless when compared with the priceless gain of knowing Christ Jesus my Lord. I have discarded everything else, counting it all as garbage, so that I may have Christ and become one with him. (Philippians 3:3-9)

OPINION POLL

"The saints are the sinners who keep on going."—*Robert Louis Stevenson*

OPINION POLL

"We must free ourselves to be filled by God. Even God cannot fill what is full."—*Mother Teresa*

Apparently Paul was a striking and persuasive speaker. He also had God-given power to heal people. At one point, he and his companion, Barnabas, were mistaken by the townspeople for the gods Zeus and Hermes. But Paul was always quick to take the focus off himself and put it on Jesus. Immediately after the previously quoted passage, Paul states his goal in life: "I want to know Christ and the power of his resurrection and the fellowship of sharing in his sufferings, becoming like him in his death, and so, somehow, to attain to the resurrection from the dead" (Philippians 3:10-11, NIV).

So it was Paul who was on the road trips, who was doing the speaking and the healing, who was starting and strengthening churches. Yet Paul did none of this for his own fame and fortune. He saw himself as a representative of Jesus and strove to live entirely for Him. Paul was merely an "ambassador" (2 Corinthians 5:20; Ephesians 6:20) who spoke and acted on behalf of someone else.

Paul was willing to do whatever it took to get his message across. He wrote:

> When I am with the Jews, I become one of them so that I can bring them to Christ. When I am with those who follow the Jewish laws, I do the same, even though I am not subject to the law, so that I can bring them to Christ. When I am with the Gentiles who do not have the Jewish law, I fit in with them as much as I can. In this way, I gain their confidence and bring them to Christ. But I do not discard the law of God; I obey the law of Christ. When I am with those who are oppressed, I share their oppression so that I might bring them to Christ. Yes, I try to find common ground with everyone so that I might bring them to Christ. (1 Corinthians 9:20-22)

Paul was creative in his attempt to find "common ground" with other people. For example, when he was roaming around Athens he came across an altar devoted "To an Unknown God" (Acts 17:23). He used the opportunity to discuss how Jesus was unknown to a lot of people. And as Paul made Him known, some of his listeners became believers.

Always, always, always Paul kept the spotlight on Jesus. If it weren't for Paul, our understanding of Jesus would be considerably impaired (and the New Testament would be much, much shorter). In order for us to better comprehend why Jesus is so special to so many people, we need to take a closer look at what Paul had to say about Him.

Yours Truly, Paul

When you look through the New Testament for the first time, the titles of the Bible books seem quite strange. But most of them are letters from Paul to various churches. So Galatians is the letter to the church in Galatia; Philippians was sent to the believers in Philippi; the two letters to the Thessalonians went to Thessalonica; and Colossians was mailed off to the church in Colosse. (We'll leave it to you to decipher Romans and the others.)

In many cases Paul had founded the church and was writing to follow up with encouragement, instruction, and reminders of spiritual truth. Several times you can tell from his writing that he was aware of specific issues within a particular church and was writing to address the problem. As you might expect, Paul says much the same thing to all the churches. And not surprisingly, his focus remains on the importance of Jesus. Yet each of his letters has a particular theme that distinguishes it from the others.

Below is a sampling of what he wrote to various churches. We don't cover all his letters, but you can get an idea of how the same devotion to Jesus is expressed in different ways depending on the specific group Paul was writing.

To the Colossians

When writing to the Colossian church, Paul emphasized the supremacy of Christ above everything else. Jesus was a visible manifestation of the supreme God that no one is allowed to see. Jesus has always existed and is supreme over all creation. He is the head of the church. "God in all his fullness" lived in Jesus (Colossians 1:15-23). Now that Christ is seated at the right hand of

168

God, we should set our sights higher than our piddly little problems. Instead, our lives should take on an exciting spiritual focus. Everything we do or say should represent Jesus (Colossians 3:1-17).

To the Galatians

Paul warned the Galatians about trying to hold on to their religious traditions to the point where they missed the freedom made possible by Jesus. People can be slaves to sin, but they can also be slaves to their religious practices. Thanks to what Jesus has done, wrote Paul, "Now you are no longer a slave but God's own child. And since you are his child, everything he has belongs to you" (Galatians 4:7). While in the past our lives had been marked with sin and various problems, Christians should be filled with love, joy, peace, patience, kindness, goodness, faithfulness, gentleness, and self-control (Galatians 5:19-23).

To the Ephesians

To the Ephesians, Paul reveals a "secret plan" devised by God: "At the right time [God] will bring everything together under the authority of Christ—everything in heaven and on earth" (Ephesians 1:9-10). Salvation is a gift from God. People can take it or leave it, but they can do nothing to improve on it or detract from it.

To the Philippians

The letter to the Philippians highlights Jesus' humility and the sheer joy that should result from comprehending what He has done for us. Jesus is God, yet didn't let His position deter Him from showing His complete love for humanity. In history's most significant act of humility, Jesus came to earth in flesh and blood and died a wretched death on the behalf of others. He had rights, but He didn't demand them. We should follow the example He set for us.

To the Corinthians

Most of Paul's letters emphasized the need for unity among believers. This teaching comes out in numerous applications described in his letters to the Corinthians. Unity and order are important in worship, marriage, settling disagreements, exercising one's spiritual gifts, and so forth. The concept of someone dying on the cross being

SOMETHING OLD,
SOMETHING NEW

Psalm 68:18 . . . Ephesians 4:4-10

As the psalm described God ascending to His throne and receiving gifts from His people, Paul applies this passage to Jesus' ascension which was "higher than all the heavens, so that his rule might fill the entire universe."

W.D.J.D.?

Sometimes people get bogged down in debates about what Jesus might have meant by this or that action while He was on earth. But according to Paul, those individual actions are somewhat incidental. Let us not miss the point that Jesus' ultimate act of humility had already taken place by the time He was laid in a manger. Jesus was God, but He chose to bring Himself down to a human level. Everything else He did helped show us how to live, but it was this original sacrifice that made all His other actions so significant.

"OUR PASSOVER LAMB"
(1 Corinthians 5:7)

Just as lambs "with no defects" were sacrificed to spare lives of male children at the first Passover in Egypt (Exodus 12), so Jesus was a perfect sacrifice—a "Passover Lamb" whose blood was shed to prevent the permanent spiritual death of those who believe in Him.

"THE HEAD OF HIS BODY, THE CHURCH" (Ephesians 4:15)
"THE HEAD OF THE CHURCH"
(Colossians 1:18)

It's amazing what parts a human body can do without and still function, but without a head it is only a corpse. Jesus is vital to the life and sustenance of the church.

a *good* thing will sound like foolishness to lots of people, says Paul. "So when we preach that Christ was crucified, the Jews are offended, and the Gentiles say it's all nonsense. But to those called by God to salvation, both Jews and Gentiles, Christ is the mighty power of God and the wonderful wisdom of God" (1 Corinthians 1:20-31). That's why we continue to celebrate the Lord's Supper, because it is "announcing the Lord's death until he comes again" (1 Corinthians 11:20-26). Christians are supposed to have "the mind of Christ" (1 Corinthians 2:16).

In 1 Corinthians, as in other places, Paul describes the church—the worldwide group of people who believe in Jesus—by using the image of a human body. Jesus is the head, and individual believers play differing roles. Just as a body needs hands, feet, eyes, ears, and all the rest to function as intended, the people within the church need to use the spiritual gifts that have been given to them. Jesus isn't looking for clones who are cookie-cutter imitations of one another. The church achieves unity only as its individuals tap into the diverse gifts at their disposal. Church members are all supposed to be like Jesus, but they need to beware trying to become too much like anyone else.

Yet the banner of unity isn't an excuse to tolerate any and every doctrine. Even as Paul was exhorting the Corinthian church to be united, he was also writing to tell them to kick out a member who was sleeping with his "father's wife" (probably his stepmother, but still a definite no-no). If Jesus is the unifying factor—the "head" of the body, so to speak—then any overt sin or anything opposed to His truth is divisive. (A single decayed tooth, out-of-joint toe, or even a hangnail can cause discomfort or worse for the entire body.) Paul's instructions were to "cast this man out of the church" with the anticipation that he would repent of his sin and return to fellowship, appropriately, with his fellow believers (1 Corinthians 5:1-8). Church should be a place where participants are encouraged and challenged to eliminate blatant sins—not to embrace them.

It's a rather fine line to walk sometimes. Paul did everything possible to reach out to a world that might want and need to hear the

Good News about Jesus. He encourages his readers and listeners to do the same. Yet he also warns new believers to be careful about falling back into old habits and sinful lifestyles. As believers are reaching out to others, Paul cautions, "Don't team up with those who are unbelievers" (2 Corinthians 6:14). A marriage or business partnership, for example, is likely to feel severe strain if one partner is pursuing Christian principles while the other isn't.

Paul's secret of success in Christian life was to "let God transform you into a new person by changing the way you think. Then you will know what God wants you to do, and you will know how good and pleasing and perfect his will really is" (Romans 12:2). Paul never promoted self-help. He readily confessed his weaknesses and inability to succeed on his own. He knew for a fact that when he was drained of strength, that's when he would feel Jesus working through him. He summarized: "Since I know it is all for Christ's good, I am quite content with my weaknesses and with insults, hardships, persecutions, and calamities. For when I am weak, then I am strong" (2 Corinthians 12:10).

I Get Knocked Down, but I Get Up Again

Persecution is a recurring theme in the writings of Paul. But he remains ever optimistic. He reminds his readers that those who unite with Jesus in His sufferings will also share in His comfort (2 Corinthians 1:5-7). And as they receive comfort from God, they are enabled to comfort others.

Although people are fragile, the Source of power within believers is strong. Paul used the image of "jars of clay" or "perishable containers" that contain great treasure. When people looked at him, Paul wanted them to see not the weak outer shell but the treasure that lay within. And the connection with Jesus is empowering. Paul wrote: "We are pressed on every side by troubles, but we are not crushed and broken. We are perplexed, but we don't give up and quit. We are hunted down, but God never abandons us. We get knocked down, but we get up again and keep going. Through

OPINION POLL

"The greatest of all weaknesses is the fear of appearing weak."—*J. B. Bossuet*

**SOMETHING OLD,
SOMETHING NEW**

Psalm 16:10; Isaiah 53:8-10 . . . 1 Corinthians 15:3-4

David wrote that God would not allow His "Holy One" to rot in the grave. And Isaiah prophesied that after the Messiah's burial, He would "enjoy a long life, and the Lord's plan will prosper in his hands." Paul was aware of these and other Old Testament references to resurrection.

suffering, these bodies of ours constantly share in the death of Jesus so that the life of Jesus may also be seen in our bodies" (2 Corinthians 4:1-12).

And connected with this train of thought is the importance of Jesus' resurrection. Paul states clearly that Christ died for our sins, that He was buried, and then was raised from the dead. Yet some people were denying the resurrection—not only of Jesus, but of anyone. Paul pressed the issue, suggesting that belief in resurrection is the fulcrum of one's faith. To those who came down on the side that didn't believe in resurrection, Paul wrote: "For if there is no resurrection of the dead, then Christ has not been raised either. And if Christ was not raised, then all our preaching is useless, and your trust in God is useless. . . . And we apostles would all be lying about God. . . . And . . . your faith is useless, and you are still under condemnation for your sins" (1 Corinthians 15:13-17).

Perhaps Paul was thinking about all the suffering he had experienced because of his stand for Jesus. He saw his eventual resurrection and eternal life with Jesus as the payoff for all the pain and anguish he faced on a regular basis. If he didn't believe something better was in his future, he had no reason to keep trying so hard. He summarized his feelings by saying, "If we have hope in Christ only for this life, we are the most miserable people in the world" (1 Corinthians 15:18).

Beatings, stonings, and shipwrecks couldn't make Paul miserable. But the possibility of an afterlife without Jesus would do it in a nanosecond. So Paul then proceeded to provide many specifics in regard to the reality of resurrection. To begin with, Jesus' resurrection would undo the harm that had been done centuries ago when Adam and Eve sinned in the Garden of Eden. All it took was one person (Adam) to bring humanity under the taint of sin, and all it took was the right person (Jesus) to provide new life—a second chance for everyone.

Jesus' resurrection was also important because it was representative of what would then take place for all believers. It is proof that Jesus has defeated His final enemy—death. Jesus was "the first of a great harvest of those who will be raised to life again" (1 Corinthians 15:20). Because He rose from the dead, believers can have faith that they will too.

Paul also provides great detail about how our physical bodies will be replaced with new and improved eternal bodies (1 Corinthians 15:35-50). Our current bodies are meant to run down, die, and decay. But it's all part of God's plan to then move on to something much better. We would be thrilled to trade in our old Pinto for a new Rolls-Royce, but the upgrade from a physical body to a spiritual body will be a much greater contrast. Just as physically our bodies are now like Adam's, in a spiritual state they will be like Christ's (1 Corinthians 15:48-49).

So Paul was pretty matter-of-fact about death. To him it was simply a gateway—even an escape. In fact, Paul had something of a death wish, but he never acted on it. At one point he explained: "For to me, living is for Christ, and dying is even better. Yet if I live, that means fruitful service for Christ. I really don't know which is better. I'm torn between two desires: Sometimes I want to live, and sometimes I long to go and be with Christ. That would be far better for me, but it is better for you that I live" (Philippians 1:21-24).

The death of believers is to be a comforting thought for those who understand Jesus' plan. Paul didn't want Christians to "be full of sorrow like people who have no hope" (1 Thessalonians 4:13). Through death, all believers will be united with each other and with Jesus forever. In connection with these thoughts, Paul speaks with assurance of the eventual return of Jesus to earth (1 Thessalonians 4:13–5:11). Though it will be "like a thief in the night," it's nothing for believers to worry about. For them, it should be something to anticipate and celebrate.

Third Floor of Paradise: Grace, Thorns, Unexpressable Visions

You may wonder how Paul came to know so much about the behind-the-scenes goings on when it came to church life, resurrection, the

SOMETHING OLD, SOMETHING NEW

Leviticus 23:9-14 . . . 1 Corinthians 15:20

One of the Old Testament celebrations was the Festival of Firstfruits. As the first of the crops were harvested, some of the initial grain was offered to God along with a sacrifice. This was done prior to eating any of the grain to acknowledge God's provision for His people. In the same way, Jesus was the "firstfruits" of people resurrected and returning to God. (This symbolism also reinforces many of the parables that used harvesting as an analogy.)

IN JESUS' NAME

"THE FIRST OF ALL WHO WILL RISE FROM THE DEAD"
(Colossians 1:18)

This title for Jesus is taken from the section of Colossians that explains how Jesus is first (preeminent) in all things.

W.D.J.D.?

Jesus had told His disciples to ask and they would receive (Matthew 7:7-7), but sometimes they didn't receive exactly what they asked for. When Paul asked that his "thorn" be removed, that's not what Jesus thought was best in his case. What Paul received instead was an unlimited supply of God's grace to get him through his suffering. The removal of the problem would have been a onetime example of Jesus' power and presence. But living with the problem would be an *ongoing* reminder.

return of Jesus, and so forth. After all, he hadn't tagged along with Jesus and the disciples. He had come to faith after the ascension of Jesus. What made him such an authority?

We don't know a lot about Paul's spiritual development. We *do* know about his conversion experience, which was quite dramatic. He clearly heard Jesus speaking to him, and he responded to the voice. In a few other places he indicates that probably Jesus spoke to him on a regular basis.

Perhaps the most telling passage is 2 Corinthians 12:1-10. Paul refers in third person to a man, which most people agree is Paul himself. He was "caught up into paradise and heard things so astounding that they cannot be told." And as a result of this experience, he writes that "I was given a thorn in my flesh, a messenger from Satan to torment me and keep me from getting proud."

Many people think Paul's "thorn" was some kind of physical limitation that hindered his ministry. (Speculation has included poor eyesight, epilepsy, and other things.) Three specific times Paul asked Jesus to remove it. But each time Jesus replied, "My gracious favor is all you need. My power works best in your weakness."

So it seems that Paul was acquiring a spiritual education beyond the norm for most people. He was receiving direct messages from Jesus and passing them on to other believers. He would make it clear whenever he was expressing his own opinion as opposed to something directly from Jesus. For example, when addressing the topic of marriage, at one point he wrote, "I have a command that comes not from me, but from the Lord" (1 Corinthians 7:10). But after passing along the instruction, he added, "Now, I will speak to the rest of you, though I do not have a direct command from the Lord" (1 Corinthians 7:12). In writing about proper procedure during the Lord's Supper, he says, "For this is what the Lord himself said, and I pass it on to you just as I received it" (1 Corinthians 11:23).

It seems that Paul and Jesus had an ongoing conversation. The same was true of other New Testament writers: John, James, Peter, and Jude. Many of them could insert eyewitness testimony into the new insights they received from Jesus. But Paul is by far the most influential of the New Testament writers.

Jesus was at the center of everything Paul wrote. Paul's imagery is extreme: "I have been crucified with Christ. I myself no longer live, but Christ lives in me" (Galatians 2:19-20). And Paul suggests the same should be true of all believers: "Our old sinful selves were crucified with Christ so that sin might lose its power in our lives. We are no longer slaves to sin. For when we died with Christ we were set free from the power of sin. And since we died with Christ, we know we will also share his new life" (Romans 6:6-8). This is the symbolism behind baptism. It represents death and new life.

Paul's letter to the Romans contains a concise explanation of most of the doctrines held by the church today: justification, sanctification, redemption, grace, freedom, and more. It also has some of Scripture's greatest promises concerning Jesus, such as this passage:

> If God is for us, who can ever be against us? Since God did not spare even His own Son but gave him up for us all, won't God, who gave us Christ, also give us everything else? . . . And I am convinced that nothing can ever separate us from his love. Death can't, and life can't. The angels can't, and the demons can't. Our fears for today, our worries about tomorrow, and even the powers of hell can't keep God's love away. Whether we are high above the sky or in the deepest ocean, nothing in all creation will ever be able to separate us from the love of God that is revealed in Christ Jesus our Lord. (Romans 8:31-32, 38-39)

SOMETHING OLD,
SOMETHING NEW
Psalm 139 . . . Romans 8:31-39

Believers have always had the promise of God's continual presence in their lives. But in the life, death, and resurrection of Jesus, the promise takes on more of a personal relationship than ever before.

That Crazy Paul!

Sometimes when a joke doesn't go as expected, or if you just don't understand what someone is trying to tell you, the person will say, "I guess you had to be there." The life and writing of Paul is proof positive that when it comes to having a good relationship with Jesus, believers don't have the excuse of not having been there.

"He is no fool, who gives what he cannot keep, to gain what he cannot lose."
—*Jim Elliot*

Jesus certainly set the model to show us how to live. But Paul is the model for what can happen when Jesus becomes the top priority in a person's life. Both models work in tandem.

It would certainly have been enlightening to sit at Jesus' feet and soak in everything He had to say . . . to witness His miracles first-hand . . . to share a meal with Him. During the 1960s many groups tried to return to this combination of communal living and spiritual quest. But Paul's model was to "clothe himself" with Jesus Christ (Romans 13:14, NIV)—to become spiritually strong by internalizing the truths of Scripture and then using that knowledge in outreach so others will benefit as well. People might look at Jesus' example and think, *He was God! I could never live like that.* But Paul was just a regular person willing to conform to Jesus' teachings, and he literally changed his world. He demonstrates what the power of Jesus can do for anyone.

This chapter has only barely begun to consider what Paul said and wrote about Jesus. But he clearly had a passion for the man he considered Savior, Lord, and King. Paul lived solely so Jesus might live through him. And he demonstrates the attitudes and actions of other martyrs who died because of their unyielding devotion to Jesus during the first century and even to this very day.

This degree of attraction to a dead man may seem ludicrous, fanatical, or mentally unstable to those who don't give any credence to the resurrection or significance of Jesus. Yet if Jesus wasn't very, very real to Paul, none of the apostle's actions make any sense. Indeed, he was even accused of being mentally unbalanced during his lifetime. One time after he told the story of his conversion experience, his listeners started screaming, "Away with such a fellow! Kill him! He isn't fit to live!" (Acts 22:22) Another time a Roman official who heard it told him, "Paul, you are insane. Too much study has made you crazy!" (Acts 26:24)

Some readers may wish to cast their votes with these people, and it's certainly your right to do so. Yet perhaps these looks into the life of Paul will help you understand the mentality of people who try to imitate his lifestyle and commitment to Jesus. Jesus was dead and gone, yet His personal influence was stronger than ever in the lives of his early followers. He was still speaking to people, still instructing them, and still ministering to them—at least, that's what they said and how they acted. It's difficult to explain their actions otherwise.

In the mystery of the Kingdom of God, the influence of Jesus was more powerful after He died than while He was alive. Go figure.

But in contrast, a look at the life of Jesus in hindsight also began to *explain* a lot of mysteries. The next chapter will focus on the book of Hebrews, which connects the New Testament figure of Jesus with a lot of Old Testament symbolism which seemed to prepare the way for Him.

Questions to Ponder and/or Discuss

1. Who do you know who has experienced the most dramatic spiritual transformation? What prompted the change? How do you determine whether the change is genuine and permanent, or just a phase?

2. When you read of Paul's intense sufferings just so he could tell more people about Jesus, what's your initial reaction?

- He's a nut!
- Go for it, Paul. Just don't ask me to join you.
- That's the kind of person I want to be.
- Other: _____

3. If Paul had spent the past six months with you and had gotten to know you well, what one thing about Jesus do you think he would stress to you in a follow-up letter?

CHAPTER SIXTEEN

Everything Old Is New Again

JESUS: A NEW LOOK AT THE OLD TESTAMENT

One of the more popular programs on PBS in recent years has been *Antiques Roadshow*. Teams of antiques appraisers show up in various towns where local people bring all sorts of old stuff to see if it might be of value. Sometimes "treasures" turn out to be junk, but more often the program shows us pleasant surprises.

Great-grandpa's old birdcage isn't worth so much in itself. Too bad. But look! He lined the bottom with a personal letter signed by Abraham Lincoln! Aunt Petunia's gaudy "costume" jewelry turns out to be made from genuine (and huge) precious stones. The jar that Cousin Clem used to mix worm medicine for his cattle is a rare and exquisite product of an Old World glass manufacturer.

The success of *Antiques Roadshow* is that we love to see people show up with old, long-overlooked possessions—and a hefty dose of hope—and be rewarded for their efforts. Our culture has a tendency to equate "old" with "worthless," and it's good to see such thinking disrupted.

The biblical book of Hebrews is a lot like *Antiques Roadshow*. No one knows for certain who the author was, but he or she was an

SOME THINGS YOU'LL DISCOVER IN THIS CHAPTER

1. When you know something about the life of Jesus, many parts of the Old Testament make a lot more sense.

2. Jesus is the perfect High Priest, who is able to deal with all our sins. His power is forever.

3. Jesus Himself created and sustains the universe.

OPINION POLL

"Man is neither angel nor beast; and the misfortune is that he who would act the angel acts the beast."—*Blaise Pascal*

IN JESUS' NAME

"THE ONE THROUGH WHOM GOD CREATED EVERYTHING"
(Colossians 1:16)

You may recall back in chapter 2 that when God spoke at Creation, He said, "Let us make people in our image" (Genesis 1:26). Here in the New Testament, both Paul and the writer of Hebrews credit Jesus (as God) with the creation of "the universe and everything in it" (Hebrews 1:2).

180

insightful "appraiser" of several portions of the "Old" Testament who brought to light the surprising value of many things we find there. We saw in chapter 2 that Jesus can be found throughout the Old Testament in the illuminating writings of the prophets. But after He came to earth as prophesied, a lot of other Old Testament symbols and events began to make a lot more sense. The author of Hebrews, who writes primarily to a Jewish-Christian audience who would be very familiar with the Old Testament, makes a lot of references that help explain the significance of Jesus. We may not be as familiar with the Old Testament as many of the original readers of Hebrews would have been, so we may need to think a bit harder to make sense out of what is being written. But in our search to better understand the biblical Jesus, Hebrews is a book we shouldn't overlook.

Different Angles on Angels

Angels have always had a lot of prestige in the Bible. They frequently serve as messengers for God, and almost every time one of them appears in Scripture, the first words out of his mouth are usually, "Don't be afraid!" It seems that most people are quite intimidated, if not downright scared, whenever angels show up.

In the Old Testament, angels were seen by Abraham, Hagar, Jacob, Balaam and his donkey, Gideon, Samson's parents, Daniel, and others. In the New Testament, we have seen that both Mary and Joseph received an angelic visit prior to Jesus' birth. An angel ministered to Jesus in His emotional distress in the Garden of Gethsemane. An angel sprang Peter from prison in a miraculous way during the early days of the new and growing church.

On the grand scale of created beings, angels are impressive in contrast to humans. Human beings can't quite stack up, and, as a human, Jesus found Himself "lower than the angels" for a while (Hebrews 2:7). But lest there be any confusion, the author of Hebrews makes it clear that Jesus had only a temporary "demotion." The rest of the story about Jesus is that "The Son reflects

God's own glory, and everything about him represents God exactly. He sustains the universe by the mighty power of his command. After he died to cleanse us from the stain of sin, he sat down in the place of honor at the right hand of the majestic God of heaven" (Hebrews 1:3).

So while people may take a backseat to angelic beings, Jesus never will. In His submission and sacrifice, He humbly lived as a human being for 33 years, but never again will He be subject to anyone or anything else.

Jesus, as the author of Hebrews points out, is the Son of God—a relationship unattainable for angels. Jesus is eternally God's Son, and human beings can be "adopted" into God's family to receive the same rights and inheritance as Jesus (Romans 8:15-17). Angels cannot.

Jesus is also credited with creating and sustaining the universe. His kingdom is forever. He is bestowed with much praise from God. No other created being has the same status—neither angel nor human. Jesus is superior to the angels.

You're Going Down, Moses!

Moses was a revered figure of the Hebrew faith. No other Old Testament figure, except perhaps Abraham, received such respect. So how does this new guy, Jesus, stack up against Moses?

Both Moses and Jesus were certainly faithful to God's plan, says the writer of Hebrews. Both were servants. Both were called to oversee people who were somewhat obstinate. But the comparisons end there.

If you were the head steward at Buckingham Palace, it would be a position of great honor, but it wouldn't make you the Queen. There is no doubt that "Moses served faithfully and was entrusted with God's entire house" (Hebrews 3:2). But Moses was *only* a servant. Jesus was "the faithful Son" who was "in charge of the entire household" (Hebrews 3:6). Therefore, "Jesus deserves far more glory than Moses."

SOMETHING OLD,
SOMETHING NEW

Psalm 2:7 ... Hebrews 1:5-6
Psalm 45:6-7 ... Hebrews 1:8-9
Psalm 102:25-27 ... Hebrews 1:10-12
Psalm 104:4 ... Hebrews 1:7
Psalm 110:1 ... Hebrews 1:13

The author of Hebrews obviously does a lot of quoting from Old Testament Scripture to back up the points he is trying to make. Perhaps his audience would be convinced by nothing less.

W.D.J.D.?

Even in retrospect, even after acknowledging the superior position of Jesus above all other people and things, Jesus' acts of service cannot be overlooked. Indeed, they are integral to His character. If Jesus is God and the Creator of all things, and if He can "stoop" to serve people who are nowhere near His level, shouldn't mere mortals be willing to do the same?

To Aaron Human, to Jesus Divine

Okay, so Moses was a great leader, yet not as great as Jesus. But how about Aaron, his brother? After all, Aaron was called specifically by God to be the first high priest. And afterward, all priests had to come from Aaron's family, the tribe of Levi. The priests did the work of God among the people. Isn't that essentially the same thing Jesus did?

Yes it is. Just as Aaron had been designated to stand between the sinful Israelites and the Holy God, so was Jesus. But again, there are some crucial differences. Aaron and all other priests had to make offerings for their own sins, but Jesus committed no sin. Still, Jesus "offered prayers and pleadings, with a loud cry and tears, to the one who could deliver him out of death" (Hebrews 5:7). Because Jesus was a sinless God who willingly became human, He qualified as "a perfect High Priest"(5:9).

Shouldn't we be somewhat intimidated by a "perfect" High Priest? After all, wouldn't you rather do your confessing and make offerings through someone who occasionally sins just like you do?

The drawback to such thinking is that it's more important for the High Priest to relate well to God than to you. In Israel's history, the nation had scores of corrupt priests who went through the motions but were just as rotten as anyone else. They had no spiritual sensitivity at all. Although the priests were praying and making sacrifices, God wasn't listening.

What makes Jesus so special is that He has been in our shoes. Of all the people who ever lived, Satan would love to have swayed Jesus into doing something against God. Jesus felt every temptation we feel, so He knows exactly how hard we struggle with sin. Yet He never gave in.

And because Jesus never sinned, He was the perfect sacrifice to God on our behalf. All debts were cancelled. The bill was paid in full. The veil in the temple was torn in two. No longer do believers need to fear God's condemnation.

Hebrews 4:14-16 is a frequently quoted passage:

IN JESUS' NAME

"GREAT HIGH PRIEST"
(Hebrews 4:14)
"THE SON OF GOD" (Hebrews 4:14)
"THE SOURCE OF ETERNAL SALVATION" (Hebrews 5:9)

As you can see by the various names being used for Jesus throughout this section, they are beginning to overlap and interrelate. As the Son of God, Jesus could be not only the High Priest but could simultaneously be the sacrifice who achieves eternal salvation for those who believe.

That is why we have a great High Priest who has gone to heaven, Jesus the Son of God. Let us cling to him and never stop trusting him. This High Priest of ours understands our weaknesses, for he faced all of the same temptations we do, yet he did not sin. So let us come boldly to the throne of our gracious God. There we will receive his mercy, and we will find grace to help us when we need it.

Of course, since people now have direct access to God and a "perfect" High Priest in Jesus, believers have run low on excuses for not getting their spiritual lives in better shape. The writer of Hebrews had to chide his readers a bit. He told them, "You have been Christians a long time now, and you ought to be teaching others. Instead, you need someone to teach you again the basic things a beginner must learn about the Scriptures. You are like babies who drink only milk and cannot eat solid food. And a person who is living on milk isn't very far along in the Christian life and doesn't know much about doing what is right" (Hebrews 5:12-13).

Mel-*Who*-zedek?

If you want to get a little more picky about all this high priest thinking (which we're sure you are begging to do), Aaron isn't even the best model to symbolize the priesthood of Jesus. Another little known Bible character came along before Aaron and is targeted by the author of Hebrews to better represent the type of priest Jesus is—a man named Melchizedek.

This mystery man Melchizedek is identified only as "the king of Salem and a priest of God Most High" (Genesis 14:18-20). He offered bread and wine to Abraham and blessed him. Then Abraham gave Melchizedek a tenth of everything he had recovered from the raiding party. That's pretty much everything Genesis tells us about him. But the author of Hebrews has much more to say about Melchizedek.

To begin with, "God designated Jesus to be a High Priest in the

SOMETHING OLD,
SOMETHING NEW
Genesis 14:18-20 ... Hebrews 7

Tucked into the saga of Abraham (Genesis 12–25) is the story of how his nephew Lot went to live in Sodom and was one of several people kidnapped and carried away after a raid on the city. When Abraham heard what had happened, he assembled a private army and rescued Lot and the others. The king of Sodom wanted to give Abraham a big reward, but Abraham refused to take anything because of Sodom's widespread reputation for sin. It is at this point that Melchizedek shows up.

line of Melchizedek" (Hebrews 5:10). It is significant that Melchizedek was both king and priest—two distinct roles that are also descriptive of Jesus. "Melchizedek" translates to "King of justice," and his domain, "Salem," means *peace*. ("Salem" would later become "Jerusalem.") Jesus, as we have seen, has titles that involve both peace and justice (righteousness). Melchizedek appears to come out of nowhere in Genesis, without the normal genealogies attached, making it seem he has "no beginning or end to his life." Even more literally, Jesus "remains a priest forever" (Hebrews 7:3).

While the symbolic connections to Jesus seem quite clear, it is much more of a challenge to figure out who this Melchizedek person was to begin with. Some people have even suggested he *was* Jesus in a pre-incarnation form.

One school of thought suggests that if Jesus has always existed just as God the Father has, then perhaps He made some "guest appearances" in the Old Testament. For example, when Abraham had three angelic visitors, one of them was later identified as "the Lord" (Genesis 18). And who was the fourth person in the fiery furnace with Shadrach, Meshach, and Abednego (Daniel 3)? The case can be made that these were merely angels doing their jobs, but some scholars speculate that such appearances were actually Jesus getting personally involved with the people and events of the Old Testament. Such manifestations are known as *theophanies*. None are recorded after the incarnation of Jesus.

Some people like to suggest that Melchizedek—the "king of justice" and "king of peace"—was actually one of these previews of Jesus. Others disagree, and point out how clearly the author of Hebrews states that Mel simply *resembled* "the Son of God" (Hebrews 7:3). Either way, the connection can't be missed.

The author of Hebrews goes on to explain how Melchizedek compares to Aaron when it comes to prestige as a high priest. Abraham paid a tithe to Melchizedek. And since Aaron was from the tribe of Levi, who was a son of Jacob (Israel), who was a son of Isaac, who was a son of Abraham ... it's as if Aaron paid a tithe to Melchizedek through Abraham (Hebrews 7:9-10). There's some other technical, legal stuff in this section that we don't need to examine too closely at this point. If you want to go deeper into the intricacies of high priests, theophanies, and obscure Old Testament figures, get some good Bible commentaries and go to it!

But let's not lose focus of the topic of this book. What does all this have to do with Jesus? Simply put, Jesus is said to be "a priest forever in the line of Melchizedek" (Hebrews 7:17). This is significant because Melchizedek served God prior to the establishment of the Old Testament legal system. He was not bound by the laws and traditions that had become so entrenched in the Hebrew culture. As Jewish people heard about Jesus and were suspicious of the new Christian movement, the author of Hebrews was taking them back to a point before their laws had even been written. In Melchizedek, he was showing them an example of a godly person, highly esteemed by even Abraham, who had showed up out of nowhere and left just as quickly, yet who continued to be worthy of respect. Jesus was this kind of High Priest, only better (Hebrews 7:15-28).

A New High for a High Priest

Apparently the author of Hebrews thought he might be getting a bit too technical for his readers. So he stops in his tracks and reestablishes his theme: "Here is the main point: Our High Priest sat down in the place of highest honor in heaven, at God's right hand. There he ministers in the sacred tent, the true place of worship that was built by the Lord and not by human hands" (Hebrews 8:1-2).

Jesus isn't just a better priest; He's operating under a whole new set of rules (Hebrews 8:6). Anyone who wanted to cling to the legal system spelled out in the Old Testament was going to miss out on something groundbreaking: a new covenant. No longer would God require blood sacrifices for an annual "rolling back" of sins until the next offering. This new covenant would involve something previously unheard of—total forgiveness of sins. In addition, it completely upgraded and replaced the previous covenant (Hebrews 8:13).

SOMETHING OLD,
SOMETHING NEW
Psalm 110:4 ... Hebrews 7:17, 21

David the psalmist knew about Melchizedek and was one of the first to make clear connections between the mysterious figure from the past and the future Messiah that everyone was expecting.

SOMETHING OLD,
SOMETHING NEW
Jeremiah 31:31-34 ... Hebrews 8:8-12

Again, remembering whom he was writing to, the author of Hebrews provided a lengthy Old Testament passage to back up what he was saying. Through the prophet Jeremiah God had promised "a new covenant with the people of Israel and Judah," the end result of which would be: "I will forgive their wrongdoings, and I will never again remember their sins."

IN JESUS' NAME

"THE ONE WHO MEDIATES THE NEW COVENANT BETWEEN GOD AND PEOPLE" (Hebrews 9:15; 12:24)

As High Priest, Jesus mediates between sinful human beings and God the Father, bringing them together with no further fear of condemnation. He is the only negotiator who can achieve a win-win settlement for the long-lasting sin problem that started in the Garden of Eden. Other translations refer to Jesus as an *intercessor* or *advocate* for humanity.

W.D.J.D.?

In the Old Testament, a priest's work was never done. Dealing with the sins of the people was a full-time job as they stood "before the altar day after day, offering sacrifices that can never take away sins" (Hebrews 10:11-12). What did Jesus do that was different? After He had made His offering, *He sat down* at God's right hand. The job was finished. Over. Done. Completed. The fact that Jesus sat down is proof.

The author of Hebrews reminds everyone of the way things used to be. The tabernacle had been built to a very specific plan supplied by God. The priests could enter the Holy Place, but only the High Priest could enter the Most Holy Place . . . and then only once a year . . . and then only to make a blood offering on the Ark of the Covenant (Hebrews 9:7). The whole system, from the structure of the tabernacle, to its furniture, to the clothing of the priests, was to symbolize the holiness of God in contrast to the sinfulness of human beings. The ceremony and animal sacrifices had been essential to the spiritual health of the Israelite community. But now, says the author of Hebrews, we can see how all those things were only symbols of what God would do through Jesus. As crucial as they were, they were "only a shadow of the things to come, not the reality of the good things Christ has done for us" (Hebrews 10:1).

Consider these two statements from this section of Hebrews: (1) "Without the shedding of blood, there is no forgiveness of sins" (9:22); and, (2) "It is not possible for the blood of bulls and goats to take away sins" (10:4). At first glance they might appear to be contradictory, but they begin to make sense in the context of a third statement: "So Christ has now become the High Priest over all the good things that have come. He has entered into that great, perfect sanctuary in heaven, not made by human hands and not part of this created world. Once for all time he took blood into that Most Holy Place, but not the blood of goats and calves. He took his own blood, and with it he secured our salvation forever" (Hebrews 9:11-12).

Jesus needed no blood sacrifice to enter God's presence, because He had done nothing sinful to separate Himself from God. That's why He was such a superior High Priest. In addition, instead of using the blood of animals to offer for the sins of His people, He offered His own blood instead. So His sacrifice was "once for all time." The annual animal sacrifices, ineffective in themselves, were arrows pointing to the ultimate sacrifice yet to come. And now that Jesus has completed the onetime sacrifice that is acceptable to God, we have no further need to slaughter animals. (PETA should be glad to hear it.)

From Blood to Behavior

But enough theological discussion. At this point the writer of Hebrews takes a very practical turn for the rest of his letter. He has made his case for the importance of Jesus and God's new covenant, and he anticipates the next question: "So what?" What difference does it make in the real world?

For one thing, he says that believers should never take Jesus' original sacrifice or His position as High Priest for granted. They have no cause for a casual attitude: "Thanks for the salvation. See you in heaven!"

The whole reason Hebrews has been so comprehensive and specific is to lay the foundation for how believers ought to respond. Indeed, the author had prefaced his comments with a question: "What makes us think that we can escape if we are indifferent to this great salvation that was announced by the Lord Jesus himself?" (Hebrews 2:3)

It is no small privilege to "go right into the presence of God, with true hearts fully trusting him" (Hebrews 10:22). Indeed, this weighty truth is accompanied by a stern warning: "Dear friends, if we deliberately continue sinning after we have received a full knowledge of the truth, there is no other sacrifice that will cover these sins. There will be nothing to look forward to but the terrible expectation of God's judgment and the raging fire that will consume his enemies. . . . It is a terrible thing to fall into the hands of the living God" (Hebrews 10:26-27, 31).

Jesus, the one who made this all possible, will one day return no longer as High Priest but as King. So in the meantime, it is imperative for believers to continue meeting together and encouraging one another to "outbursts of love and good deeds" (Hebrews 10:23-25).

And now a riddle. What do the following people have in common: Abel, Enoch, Noah, Abraham, Sarah, Isaac, Jacob, Joseph, Moses, Joshua, Rahab, Gideon, Samson, David, Samuel, and a few others? You may not even know who all these people are, but they have a common bond. For one thing, they were all Old Testament characters. But more importantly, they showed a lot of faith in their

"Christ is the great central fact in the world's history. To him everything looks forward or backward. All the lines of history converge upon him."
—*C. H. Spurgeon*

IN JESUS' NAME
"THE AUTHOR AND PERFECTER OF OUR FAITH" (Hebrews12:2, NIV)

Translated another way, Jesus is the one "on whom our faith depends from start to finish." He not only originated our faith, but He also sees His followers through the whole lifelong process of spiritual maturity and growth.

lives (for the most part) and were singled out (with a few others) in a sort of "Faith Hall of Fame" in Hebrews 11. They had been promised a Messiah, a deliverer, a better way of life but had not lived to see the prophecies come to pass. Even so, they had lived with a great amount of trust in God and His timing.

The author of Hebrews points out that all the Old Testament people of faith had died (some by horrible deaths) looking forward to God's promised Savior. New Testament believers, however, can look *back* to Jesus and see the fulfillment of centuries of expectation. Therefore, it is imperative for them to act on what they have seen with their own eyes and heard with their own ears.

It's as if the Old Testament people were running the first legs of a relay, and had "passed the baton" to New Testament believers. Only by responding to Jesus would the race be completed, and then the whole "team" would be victorious (Hebrews 11:40).

And it is essential in any race to "strip off every weight that slows us down" (Hebrews 12:1). In a spiritual sense, sin is an ankle weight in any Christian's marathon. Believers will do well to remove all such weights, work on endurance in the Christian life, and keep their eyes on the finish line where Jesus awaits (Hebrews 12:1-4). The Old Testament people of faith are "a huge crowd of witnesses" cheering them on toward completion of the race and ultimate victory.

Faith is just as important as it ever was, even though it should come a bit easier now. What Jesus told Thomas still holds true: "You believe because you have seen me. Blessed are those who haven't seen me and believe anyway" (John 20:29). When times get tough, it's faith that can make a positive difference. Jesus may not be physically present, but faith is "the confident assurance that what we hope for is going to happen" and "the evidence of things we cannot yet see" (Hebrews 11:1).

As his letter winds down to the end, the author of Hebrews reminds us: "Jesus Christ is the same yesterday, today, and forever" (Hebrews 13:8). Jesus hadn't changed a bit from the time the world was created until His post-resurrection appearances, and He hasn't changed from His first-century life and death until our 21st-century musings about Him. It may be that we understand Him better and can see certain things more clearly, but that doesn't mean Jesus is changing.

Indeed, it is quite enlightening to look back into the Old Testament and see how much about Jesus is there in one way or another. Prophecy. The structure and furnishings of the tabernacle. Blood sacrifices. Faithful men and women. Priests. Atonement for sins. The author of Hebrews looks at all these "old" things and reveals their new meaning and value in the context of Jesus. And then he changes direction and looks into the future to a time when our current understanding of Jesus will be "old" and will be replaced by a much clearer understanding of who He is.

And if you want an even better look into the future, keep reading. The next chapter will look at Jesus as He is portrayed in the book of Revelation. In our ongoing examination of the biblical Jesus, there are a few more surprises in store.

Questions to Ponder and/or Discuss

1. Of all the arguments recorded in Hebrews, which seems the most convincing to prove that Jesus was someone quite special?

2. If you were nominating someone in the Old Testament for "Person with the Most Faith," whom would you choose? Why?

3. Do you know people who seem to take their Christian faith for granted? In what ways?

CHAPTER SEVENTEEN

You Say You Want a Revelation

JESUS: A LOOK INTO THE FUTURE

Have you ever been flipping through someone's photo album and seen a decline in the number of pictures as the person became older? It's a common occurrence. Proud parents always take lots of baby pictures. Schools see to it that student photos are taken each year. Special childhood events create natural photo opportunities. But along the way, the camera gets put aside and years go by between pictures.

In a sense, this book has presented a number of biblical "snapshots" of Jesus. We saw Him as He appeared in prophecy. We got some very detailed baby pictures. His teenage years and early adulthood are somewhat sketchy, but His ministry years are amply documented. And we've even seen a number of post-resurrection appearances to round out our perspective. But we still have one very important section of this album to examine before we have a total picture of the "growth" of Jesus throughout history.

In this chapter we want to peer into the future, using the book of Revelation as our guide, and see what part Jesus will play. And surprisingly, this section will contain some of the most vivid portraits

SOME THINGS YOU'LL DISCOVER IN THIS CHAPTER

1. Though many events in the book of Revelation appear frightening, they are really meant to comfort God's people and prepare them for the return of Jesus.

2. The Beast, or Antichrist, is a major spiritual adversary in the final conflict at the end of the world.

3. There are literally "pearly gates" in the New Jerusalem, along with other wonderful things to experience in heaven.

191

OPINION POLL

"Revelation has as many mysteries as it does words."—*Jerome*

IN JESUS' NAME

"THE ALPHA AND THE OMEGA"
(Revelation 1:8)
"THE FIRST AND THE LAST"
(Revelation 1:17)

When Jesus first appeared to John, He used a couple of names that suggested He will finish what He has begun. The events He described are potentially frightening, but He will be in control to the very last.

of Jesus that we've seen so far. The Bible may leave us scratching our heads in regard to certain future events, but it makes one thing clear: Jesus will continue to be the central character whenever and however those events take place.

Jesus: Live in Exile Vision!

Let's set the scene first. Jesus' disciple John is the only one of the original apostles (other than Judas) thought to avoid dying as a martyr. However, he was still unpopular with the leadership of Rome and found himself exiled to a small island called Patmos in the Aegean Sea. While there, he took a little trip into the future. Jesus appeared to him in a vision and gave him the job of recording what he saw. John's record became the final book of the Bible: Revelation. And John was an excellent witness and scribe, even though it is difficult to make sense of many of the things he describes. It will not be the goal of this chapter to examine the whole of the book of Revelation, yet the images it gives us of Jesus are not to be missed in the context of those we have already seen.

Before John saw Jesus, he heard Him. A loud voice that sounded like a trumpet blast told him to write down everything he saw and send the message to seven different churches in the area. When John turned to see who had spoken, it wasn't anyone who could be mistaken for the other convicts on the island:

> When I turned to see who was speaking to me, I saw seven gold lampstands. And standing in the middle of the lampstands was the Son of Man. He was wearing a long robe with a gold sash across his chest. His head and his hair were white like wool, as white as snow. And his eyes were bright like flames of fire. His feet were as bright as bronze refined in a furnace, and his voice thundered like mighty ocean waves. He held seven stars in his right hand, and a sharp two-edged sword came from his mouth. And his face was as bright as the sun in all its brilliance. (Revelation 1:12-16)

John had been one of Jesus' closest disciples. He had even seen Jesus several times after His resurrection—but apparently never like this! When John saw this image of Jesus, he fell down in sheer terror. But Jesus told him not to be afraid. Even though Jesus had previously died, He now made His resurrection clear by saying, "I am alive forever and ever! And I hold the keys of death and the grave" (Revelation 1:18). He also explained what John was seeing: "The seven stars are the angels of the seven churches, and the seven lampstands are the seven churches" (Revelation 1:20).

Church Chat

Then Jesus began a lengthy dictation to each of the seven churches. While these particular churches were literal locations of that day, perhaps they also represent a timeline of the church throughout history, a representation of various types of churches, or something else. In this case, as with most of the content of Revelation, you can find a number of interpretations—some of them quite bizarre. But in spite of any symbolism, Jesus made it clear that He saw what was going on and planned to reward those who remained faithful to Him in spite of false doctrines, persecution, a decline of spiritual commitment, and other problems.

If you know the history and culture of these first-century churches, many of Jesus' comments make more sense. But suffice it to say that in each case, He offered praise for the good things they were doing, correction for their shortcomings, and encouragement for them to remain victorious in their spiritual struggles. Each "letter" to the churches (Revelation 2–3) follows the same format.

One of the harshest letters is the last one, which is the one written to the church in Laodicea. Jesus condemns the "lukewarm" commitment they had toward Him, saying, "I know the things you do, that you are neither hot nor cold. I wish you were one or the other! But since you are like lukewarm water, I will spit you out of my mouth!" (Revelation 3:15-16) He has little positive affirmation for this particular church. Yet He also makes it clear He has not given up on them, and that He is still hopeful they will turn to Him with full devotion instead of offering only a halfhearted faithfulness.

W.D.J.D.?

Surely Jesus realized that many people reading the message of Revelation would become quite frightened, which wasn't His intent. So what did He do? He prefaced all the "bad stuff" with one of the most comforting promises in Scripture. Anyone uncertain about his or her salvation or status has Jesus' reassurance: "Look! Here I stand at the door and knock. If you hear me calling and open the door, I will come in, and we will share a meal as friends" (Revelation 3:20). No one who responds to this invitation (which is directed to the worst of the seven churches) need fear the coming wrath of God described later in Revelation.

IN JESUS' NAME
"THE LION OF THE TRIBE OF JUDAH" (Revelation 5:5) "A LAMB THAT HAD BEEN KILLED" (Revelation 5:6)

The basic natures of lions and lambs are about as diverse as any two animals can get. Yet both of these names are applied to Jesus with equal accuracy and insight. Jesus the servant/sacrifice is also Jesus the king.

194

The book of Revelation is not meant to be a frightfest, but rather a message of comfort for those who faithfully look forward to the return of Jesus. Jesus' prelude to the churches makes the events that follow more relevant. This apocalyptic book isn't meant to scare people into heaven. Jesus' offer of love, mercy, and forgiveness is still the "good news" of the Bible. After everything Jesus went through, He prefers that people respond to God's present love rather than His future wrath. Revelation is a scary book, but only for those who fanatically reject Jesus—and more to the point, for those who relentlessly persecute those who *do* respond to Him.

What in Heaven Are You Looking At?!

After hearing the messages to the churches, John saw a door open in heaven and heard an invitation to "come up here" (Revelation 4:1). The first thing he saw was the throne of God, surrounded by brilliance, angels, and elders offering worship. The figure on the throne was holding a scroll, sealed with seven seals. A strong angel shouted: "Who is worthy to break the seals on this scroll and unroll it?" But no one answered.

John was moved to tears, but a heavenly being told him to stop crying because, "Look, the Lion of the tribe of Judah, the heir to David's throne, has conquered. He is worthy to open the scroll and break its seven seals" (Revelation 5:5). Yet when John looked, he didn't see a lion. Instead, he saw "a Lamb that had been killed but was now standing." And this was an unusual Lamb. It had seven horns and seven eyes, explained as "the seven spirits of God that are sent into every part of the earth" (Revelation 5:6).

As the Lamb took the scroll, everyone fell down before Him and sang His praises: "The Lamb is worthy—the Lamb who was killed. He is worthy to receive power and riches and wisdom and strength and honor and glory and blessing" (Revelation 5:11-12).

Then the Lamb started popping the seals on the scroll. Each of the first four seals released a horse and rider—conquest, bloodshed, famine, and death. These figures have come to be known as "The Four Horsemen of the Apocalypse" because they rode out to destroy one-fourth of the earth "with the sword and famine and disease and wild animals" (Revelation 6:8). Yet according to Scripture, it is Jesus who is in control of these events, unleashing them in His own timing.

The fifth seal revealed a horde of martyrs eager for revenge, who were told to be patient "a little longer." The breaking of the sixth seal triggered a great earthquake, which resulted in the darkening of the sky, the moon becoming "as red as blood," and the devastation of numerous mountains and islands. The people of earth attributed these catastrophes to the wrath of God.

Meanwhile, John witnessed an enormous crowd of people shouting praises to God and to the Lamb. They were dressed in white and waving palm branches. Someone identified these people to John as "the ones coming out of the great tribulation. They washed their robes in the blood of the Lamb and made them white. That is why they are standing in front of the throne of God, serving him day and night in his Temple. . . . For the Lamb who stands in front of the throne will be their Shepherd. He will lead them to the springs of life-giving water. And God will wipe away all their tears" (Revelation 7:14-17).

Again, notice the contrasts. The "Lion" was the "Lamb," and now the "Lamb" is also the "Shepherd." We tend to have trouble juxtaposing such images, but no one seemed to have problems doing so in this heavenly context.

SOMETHING OLD, SOMETHING NEW

1 Chronicles 29:10-13 . . . Revelation 5:11-14

The praise in heaven is not unlike the praise offered by David as Solomon's temple was being dedicated. To David, *that* was a special occasion. John, however, is witnessing events that are unprecedented.

The Silence of the Lamb

If you read through this portion of Revelation, you will see how severe are the events taking place on earth during the "tribulation period"—an end-times span of unprecedented hostility and aggression toward believers in Jesus. Yet much worse things are still to come, according to John's vision. When Jesus, the Lamb, opened the seventh seal, there was dead silence throughout heaven "for about half an hour" (Revelation 8:1). Apparently the songs, prayers, and praises stopped for a somber period of time, after which followed a series of angelic trumpet blasts.

OPINION POLL

"We are heading towards catastrophe. I think the world is going to pieces. I am very pessimistic. Why? Because the world hasn't been punished yet, and the only punishment that could be adequate is the nuclear destruction of the world."
—*Elie Wiesel*

W.D.J.D.?

Even in the face of the utmost opposition, Jesus provides a source of truth—unpopular though His two witnesses were. Anyone desiring to cease loyalty to Satan and his minions will have an opportunity to do so even at this late date in the history of the earth.

The trumpets summoned greater devastation than any of the previous seals. A third of the earth was burned. A third of everything in the sea died. A third of the fresh water was contaminated. The light from the heavens diminished by a third. A special breed of locust—perhaps demonic—invaded the human race, stinging like scorpions and able to torture people. Massive armies assembled. And as a result of these plagues, a third of the people on earth were killed. But the mood of those who remained alive was a rebellious one: "They continued to worship demons and idols made of gold, silver, bronze, stone, and wood. . . . And they did not repent of their murders or their witchcraft or their immorality or their thefts" (Revelation 9:20-21).

But in the midst of all this turmoil, Jesus also had His representatives. Two men identified only as "prophets" or "witnesses" were empowered to speak on His behalf for "1,260 days" (Revelation 11:3). They had supernatural abilities to protect themselves, to prevent rainfall, to turn the waters to blood, and to originate plagues (as if things weren't already bad enough). At the end of their designated time, however, they were killed and lay dead in the streets of Jerusalem for three and a half days, seen by "all peoples, tribes, languages, and nations." But after that three and a half days, "the spirit of life from God entered them, and they stood up!" A voice from heaven told them, "Come up here!" and they did. They rose to heaven in a cloud as everyone watched.

The Beast Is Yet to Come

The turbulence on earth was only part of the picture in John's vision. The conflict extended even into heaven. First John saw a pregnant woman, who was "clothed with the sun, with the moon beneath her feet, and a crown of twelve stars on her head" (Revelation 12:1-2). She was being stalked by a large red dragon who intended to devour the baby as soon as it was born. But instead, the newborn male child was "snatched away from the dragon and was caught up to God and to his throne," and was destined to "rule all nations with an iron rod."

Following this event there was "war in heaven" with Michael (an archangel) and his angels fighting the dragon and his angels. The dragon lost and was thrown out of heaven, with his supporters, down to earth. But he wasn't through fighting. He turned his attention to the woman who had given birth to the child, hoping to drown or otherwise kill her. But God intervened and protected her. So the dragon then "declared war against the rest of her children—all who keep God's commandments and confess that they belong to Jesus" (Revelation 12:17).

Interpreters of such passages can get as political and/or theological as they wish, and many do. But regardless of specifics, it seems clear that the dragon represents Satan, the child represents Jesus, and the woman is likely an image of Israel—the Jewish people. For our purposes, let us simply note that, according to Revelation, the horrendous events taking place on earth are the by-products of an ongoing spiritual battle. Jesus isn't taking a stand against people who don't see eye to eye with Him. His battle is against the great red dragon, Satan. Of course, those who support the dragon and his efforts are going to be in the line of fire. And as we will see, the spiritual conflagration will continue throughout the book of Revelation.

It is at this point of the narrative that we meet "the beast," who is more frequently referred to as the Antichrist. He is the (apparently) human representative of the dragon on earth, leading people in worship of the dragon. The beast has tremendous miraculous power, speaks great blasphemies against God, and wages war against anyone proclaiming belief in Jesus. The beast has a partner in crime, frequently referred to as the "false prophet." It is this partner who requires all people to receive a special mark that is "either the name of the beast or the number representing his name" (Revelation 13:11-18). The number is 666, which again has been a source

SOMETHING OLD,
SOMETHING NEW
Daniel 12:1-4 ... Revelation 12

Much of the last half of the book of Daniel is helpful in understanding the events in Revelation. In this passage is found the prophecy that Michael, "the archangel who stands guard over your nation," will arise during a time of great anguish.

"JUDGE OF THE LIVING AND THE DEAD" (2 Timothy 4:1)

Paul had written that we must all appear before Jesus to be judged (2 Corinthians 5:10). Yet this image of Jesus as judge with sickle in hand is far removed from our mahogany courtrooms and jury deliberations. When the time of judgment comes, the verdict will already be determined.

OPINION POLL

"Only our concept of time makes it possible for us to speak of the Day of Judgment; in reality it is a constant court in perpetual session."—*Franz Kafka*

of great speculation among people eager to peer into the future through the descriptions provided in Revelation.

Where Is Jesus?

So where was Jesus during all this activity? It seems He was biding His time. When on earth He seemed to operate on a timeline known only to Himself as His own end approached. Now He seems to be patiently waiting until the time is right for the end of the world as we know it. For example, right after we read about the rise of the beast and all his power, we see Jesus the Lamb standing with 144,000 specially designated believers. The beast and false prophet had been requiring people to label their right hands or foreheads with a special mark, but this group of people had the names of God and Jesus on their foreheads instead. They are identified as "spiritually undefiled, pure as virgins, following the Lamb wherever he goes. They have been purchased from among the people on the earth as a special offering" (Revelation 14:4-5). So even as bad as the world situation has become, it seems that Jesus has faithful representatives who don't buckle to the pressure being applied by dragons, beasts, false prophets, and other rotten influences. In fact, it's shortly after this that John hears a voice from heaven say, "Blessed are those who die in the Lord from now on . . . for they will rest from all their toils and trials; for their good deeds follow them!" (Revelation 14:13)

It Ain't Over till the Sharp Sickle Swings

Another image of Jesus follows—this one more intense than many of the previous ones. John saw Him sitting on a white cloud with a gold crown on His head and a sharp sickle in His hand. When an angel announced that the time had come, Jesus swung the sickle over the earth, "and the whole earth was harvested" (Revelation 14:14-20). The "grapes" that were gathered from this crop were fed into "the great winepress of God's wrath" because "they are fully ripe for judgment." As a result of this judgment, a river of blood flowed in a stream about 180 miles long, and as high as a horse's bridle.

This image of Jesus "harvesting the earth" is followed by yet another series of judgments on the still-rebellious people of earth. After seven seals and seven trumpets, next came seven "bowls," each containing a plague to be "poured out" on humanity: horrible sores, the death of everything in the sea, fierce blasts of heat from the sun, darkness, hailstones the size of German shepherds, and more. In addition, armies gathered at a place called Armageddon for a large-scale battle the likes of which has never been seen.

John also devotes two chapters (Revelation 17–18) to wrapping up some old business. Starting at the Tower of Babel, and continuing throughout the Old Testament, the name "Babylon" was synonymous with sin and firm opposition to God. Numerous prophets predicted its ultimate downfall. Here, in Revelation, in the context of other judgments, two entire chapters are devoted to its demise. In John's vision, Babylon is personified as a woman dressed in purple and scarlet clothing, wearing expensive jewelry and riding a scarlet beast. Her identity is clear, however, based on the name on her forehead: "Babylon the Great, Mother of All Prostitutes and Obscenities in the World."

IN JESUS' NAME

"LORD OVER ALL LORDS AND KING OVER ALL KINGS" (Revelation 17:14) "KING OF KINGS AND LORD OF LORDS" (Revelation 19:16)

As John's account of his revelation nears an end and as the wicked systems of the earth are being uprooted and demolished for the first time in centuries, this telling name of Jesus is used. The collective sinful powers will go to war against Jesus, but will be easily defeated by the King of kings and Lord of lords.

Saddle Up!

John's narrative takes a dramatic turn at this point. He writes that shouts of praise filled the heavens, sounding "like the shout of a huge crowd, or the roar of mighty ocean waves, or the crash of loud thunder" (Revelation 19:1-6). Heavenly beings were cheering the fall of Babylon, the glory of God, and the announcement that, at last, it was time "for the wedding feast of the Lamb."

John saw the heavens open, revealing a white horse with a rider who can be none other than Jesus. This is one of the last detailed descriptions of Jesus in Scripture, and it is far different than anything so far:

> The one sitting on the horse was named Faithful and True. For he judges fairly and then goes to war. His eyes were bright like flames of fire, and on his head were many

IN JESUS' NAME
THE UNKNOWN NAME
(Revelation 19:12)

Throughout this book we have seen a lot of different names for Jesus. Several are used in this very section, including "Faithful and True," "the Word of God," and "King of kings and Lord of lords." Jesus' many names help us understand the width of His influence and the depth of His character. Yet John notes another mysterious name that was significant only to Jesus. This unknown name reminds us that there is still much about Jesus we do not fathom. No matter how many names we hear to describe Him, we can never comprehend His totality.

crowns. A name was written on him, and only he knew what it meant. He was clothed with a robe dipped in blood, and his title was the Word of God. The armies of heaven, dressed in pure white linen, followed him on white horses. From his mouth came a sharp sword, and with it he struck down the nations. He ruled them with an iron rod, and he trod the winepress of the fierce wrath of almighty God. On his robe and thigh was written this title: King of kings and Lord of lords. (Revelation 19:11-16)

Jesus and his army rode off to battle the beast and his armies, but it was no contest. The beast and false prophet were captured and immediately sentenced: "Both the beast and his false prophet were thrown alive into the lake of fire that burns with sulfur." As for their supporters, "their entire army was killed by the sharp sword that came out of the mouth of the one riding the white horse. And all the vultures of the sky gorged themselves on the dead bodies" (Revelation 19:20-21).

Satan himself was taken prisoner and "bound . . . in chains for a thousand years" (Revelation 20:1-3). During this time, righteous people who had not pledged allegiance to the beast during the time of tribulation were resurrected and "reigned with Christ for a thousand years." Afterward Satan was released and went right back to his opposition to Jesus. But apparently his time had run out. Fire fell from heaven to consume his followers. At long last, the Devil is finally cast into the lake of fire to join the beast and false prophet.

And according to Revelation, Satan is not the pompous ruler of hell that we see parodied so often. According to John's narrative, he and his supporters "will be tormented day and night forever and ever" (Revelation 20:10). John also describes a final judgment around "a great white throne." The records are all consulted—especially the Book of Life. Anyone whose name isn't found in this book is also thrown into the lake of fire.

Now for the Good "New"s

Reading through John's account of the wars, conflicts, and judgments of the last days can be a bit brutal. But the final two chapters of Revelation contain enough good news to counterbalance all the horror up to this point. Just as John was shown the gory specifics of what would happen to those who oppose Jesus, he was also shown what happens to the ones who remain faithful.

Everything old had disappeared—heaven, earth, and the sea. In its place John saw a new heaven and new earth. The city of Jerusalem was new as well, and descended out of heaven "like a beautiful bride prepared for her husband." The significance of this event was announced from heaven: "Look, the home of God is now among his people! He will live with them, and they will be his people. God himself will be with them. He will remove all of their sorrows, and there will be no more death or sorrow or crying or pain. For the old world and its evils are gone forever" (Revelation 21:3-4).

New heaven. New earth. New Jerusalem. All this will take some getting used to. From this point on, God will be the light. There will be no sun, moon, or stars. Instead of dirt, the streets are made of "pure gold, as clear as glass," as is the city itself. The "pearly gates" literally exist. The city walls are inlaid with all sorts of precious stones (Revelation 22:18-27). A crystal river flows from the throne of God and Jesus right down Main Street. The tree of life, last seen in the Garden of Eden, flourishes in this new city. There is no more night, no more tears, and no more pain.

The book of Revelation (and the Bible) concludes with an invitation: "Let the thirsty ones come—anyone who wants to. Let them come and drink the water of life without charge. . . . He who is the faithful witness to all these things says, "Yes, I am coming soon!" (Revelation 22:17, 20)

Of course, it has been almost 2,000 years since John recorded this promise of Jesus to come "soon." Some people are convinced that the whole Revelation mystique is a myth, a hoax, or worse. Others point to the insight provided by Peter: "You must not forget, dear

SOMETHING OLD,
SOMETHING NEW

Genesis 1–2 . . . Revelation 21–22

The first two chapters of the Bible, as well as the last two chapters, describe a fresh new creation of God. But when we get to Revelation, the physical Garden of Eden has been replaced by a spiritual and eternal home with God. And this time the tempter who showed up in the Garden is no longer free to impose himself on those who believe in Jesus.

IN JESUS' NAME

"THE BRIGHT MORNING STAR" (Revelation 22:16)

As Jesus gives one more reminder that the message of Revelation is "for the churches," He refers to Himself by this name. While it isn't always easy to detect His brightness now, believers are promised that someday everything will reflect His brilliance.

W.D.J.D.?

Jesus has just delivered a weighty message to the churches. The prophecy contained in Revelation has been plenty grim, so Jesus doesn't attempt to add guilt or threats to attract people. Instead, He sends out an open invitation and welcomes anyone willing to respond. And to sweeten the deal, three times He reminds His listeners that He is returning soon (Revelation 22:7, 12, 20). In fact, these are the last quoted words of Jesus in Scripture.

OPINION POLL

"I've read the last page of the Bible. It's all going to turn out all right."
—*Billy Graham*

friends, that a day is like a thousand years to the Lord, and a thousand years is like a day. The Lord isn't really being slow about his promise to return, as some people think. No, he is being patient for your sake. He does not want anyone to perish, so he is giving more time for everyone to repent" (2 Peter 3:8-9).

So, on God's timetable, suggests Peter, only a couple of days have passed since Jesus' promise to return "soon." But Peter also reminds us that Jesus will return "as unexpectedly as a thief" (2 Peter 3:10). The Bible writers all agree that if we want to respond to the invitation of Jesus, sooner is definitely better than later. One day it will be *too* late.

(We should reemphasize at this point that there are numerous ways to interpret the events described in Revelation. Many good people consider them to be literal, for the most part. Other good people feel they are primarily symbolic. Again, we haven't tried to take a position, but have instead tried to keep the focus on the descriptions of Jesus. If you wish further explanation, other books are available that will take you deeper into this mysterious and wonderful book of the Bible.)

The good news of the gospel of Jesus is that the Good News holds up—no matter what. According to Revelation, it's not correct to say it holds up to the end, because there *isn't* an end. The Good News just keeps going and going and going.

No matter how bad the situation might get, believers have God's Word—the bad stuff isn't going to last forever. And no matter how good things are now, they're only going to get better. That's a revelation worth thinking about!

Questions to Ponder and/or Discuss

1. When you think about the last days, the tribulation period, the return of Jesus, and other events described in Revelation, what is your overriding reaction?

- Skepticism
- Confusion
- Wonder
- Confidence
- Desire to know more
- Fear
- Anticipation
- Anxiety/Stress

2. What questions about the end times do you have? How do such questions affect your here-and-now relationship with Jesus?

3. Why do you think Jesus would prefer for someone to be spiritually "cold" rather than merely lukewarm?

CHAPTER EIGHTEEN

Jesus: Here and Now?

JESUS IN THE 21ST CENTURY

"What should I do with Jesus who is called the Messiah?"

Good question. Pontius Pilate asked it first (Matthew 27:22), but a lot of people are still wondering.

We've come a long way since we started this book. Our search for the biblical Jesus has taken us from creation, to the Garden of Eden (where we saw the first promise that He would come), through the prophecies of the Old Testament, to the flurry of activity that took place during the first century. But now that we're almost 2,000 years beyond those events, what's the buzz about Jesus?

In one sense, Jesus is bigger than ever. A lot of people are speaking on His behalf, and His name is well-known around the world. Yet in another sense, His significance has become quite diluted in our culture. With so many people speaking up for Him, it stands to reason that not everyone is equally well informed.

Even the most inexperienced Internet user quickly realizes the great wealth of information at his or her fingertips, yet just as quickly discovers what a cornucopia of *mis*-information the Internet can be. Intelligent people don't dare believe everything

SOME THINGS YOU'LL DISCOVER IN THIS CHAPTER

1. Many people today feel a great spiritual hunger to know more about Jesus.

2. According to certain data, religious attitudes haven't changed much over the last century.

3. The Bible contains many comforting promises for those who commit themselves to Jesus.

they find online. The Internet allows everyone to be an "expert," which can be a frightening thought. If you post a question, you are likely to get a lot of answers—but that doesn't mean the respondents have any clue what they're talking about.

The Messiah: Complex

This same "everyone's-an-expert" mentality has spread to religious topics. People who haven't cracked a Bible in decades speak with great authority about Jesus. Some who are quite emphatic have no spiritual foundation other than a strong opinion. Others have theological opinions that were established during late night high school "rap sessions" and haven't been updated since. And while such individuals may not be completely wrong about what they profess, they aren't likely to be entirely correct, either.

Adding to this mentality is our cultural tendency to prefer films to books. A few people are still big readers, but most would usually rather "wait for the movie." So while the biblical account of Jesus remains unread, we see regular updates of what Hollywood has to say about Him. At one time Jesus' life was *The Greatest Story Ever Told*. More recently, however, we've seen Him in less flattering portrayals. We've seen Him wearing a clown nose and Superman T-shirt as one of many participants on a schoolyard playground (*Godspell*), as a celebrity (*Jesus Christ Superstar*), as a good ol' Southern boy (*Cotton Patch Gospel*), as someone who fantasized about love, sex, marriage, and fatherhood from the cross (*The Last Temptation of Christ*), and more. We've seen accounts of His life in animation, live action, and even Claymation.

And yet our fascination with Jesus doesn't seem to be waning. As this is being written, the ABC game show *Who Wants to Be a Millionaire?* is less than a year old and finding tremendous popularity among viewers. The other networks are currently scrambling (and failing) to find something—including dramas, comedies, and rival game shows —to successfully compete with it. One of the first shows to succeed in attracting more viewers was the initial installment of a four-hour miniseries that highlighted the human aspects of Jesus. So in spite of all that has been written and said to date, our society still seems to have a lot of interest in better understanding who Jesus was.

We've seen hundreds of different faces for Jesus as conceived by the greatest artists of the past two millennia—from His birth to death to resurrection. We've seen thousands of "Christ figures" in literature. Who knows how many songs have been written about Jesus—both pro and con? People have attempted to describe Him with almost every label possible. Sage. Cynic. Mystic. Rebel. Seeker. And yet, in spite of all the things we know (or think we know) about Jesus, there is always much more that we *don't* know.

And that's okay. Jesus repeatedly hinted that the kingdom of God was something of a *mystery*. If we could fully understand it all, there would be no need for faith. And faith is something He always encouraged among His followers.

OPINION POLL

"He who has the judge for his father, goes into court with an easy mind."
—*Miguel Cervantes*

The Mystery Continues

As we have seen, even limiting ourselves to the biblical description of Jesus has been eye-opening and mentally challenging. We've seen Jesus described as a man of sorrows, a suffering servant, a shepherd, a counselor, a lord and king, a judge, the Son of Man, the Son of God, a Prince of Peace, an advocate for His people, and more. The biblical Jesus is *all* of these things—most of them simultaneously. Is it strange, therefore, that even our best-produced portrayals of Jesus are somewhat shallow in comparison? If you want to produce a four-hour (or even much longer) program on the life of Jesus, you have to choose one or two aspects to focus on. Otherwise, Jesus will come across as little more than a schizophrenic personality, and that isn't an accurate biblical portrayal.

We can hardly mentally conceive of—much less reenact the life of—a single figure who is both sacrifice and Savior, Intercessor and Judge, sheep and Shepherd, present and eternal, God and human. The real Jesus remains outside our boundaries of reason, logic, and understanding. According to the Bible, He's as close as a best friend

but Lord of the Universe. He was willing to submit to the ultimate act of humility yet was rewarded with more glory than any other being. He urges everyone to follow Him, and still allows anyone to casually reject Him and walk away if he or she so wills.

If we really believe Jesus is all of the things He said He was, we can't help but contend with an element of mystery. Most people struggle to make sense of these things. Some eventually lose faith. For others, the struggle results in a greater degree of strength. Either way, as we continually try to strip away the layers of myth-information to get to the truth, we begin to confront Jesus, the real person.

Seekers, Skeptics, and Scientists

As we have previously suggested, one way to sidestep the biblical Jesus is to question the authority of the Bible. Throughout history, individuals and groups have certainly challenged various aspects of inspiration, translation, canonization, and more. Others have just as zealously and intelligently defended such things. Where there are believers, there will almost certainly continue to be skeptics.

The Jesus Seminar, sponsored by the Westar Institute, is one current large-scale discussion. More than a hundred Bible scholars have been meeting twice a year since 1985 to challenge the quotations and actions attributed to Jesus and then vote on whether or not they believe Jesus actually said and did those things. They vote using colored beads: red to indicate He definitely said it, black for definitely not, pink for probably, and gray for possibly, but not likely.

Though sincere and scholarly in their approach, the Jesus Seminar has received a lot of criticism—much of it for being quite subjective in their determinations. In an interview, the founder, Robert W. Funk, discounted the likelihood of Jesus being able to, for instance, walk on water. He said, "I want a teacher who experiences and understands the world and its problems the same way that I do and with the same set of limitations that I have." Critics of the Jesus

Seminar might argue that such a mindset tends to skew objectivity—that if God is bound by the same limitations we have, it will never allow for much of a God. (Consequently, the Jesus Seminar has so far estimated that less than twenty percent of the quotations and actions attributed to Jesus in the Bible are historically accurate.)

The debate will certainly continue. Let it. But as it does, we might do well to remember that one of Jesus' names for Himself was "The Truth" (John 14:6). Anything that can be proven true is of God. The rest is subject to skepticism . . . or faith. And each person has the choice of whether to place his or her faith in what the Bible says or in what other people say.

OPINION POLL

"The truth is rarely pure, and never simple."—*Oscar Wilde*

Mystery, speculation, and faith are necessary whether we want to discuss religion, politics, science, or essentially any topic. We accumulate a few irrefutable facts, and it is our natural desire to want to fill in the gaps and make sense of those pieces of factual information. This is true of scientists as well as theologians.

In 1916, a survey was conducted by a devout atheist named James Leuba, who selected 1,000 scientists at random and asked if they believed in God. For the purposes of his survey, "God" was defined as a being who actively communicates with people and to whom one can pray and expect to receive an answer. About 40 percent of the biologists, physicists, and mathematicians who responded affirmed a belief in God. Fifteen percent claimed to be agnostic, with "no definite belief." And about 42 percent said they did not believe in God as He was defined in the questionnaire. (Curiously, while only 40 percent expressed belief in God, 50 percent of the respondents indicated they believed in personal immortality.) James Leuba predicted that as knowledge and education spread, disbelief in God would also grow.

A few years ago a man at the University of Georgia named Edward Larson repeated Leuba's survey—verbatim. He didn't know whether his randomly selected respondents were Christians, Jews, Muslims, or of any other faith, or if they ever participated in any sort of religious traditions. He announced the results of his survey

"Men occasionally stumble over the truth, but most of them pick themselves up and hurry off, as if nothing had happened."—*Winston Churchill*

"To present Christ's lordship as an option leaves it squarely in the category of stereo equipment for a new car." —*Dallas Willard*

in 1997: 40 percent expressed a belief in God, 15 percent were self-defined agnostics, and about 45 percent said they didn't believe in God. Based on this research, changes in religious attitudes within the scientific community had been inconsequential over the previous 80 years. In his summary, Larson wrote, "Leuba misjudged either the human mind or the ability of science to satisfy all human needs."

So while a higher percentage of scientists reject a belief in God than express faith in Him, it's still not too difficult to find an enlightened mind open to spiritual seeking. And the search for truth can take place in hearts as well as in minds. If you want to consider that the biblical Jesus may have been someone more significant than you've been giving Him credit for, you're in good company. Like anything else, you start with what you are convinced to be true and build your faith from there.

For those who *do* believe the Bible, Jesus Christ is the same yesterday, today, and forever (Hebrews 13:8). The God of creation is the same as the first-century Jesus, who is the same as the 21st-century Jesus. Therefore, people today have the same decision to make as people throughout history: "What should I do with Jesus who is called the Messiah?"

Jesus Knows Me, This I Love

As long as there is more than one person on earth, we're probably never going to reach complete unity in regard to our feelings about Jesus. Even within the Christian church are dozens of various denominations who differ on one or another aspect of faith.

But again, that's okay. As we saw in the Christmas story, some people find their way to Jesus through intellect, others run primarily on emotion, and some display simple, persistent, ongoing faithfulness. The Jesus we have seen is plenty big enough to accommodate all sincere efforts of people to relate to Him.

Perhaps in the past, your image of Jesus has been incomplete due to imperfect people or churches who presented Him to you. Maybe you've been barraged by one too many pushy Christians thrusting pamphlets in your face, or by those whose humor and compassion were undetectable, if present at all.

While churches sometimes tend to focus on quantity—the number of people in the pews—Jesus keeps the focus on the quality of a one-to-one relationship. He came to save the world, to be sure, but He does it one soul at a time. If the 99 sheep in the fold are already safe, it's the one straying out in the dangerous world that He will continue to pursue. It's the Pharisee who seeks Him out late in the night. It's the outcast woman at the well, or the one standing in shame before Him. It's the self-critical little man up a tree, desperate for a bit of recognition. It's the prodigal child who has grown weary of "wild living" and is ready to come home. And perhaps it's the 21st-century man or woman who just hasn't been able to make sense out of life—at least, not yet.

We might never know Jesus to the extent we would like to, yet we can be sure that He knows us completely. Jesus assures us that "the very hairs on your head are all numbered" (Matthew 10:30). Once we get past the spooky realization that Jesus knows all the bad stuff about us and loves us anyway, we can experience His fascinating forgiveness and absolute acceptance. If we don't get bogged down in Bible trivia and dry theology, we can move on to a personal relationship with the Jesus of the Scriptures that can be as intense and intimate as any relationship with a best friend or spouse.

If you desire a better understanding of Scripture or help with how to go about bringing the reality of Jesus into your 21st-century life, other books in this series cover those very topics in more detail. But as far as the authors are concerned, the one book you need to begin with is the Bible. If it's been a while since you checked it out to see what it has to say about Jesus (or about you), we urge you to get back in the habit. (Small doses of reading on a regular basis will be far more effective than "cramming" to make up for lost time.)

The Bible is God's Word and has great power, but only as it successfully connects you with God Himself. A lot of people can quote

OPINION POLL

"From somber, serious, sullen saints, deliver us, O Lord, hear our prayer." —*Teresa of Avila*

Scripture—but often do so thoughtlessly, maliciously, or in an otherwise inappropriate manner. Yet for those willing to read the Bible sincerely and take it to heart, Jesus offers numerous promises.

Promises, Promises

As we bring this book to a close, we want to review a number of promises Jesus made to His followers. There are more, and we encourage you to seek out others on your own. But below are a few to get you started.

"Keep on asking, and you will be given what you ask for. Keep on looking, and you will find. Keep on knocking, and the door will be opened. For everyone who asks, receives. Everyone who seeks, finds. And the door is opened to everyone who knocks" (Matthew 7:7-8).

"If you welcome a prophet as one who speaks for God, you will receive the same reward a prophet gets. And if you welcome good and godly people because of their godliness, you will be given a reward like theirs. And if you give even a cup of cold water to one of the least of my followers, you will surely be rewarded" (Matthew 10:41-42).

"If two of you agree down here on earth concerning anything you ask, my Father in heaven will do it for you. For where two or three gather together because they are mine, I am there among them" (Matthew 18:19-20).

"Be sure of this: I am with you always, even to the end of the age" (Matthew 28:20).

"If you try to keep your life for yourself, you will lose it. But if you give up your life for my sake and for the sake of the Good News, you will find true life" (Mark 8:35).

"Everything is possible with God" (Mark 10:27).

"If you give, you will receive. Your gift will return to you in full measure, pressed down, shaken together to make room for more, and running over. Whatever measure you use in giving—large or small—it will be used to measure what is given back to you" (Luke 6:38).

"Be sure to pay attention to what you hear. To those who are open to my teaching, more understanding will be given. But to those who are not listening, even what they think they have will be taken away from them" (Luke 8:18).

"You are truly my disciples if you keep obeying my teachings. And you will know the truth, and the truth will set you free" (John 8:31-32).

"My purpose is to give life in all its fullness" (John 10:10).

"I am the resurrection and the life. Those who believe in me, even though they die like everyone else, will live again. They are given eternal life for believing in me and will never perish" (John 11:25-26).

"When everything is ready, I will come and get you, so that you will always be with me where I am" (John 14:3).

"I am leaving you with a gift—peace of mind and heart. And the peace I give isn't like the peace the world gives. So don't be troubled or afraid" (John 14:27).

When it comes to building relationships, Jesus never holds back. He has literally done all He can do on our behalf. Since He never changes, the promises He made in the first century are just as true today. He's still at the door, knocking. What are *you* going to do with Jesus who is called the Messiah? And just as important: What would you like Him to do with you?

OPINION POLL

"We only tarnish the shining promises of God if we persist in dwelling on our own sinfulness."—*J. B. Phillips*

Questions to Ponder and/or Discuss

1. Has your understanding of Jesus changed at all during the course of reading this book? If so, in what ways?

2. If you wish to continue your pursuit of knowledge concerning Jesus and the kingdom of God, what are some steps you can take? (Consider available resources, church attendance, Bible study groups, pastoral counseling, etc.)

3. If you had a stronger personal relationship with the biblical Jesus, what long-range changes do you think you could expect for your life?

A Concise Timeline of the Life of Jesus Christ

JESUS' BIRTH AND EARLY YEARS

Jesus' birth is foretold to His mother Mary (Luke 1:26-38).

Jesus' birth is foretold to Mary's fiancé, Joseph (Matthew 1:18-25).

(about 5 B.C.)* Jesus is born (Luke 2:1-20).

Jesus is presented at the temple (Luke 2:22-38).

(about 3 B.C.) The Magi visit young Jesus (Matthew 2:1-12).

Jesus is taken to Egypt to escape King Herod (Matthew 2:13-18).

Jesus and His family return to Nazareth (Matthew 2:19-23).

Jesus attends Passover in Jerusalem and amazes the teachers of religious law with His understanding (Luke 2:41-50).

* Strange as it sounds, Jesus was probably born "B.C." (Before Christ). This is because our modern method of marking time (A.D./B.C.) was not developed until several hundred years *after* Jesus lived on earth, and the guy who invented this new system was probably off by about five years.

JESUS' MINISTRY

Jesus is baptized by John, and the Holy Spirit descends on Him (Matthew 3:13-17; Mark 1:9-11; Luke 3:21-22).

Jesus is tempted in the desert by Satan (Matthew 4:1-11; Mark 1:12-13; Luke 4:1-13).

Jesus performs His first miracle: turning water in wine at a wedding feast (John 2:1-11).

Jesus cleanses the temple (John 2:13-22).

Jesus speaks with Nicodemus (John 3:1-21).

Jesus speaks with a Samaritan woman (John 4:5-26).

Jesus is rejected at Nazareth, His hometown (Luke 4:16-30).

Jesus heals a man with leprosy (Matthew 8:2-4; Mark 1:40-45; Luke 5:12-16).

Jesus forgives and heals a paralytic (Matthew 9:1-8; Mark 2:1-12; Luke 5:17-26).

Jesus heals a man's shriveled hand on the Sabbath (Matthew 12:9-14; Mark 3:1-6; Luke 6:6-11).

Jesus chooses the 12 disciples (Mark 3:13-19; Luke 6:12-16).

Jesus delivers the Sermon on the Mount (Matthew 5:1–7:29; Luke 6:12-49).

Jesus heals a centurion's servant (Matthew 8:5-13; Luke 7:1-10).

Jesus raises a widow's dead son at Nain (Luke 7:11-17).

Jesus is anointed by a sinful woman (Luke 7:36-50).

Jesus tells several parables about the kingdom of God (Matthew 13:1-52; Mark 4:1-34; Luke 8:4-18).

Jesus calms a storm (Matthew 8:18, 23-27; Mark 4:35-41; Luke 8:22-25).

Jesus casts out demons (Matthew 8:28-34; Mark 5:1-20; Luke 8:26-39).

Jesus heals a woman who touches his garment and raises Jairus's dead daughter (Matthew 9:18-26; Mark 5:21-43; Luke 8:40-56).

Jesus sends out the 12 disciples to preach about the kingdom of God and minister to others (Matthew 10:1-42; Mark 6:7-11; Luke 9:1-5).

Jesus walks on water (Matthew 14:24-33; Mark 6:47-52; John 6:16-21).

Jesus ministers to a Gentile woman in Tyre and Sidon (Matthew 15:21-28; Mark 7:24-30).

Jesus heals a blind man at Bethsaida (Mark 8:22-26).

Peter correctly identifies Jesus as the Messiah (Matthew 16:13-20; Mark 8:27-30; Luke 9:18-21).

Jesus is transfigured on a high mountain (Matthew 17:1-8; Mark 9:2-8; Luke 9:28-36).

Jesus heals a man born blind (John 9:1-7).

Jesus sends out the 72 followers to preach about the kingdom of God and minister to others (Luke 10:1-16).

Jesus tells the story of the Good Samaritan (Luke 10:25-37).

Jesus visits with Mary and Martha (Luke 10:38-42).

Jesus raises Lazarus from the dead (John 11:17-44).

The Jewish High Council makes plans to put Jesus to death (John 11:45-54).

Jesus heals 10 lepers while passing through Samaria and Galilee (Luke 17:11-19).

Jesus heals blind Bartimaeus and his friend (Matthew 20:29-34; Mark 10:46-52; Luke 18:35-43).

Jesus talks with Zacchaeus (Luke 19:1-10).

Jesus triumphantly enters Jerusalem (Matthew 21:1-17; Mark 11:1-11; Luke 19:28-44; John 12:12-19).

Jesus curses a fig tree (Matthew 21:18-19; Mark 11:12-14).

Jesus cleanses the temple [again?] (Matthew 21:12-13; Mark 11:15-18; Luke 19:45-48).

Jesus is questioned by the Pharisees and Herodians about paying taxes (Matthew 22:15-22; Mark 12:13-17; Luke 20:20-26).

Jesus weeps over Jerusalem (Matthew 23:37-39).

Jesus commends the offering of a poor widow (Mark 12:41-44; Luke 21:1-4).

Jesus delivers the Olivet Discourse about His eventual return (Matthew 24:1–25:46; Mark 13:1-37; Luke 21:5-36).

JESUS' FINAL DAYS IN JERUSALEM

(about A.D. 30) The Jewish High Council makes plans to have Jesus arrested and killed (Matthew 26:1-5; Mark 14:1-2; Luke 22:1-2).

Another woman anoints Jesus (Matthew 26:6-13; Mark 14:3-9; John 12:2-8).

Judas agrees to betray Jesus (Matthew 26:14-16; Mark 14:10-11; Luke 22:3-6).

Jesus and His disciples share the Last Supper together, and the Lord's Supper is instituted (Matthew 26:20-35 ; Mark 14:17-31; Luke 22:7-38; John 13:1-38).

Jesus prays in the Garden of Gethsemane (Matthew 26:36-46; Mark 14:32-42; Luke 22:39-46).

JESUS' ARREST, TRIAL, AND CRUCIFIXION

Jesus is arrested at Gethsemane (Matthew 26:47-56; Mark 14:43-52; Luke 22:47-53; John 18:2-12).

Jesus is taken before Annas (John 18:13-14, 19-23).

Jesus is taken before Caiaphas and the Jewish High Council (Matthew 26:57-68; Mark 14:53-65; Luke 22:63-65; John 18:24).

Jesus is taken before the Jewish High Council again (Matthew 27:1; Mark 15:1; Luke 22:66-71).

Jesus is taken before Pilate (Matthew 27:11-14; Mark 15:1-5; Luke 23:1-5; John 18:28-38).

Jesus is taken before Herod Antipas (Luke 23:6-12).

Jesus is taken before Pilate again (Matthew 27:15-26; Mark 15:6-15; Luke 23:13-25; John 18:28–19:16).

Jesus is handed over to be crucified (Matthew 27:27-44; Mark 15:16-32; Luke 23:26-43; John 19:16-27).

Jesus dies on the cross (Matthew 27:45-50; Mark 15:33-37; Luke 23:44-46; John 19:28-30).

Jesus' body is placed in a tomb (Matthew 27:59-60; Mark 15:46; Luke 23:53-54; John 19:39-42).

JESUS' RESURRECTION AND ASCENSION

Jesus is raised from the dead and appears to several women at the tomb (Matthew 28:1-10; Mark 16:1-8; Luke 24:1-8; John 20:1-18).

Jesus appears to two followers traveling to Emmaus (Luke 24:13-32).

Jesus appears to several of the disciples (Matthew 28:16-20; Luke 24:36-49; John 20:19–21:25; Acts 1:3-8).

Jesus ascends to heaven (Acts 1:9-12).

What Jesus Says About...

Asking for Miraculous Signs

As the crowd pressed in on Jesus, he said, "These are evil times, and this evil generation keeps asking me to show them a miraculous sign. But the only sign I will give them is the sign of the prophet Jonah. What happened to him was a sign to the people of Nineveh that God had sent him. What happens to me will be a sign that God has sent me, the Son of Man, to these people. The queen of Sheba will rise up against this generation on judgment day and condemn it, because she came from a distant land to hear the wisdom of Solomon. And now someone greater than Solomon is here—and you refuse to listen to him." (Luke 11:29-31)

Being Born Again

Jesus replied, "I assure you, unless you are born again, you can never see the Kingdom of God." (John 3:3)

Bread of Life

Jesus replied, "I am the bread of life. No one who comes to me will ever be hungry again. Those who believe in me will never thirst." (John 6:35)

221

Children

Then Jesus called for the children and said to the disciples, "Let the children come to me. Don't stop them! For the Kingdom of God belongs to such as these. I assure you, anyone who doesn't have their kind of faith will never get into the Kingdom of God." (Luke 18:16-17)

Church and State

"Well then," he said, "give to Caesar what belongs to him. But everything that belongs to God must be given to God." (Luke 20:25)

Debt of Love

Then Jesus told him this story: "A man loaned money to two people—five hundred pieces of silver to one and fifty pieces to the other. But neither of them could repay him, so he kindly forgave them both, canceling their debts. Who do you suppose loved him more after that?" Simon answered, "I suppose the one for whom he canceled the larger debt." "That's right," Jesus said. (Luke 7:41-43)

Discipleship

"If you want to be my follower you must love me more than your own father and mother, wife and children, brothers and sisters—yes, more than your own life. Otherwise, you cannot be my disciple. And you cannot be my disciple if you do not carry your own cross and follow me." (Luke 14:26-27)

Divorce

"You have heard that the law of Moses says, 'A man can divorce his wife by merely giving her a letter of divorce.' But I say that a man who divorces his wife, unless she has been unfaithful, causes her to commit adultery. And anyone who marries a divorced woman commits adultery." (Matthew 5:31-32)

Enemies

"But if you are willing to listen, I say, love your enemies. Do good to those who hate you. Pray for the happiness of those who curse you. Pray for those who hurt you. If someone slaps you on one cheek, turn the other cheek. If someone demands your coat, offer your shirt also. Give what you have to anyone who asks you for it; and when things are taken away from you, don't try to get them back. Do for others as you would like them to do for you." (Luke 6:27-31)

Faith

"Even if you had faith as small as a mustard seed," the Lord answered, "you could say to this mulberry tree, 'May God uproot you and throw you into the sea,' and it would obey you!" (Luke 17:6)

Faithfulness

"Be dressed for service and well prepared, as though you were waiting for your master to return from the wedding feast. Then you will be ready to open the door and let him in the moment he arrives and knocks. There will be special favor for those who are ready and waiting for his return. I tell you, he himself will seat them, put on an apron, and serve them as they sit and eat! He may come in the middle of the night or just before dawn. But whenever he comes, there will be special favor for his servants who are ready!" (Luke 12:35-38)

Fasting

"And when you fast, don't make it obvious, as the hypocrites do, who try to look pale and disheveled so people will admire them for their fasting. I assure you, that is the only reward they will ever get. But when you fast, comb your hair and wash your face. Then no one will suspect you are fasting, except your Father, who knows what you do in secret. And your Father, who knows all secrets, will reward you." (Matthew 6:16-18)

Fear of God

"Dear friends, don't be afraid of those who want to kill you. They can only kill the body; they cannot do any more to you. But I'll tell you whom to fear. Fear God, who has the power to kill people and then throw them into hell." (Luke 12:4-5)

Forgiveness

"I am warning you! If another believer sins, rebuke him; then if he repents, forgive him. Even if he wrongs you seven times a day and each time turns again and asks forgiveness, forgive him." (Luke 17:3-4)

Forgiving Sins

Jesus knew what they were thinking, so he asked them, "Why do you think this is blasphemy? Is it easier to say, 'Your sins are forgiven' or 'Get up and walk'? I will prove that I, the Son of Man, have the authority on earth to forgive sins." Then Jesus turned to the paralyzed man and said, "Stand up, take your mat, and go on home, because you are healed!" (Luke 5:22-24)

Generosity

"I assure you," he said, "this poor widow has given more than all the rest of them. For they have given a tiny part of their surplus, but she, poor as she is, has given everything she has." (Luke 21:3-4)

Giving

"If you give, you will receive. Your gift will return to you in full measure, pressed down, shaken together to make room for more, and running over. Whatever measure you use in giving—large or small—it will be used to measure what is given back to you." (Luke 6:38)

God's Concern for Children

One day Jesus said to his disciples, "There will always be temptations to sin, but how terrible it will be for the person who does the tempting. It would be better to be thrown into the sea with a large millstone tied around the neck than to

face the punishment in store for harming one of these little ones." (Luke 17:1-2)

God's Love for Sinners
"In the same way, heaven will be happier over one lost sinner who returns to God than over ninety-nine others who are righteous and haven't strayed away!" (Luke 15:7)

God's Love for the World
"For God so loved the world that he gave his only Son, so that everyone who believes in him will not perish but have eternal life. God did not send his Son into the world to condemn it, but to save it. There is no judgment awaiting those who trust him. But those who do not trust him have already been judged for not believing in the only Son of God." (John 3:16-18)

God's Open Door
"And so I tell you, keep on asking, and you will be given what you ask for. Keep on looking, and you will find. Keep on knocking, and the door will be opened. For everyone who asks, receives. Everyone who seeks, finds. And the door is opened to everyone who knocks." (Luke 11:9-10)

Golden Rule
"Do for others what you would like them to do for you. This is a summary of all that is taught in the law and the prophets." (Matthew 7:12)

Good Gifts of God
"If you sinful people know how to give good gifts to your children, how much more will your heavenly Father give good gifts to those who ask him." (Matthew 7:11)

Good Shepherd
"I am the good shepherd. The good shepherd lays down his life for the sheep. A hired hand will run when he sees a wolf coming. He will leave the sheep because they aren't his and

225

he isn't their shepherd. And so the wolf attacks them and scatters the flock. The hired hand runs away because he is merely hired and has no real concern for the sheep." (John 10:11-13)

Greed

Then he said, "Beware! Don't be greedy for what you don't have. Real life is not measured by how much we own." (Luke 12:15)

Heart

"A good person produces good deeds from a good heart, and an evil person produces evil deeds from an evil heart. Whatever is in your heart determines what you say." (Luke 6:45)

His Commands

"When you obey me, you remain in my love, just as I obey my Father and remain in his love. I have told you this so that you will be filled with my joy. Yes, your joy will overflow!" (John 15:10-11)

His Kingdom

Pilate replied, "You are a king then?" "You say that I am a king, and you are right," Jesus said. "I was born for that purpose. And I came to bring truth to the world. All who love the truth recognize that what I say is true." (John 18:37)

His Own Death

"For I, the Son of Man, must suffer many terrible things," he said. "I will be rejected by the leaders, the leading priests, and the teachers of religious law. I will be killed, but three days later I will be raised from the dead." (Luke 9:22)

His Relationship to the Father

Jesus replied, "I assure you, the Son can do nothing by himself. He does only what he sees the Father doing. Whatever

the Father does, the Son also does. For the Father loves the Son and tells him everything he is doing, and the Son will do far greater things than healing this man. You will be astonished at what he does." (John 5:19-20)

His Return
"So when all these things begin to happen, stand straight and look up, for your salvation is near!" (Luke 21:28)

His Role
"The Spirit of the Lord is upon me, for he has appointed me to preach Good News to the poor. He has sent me to proclaim that captives will be released, that the blind will see, that the downtrodden will be freed from their oppressors, and that the time of the Lord's favor has come." (Luke 4:18-19)

His Teaching
So Jesus told them, "I'm not teaching my own ideas, but those of God who sent me. Anyone who wants to do the will of God will know whether my teaching is from God or is merely my own." (John 7:16-17)

Holy Spirit
"But it is actually best for you that I go away, because if I don't, the Counselor won't come. If I do go away, he will come because I will send him to you." (John 16:7)

Humility
"Do this instead—sit at the foot of the table. Then when your host sees you, he will come and say, 'Friend, we have a better place than this for you!' Then you will be honored in front of all the other guests. For the proud will be humbled, but the humble will be honored." (Luke 14:10-11)

Hypocrites
Meanwhile, the crowds grew until thousands were milling about and crushing each other. Jesus turned first to his disciples and warned them, "Beware of the yeast of the

Pharisees—beware of their hypocrisy. The time is coming when everything will be revealed; all that is secret will be made public. Whatever you have said in the dark will be heard in the light, and what you have whispered behind closed doors will be shouted from the housetops for all to hear!" (Luke 12:1-3)

John the Baptist

"Were you looking for a prophet? Yes, and he is more than a prophet. John is the man to whom the Scriptures refer when they say, 'Look, I am sending my messenger before you, and he will prepare your way before you.' I tell you, of all who have ever lived, none is greater than John. Yet even the most insignificant person in the Kingdom of God is greater than he is!" (Luke 7:26-28)

Judging Others

"Stop judging others, and you will not be judged. Stop criticizing others, or it will all come back on you. If you forgive others, you will be forgiven." (Luke 6:37)

Kingdom of God

One day the Pharisees asked Jesus, "When will the Kingdom of God come?" Jesus replied, "The Kingdom of God isn't ushered in with visible signs. You won't be able to say, 'Here it is!' or 'It's over there!' For the Kingdom of God is among you." (Luke 17:20-21)

Law of Abundance

Then he explained to them, "You have been permitted to understand the secrets of the Kingdom of Heaven, but others have not. To those who are open to my teaching, more understanding will be given, and they will have an abundance of knowledge. But to those who are not listening, even what they have will be taken away from them." (Matthew 13:11-12)

Law of Moses

"Until John the Baptist began to preach, the laws of Moses and the messages of the prophets were your guides. But now

the Good News of the Kingdom of God is preached, and eager multitudes are forcing their way in. But that doesn't mean that the law has lost its force in even the smallest point. It is stronger and more permanent than heaven and earth." (Luke 16:16-17)

Light of the World
Jesus said to the people, "I am the light of the world. If you follow me, you won't be stumbling through the darkness, because you will have the light that leads to life." (John 8:12)

Living Water
Jesus replied, "People soon become thirsty again after drinking this water. But the water I give them takes away thirst altogether. It becomes a perpetual spring within them, giving them eternal life." (John 4:13-14)

Loving God
Jesus replied, "'You must love the Lord your God with all your heart, all your soul, and all your mind.' This is the first and greatest commandment. A second is equally important: 'Love your neighbor as yourself.' All the other commandments and all the demands of the prophets are based on these two commandments." (Matthew 22:37-40)

Loving Others
"So now I am giving you a new commandment: Love each other. Just as I have loved you, you should love each other. Your love for one another will prove to the world that you are my disciples." (John 13:34-35)

Need for Workers
These were his instructions to them: "The harvest is so great, but the workers are so few. Pray to the Lord who is in charge of the harvest, and ask him to send out more workers for his fields." (Luke 10:2)

Nonresistance

"You have heard that the law of Moses says, 'If an eye is injured, injure the eye of the person who did it. If a tooth gets knocked out, knock out the tooth of the person who did it.' But I say, don't resist an evil person! If you are slapped on the right cheek, turn the other, too." (Matthew 5:38-39)

Our Lives

"Those who love their life in this world will lose it. Those who despise their life in this world will keep it for eternal life." (John 12:25)

Our Power over Satan

"Yes," he told them, "I saw Satan falling from heaven as a flash of lightning! And I have given you authority over all the power of the enemy, and you can walk among snakes and scorpions and crush them. Nothing will injure you. But don't rejoice just because evil spirits obey you; rejoice because your names are registered as citizens of heaven." (Luke 10:18-20)

Peace

"I am leaving you with a gift—peace of mind and heart. And the peace I give isn't like the peace the world gives. So don't be troubled or afraid." (John 14:27)

Persecution

"Do you remember what I told you? 'A servant is not greater than the master.' Since they persecuted me, naturally they will persecute you. And if they had listened to me, they would listen to you! The people of the world will hate you because you belong to me, for they don't know God who sent me." (John 15:20-21)

Prayer

"But when you pray, go away by yourself, shut the door behind you, and pray to your Father secretly. Then your Father, who knows all secrets, will reward you." (Matthew 6:6)

Prudence

"Don't give what is holy to unholy people. Don't give pearls to swine! They will trample the pearls, then turn and attack you." (Matthew 7:6)

Putting the Word into Practice

"I will show you what it's like when someone comes to me, listens to my teaching, and then obeys me. It is like a person who builds a house on a strong foundation laid upon the underlying rock. When the floodwaters rise and break against the house, it stands firm because it is well built. But anyone who listens and doesn't obey is like a person who builds a house without a foundation. When the floods sweep down against that house, it will crumble into a heap of ruins." (Luke 6:47-49)

Reconciliation

"So if you are standing before the altar in the Temple, offering a sacrifice to God, and you suddenly remember that someone has something against you, leave your sacrifice there beside the altar. Go and be reconciled to that person. Then come and offer your sacrifice to God." (Matthew 5:23-24)

Repentance

"Do you think those Galileans were worse sinners than other people from Galilee?" he asked. "Is that why they suffered? Not at all! And you will also perish unless you turn from your evil ways and turn to God." (Luke 13:2-3)

Resurrection

"For it is my Father's will that all who see his Son and believe in him should have eternal life—that I should raise them at the last day." (John 6:40)

Resurrection and the Life

Jesus told her, "I am the resurrection and the life. Those who believe in me, even though they die like everyone else, will live again. They are given eternal life for believing in me and will never perish. Do you believe this, Martha?" (John 11:25-26)

Rewards

"Yes," Jesus replied, "and I assure you, everyone who has given up house or wife or brothers or parents or children, for the sake of the Kingdom of God." (Luke 18:29)

Rewards in the Kingdom

Jesus replied, "I assure you that when I, the Son of Man, sit upon my glorious throne in the Kingdom, you who have been my followers will also sit on twelve thrones, judging the twelve tribes of Israel. And everyone who has given up houses or brothers or sisters or father or mother or children or property, for my sake, will receive a hundred times as much in return and will have eternal life. But many who seem to be important now will be the least important then, and those who are considered least here will be the greatest then." (Matthew 19:28-30)

Rich

Jesus watched him go and then said to his disciples, "How hard it is for rich people to get into the Kingdom of God! It is easier for a camel to go through the eye of a needle than for a rich person to enter the Kingdom of God!" (Luke 18:24-25)

Right Way to God

"The door to heaven is narrow. Work hard to get in, because many will try to enter." (Luke 13:24)

Scripture

Jesus told him, "No! The Scriptures say, 'People need more than bread for their life; they must feed on every word of God.' " (Matthew 4:4)

Seeking Sinners

Jesus answered them, "Healthy people don't need a doctor—sick people do. I have come to call sinners to turn from their sins, not to spend my time with those who think they are already good enough." (Luke 5:31-32)

Stewardship

"Unless you are faithful in small matters, you won't be faithful in large ones. If you cheat even a little, you won't be honest with greater responsibilities. And if you are untrustworthy about worldly wealth, who will trust you with the true riches of heaven? And if you are not faithful with other people's money, why should you be trusted with money of your own? No one can serve two masters. For you will hate one and love the other, or be devoted to one and despise the other. You cannot serve both God and money." (Luke 16:10-13)

Storing Up Possessions

"So he said, 'I know! I'll tear down my barns and build bigger ones. Then I'll have room enough to store everything. And I'll sit back and say to myself, My friend, you have enough stored away for years to come. Now take it easy! Eat, drink, and be merry!' But God said to him, 'You fool! You will die this very night. Then who will get it all?' Yes, a person is a fool to store up earthly wealth but not have a rich relationship with God." (Luke 12:18-21)

Temple

Jesus entered the Temple and began to drive out the merchants from their stalls. He told them, "The Scriptures declare, 'My Temple will be a place of prayer,' but you have turned it into a den of thieves." (Luke 19:45-46)

Those in Need

Jesus turned to his disciples and said, "God blesses you who are poor, for the Kingdom of God is given to you. God blesses you who are hungry now, for you will be satisfied.

God blesses you who weep now, for the time will come when you will laugh with joy. God blesses you who are hated and excluded and mocked and cursed because you are identified with me, the Son of Man. When that happens, rejoice! Yes, leap for joy! For a great reward awaits you in heaven. And remember, the ancient prophets were also treated that way by your ancestors." (Luke 6:20-23)

Those Not in Need

"What sorrows await you who are rich, for you have your only happiness now. What sorrows await you who are satisfied and prosperous now, for a time of awful hunger is before you. What sorrows await you who laugh carelessly, for your laughing will turn to mourning and sorrow. What sorrows await you who are praised by the crowds, for their ancestors also praised false prophets." (Luke 6:24-26)

Those Who Follow Him

Then he said to the crowd, "If any of you wants to be my follower, you must put aside your selfish ambition, shoulder your cross daily, and follow me. If you try to keep your life for yourself, you will lose it. But if you give up your life for me, you will find true life. And how do you benefit if you gain the whole world but lose or forfeit your own soul in the process?" (Luke 9:23-25)

True Wealth

"So don't be afraid, little flock. For it gives your Father great happiness to give you the Kingdom. Sell what you have and give to those in need. This will store up treasure for you in heaven! And the purses of heaven have no holes in them. Your treasure will be safe—no thief can steal it and no moth can destroy it. Wherever your treasure is, there your heart and thoughts will also be." (Luke 12:32-34)

Trust

"Don't be troubled. You trust God, now trust in me. There are many rooms in my Father's home, and I am going to prepare a place for you. If this were not so, I would tell you

plainly. When everything is ready, I will come and get you, so that you will always be with me where I am."
(John 14:1-3)

Unity
"I in them and you in me, all being perfected into one. Then the world will know that you sent me and will understand that you love them as much as you love me." (John 17:23)

Vine and the Branches
"Yes, I am the vine; you are the branches. Those who remain in me, and I in them, will produce much fruit. For apart from me you can do nothing." (John 15:5)

Violence
"Put away your sword," Jesus told him. "Those who use the sword will be killed by the sword. Don't you realize that I could ask my Father for thousands of angels to protect us, and he would send them instantly?" (Matthew 26:52-53)

Way to God
"You can enter God's Kingdom only through the narrow gate. The highway to hell is broad, and its gate is wide for the many who choose the easy way. But the gateway to life is small, and the road is narrow, and only a few ever find it." (Matthew 7:13-14)

Wisdom from the Spirit
"And when you are brought to trial in the synagogues and before rulers and authorities, don't worry about what to say in your defense, for the Holy Spirit will teach you what needs to be said even as you are standing there." (Luke 12:11-12)

Word of God Taking Root
"This is the meaning of the story: The seed is God's message. The seed that fell on the hard path represents those who hear the message, but then the Devil comes and steals

it away and prevents them from believing and being saved. The rocky soil represents those who hear the message with joy. But like young plants in such soil, their roots don't go very deep. They believe for a while, but they wilt when the hot winds of testing blow. The thorny ground represents those who hear and accept the message, but all too quickly the message is crowded out by the cares and riches and pleasures of this life. And so they never grow into maturity. But the good soil represents honest, good-hearted people who hear God's message, cling to it, and steadily produce a huge harvest." (Luke 8:11-15)

Word Put into Practice
"Anyone who listens to my teaching and obeys me is wise, like a person who builds a house on solid rock. Though the rain comes in torrents and the floodwaters rise and the winds beat against that house, it won't collapse, because it is built on rock. But anyone who hears my teaching and ignores it is foolish, like a person who builds a house on sand. When the rains and floods come and the winds beat against that house, it will fall with a mighty crash." (Matthew 7:24-27)

Words He Speaks
"It is the Spirit who gives eternal life. Human effort accomplishes nothing. And the very words I have spoken to you are spirit and life." (John 6:63)

Worry
Then turning to his disciples, Jesus said, "So I tell you, don't worry about everyday life—whether you have enough food to eat or clothes to wear. For life consists of far more than food and clothing. Look at the ravens. They don't need to plant or harvest or put food in barns because God feeds them. And you are far more valuable to him than any birds! Can all your worries add a single moment to your life? Of course not! And if worry can't do little things like that, what's the use of worrying over bigger things?" (Luke 12:22-26)

Worship

*"But the time is coming and is already here when true wor-
shipers will worship the Father in spirit and in truth. The
Father is looking for anyone who will worship him that
way. For God is Spirit, so those who worship him must
worship in spirit and in truth." (John 4:23-24)*